FOREWORD

I first read *Finn the Wolfhound* when I was about eleven years old, shortly after it was first published; and I read it again in my early teens. On each occasion I thought it was the most wonderful dog story of all. I still think so after all these years, having now read it for a third time in its present shorter form.

The original version was some twenty thousand words longer than this and contained material which is not so interesting to readers today. A splendid job of preparing this edition has been done by Antony Kamm, for while the story and language are exactly as they were, I cannot tell for certain, allowing for the passing of the years, just where it has been pruned.

This is not just a tale about a dog; it is an adventure story of high degree as well. There is excitement, tension, and action in every chapter. But perhaps the most remarkable aspect of *Finn the Wolfhound* is its fine account of the relationship between dog and master; and also of all that can happen if a champion youngster by ill fortune goes back to the wild. This was no easy story to write without overpainting the picture; yet A. J. Dawson managed to do it without sentimentality. Sentiment and sympathy and real understanding of a dog's mind are here in plenty; but there is nothing feeble or wishy-washy in the story.

This story is strong meat in places, but the grimmer incidents—fights, hunting for food, starvation, and loss of friends—never seem to be dragged in for effect. They are a logical part of the action. However, it is only fair to remind readers that circuses like the one that figures in this book would not last for two days now. Remember that *Finn the Wolfhound* was written nearly sixty years ago. Times have changed but not the charm and attraction of this adventure story, which can hold its own even against the stories of Jack London.

A. J. Dawson, M.B.E., died in 1951 at the age of seventy-nine. When still a boy, he went to sea as an apprentice but after a couple of voyages jumped his ship when it docked in Australia. For a time he was a farmer but later joined the staff of a Melbourne newspaper. After about five years he decided to become an author. He traveled about for several years and finally returned to England. He served in World War I and was afterwards chosen for a number of government missions abroad. In all, he wrote thirty-five books, mainly novels.

Dawson was well known, too, as a breeder of bloodhounds and, of course, wolfhounds. Finn himself is based on one of Dawson's own dogs, to the extent that he was the biggest and finest hound bred up to that time. In the book Finn's mother is Tara. In real life she was Tynagh, and the manner of her death as described in *Finn the Wolfhound* is actually true. And Tynagh's father (i.e., Finn's grandfather) was the famous Champion O'Leary, whose skeleton is still today in the Natural History Museum in London.

That is guarantee enough that Dawson knew what he was talking about. If all the new readers of this edition of *Finn the Wolfhound* enjoy it half as much as I have done, they should be more than satisfied.

MAXWELL KNIGHT

CONTENTS

1: THE MOTHER OF HEROES

FOR a man whose thirtieth year was still not far behind him, his face was very careworn. It suggested that he felt life's difficulties more keenly than a man should at that age.

He rose from his writing table and straightened his back with a long sigh, clenching both hands tightly and stretching both arms over his shoulders as he moved across the little room to its window. The window gave him an extensive view of dully gleaming roofs and chimney pots, seen through driving sleet, toward the end of a raw forenoon in February.

He turned away from the dripping window and looked around this den in which he worked. Its walls were covered mostly by bookshelves, but in the gaps between the shelves there were pictures; a rather odd mixture of pictures, of men and women and dogs. The men and women were mostly people who had written books, and the dogs were without exception Irish wolfhounds; those fine animals that combine in themselves the fleetness of the greyhound, the strength of the boarhound, and the picturesque, wiry shagginess of the deerhound; those animals whose history goes back to the beginning of the Christian era, through all the storied ages in which they were the friends and companions of kings and princes, great chieftains, and mighty hunters.

For several minutes the man paused before a picture, underneath which was written: "The Mistress of the Kennels." This picture showed a girl with wind-blown hair, a happy face, and laughing eyes, standing, with a small puppy in her arms, in the midst of a wide kennel enclosure on the sloping rise of an upland meadow. When the man had looked his fill at this picture and at other pictures of various Irish wolf-

hounds, each marked with the name and age of the hound
depicted, he sighed and went to the window again. While he
stood there, looking out through the sleet, the door of the
den opened, and the Mistress of the Kennels came in. Her
face had not quite the color the picture made one feel it
must have had when she stood in that wide, windy kennel enclosure; but it was still a sunny face; the eyes were still laughing eyes. She walked up to the man's side, and seeing the
expression on his face as he gazed out over the wet roofs, she
said, "Yes, it is, rather—isn't it?—after Croft."

"Oh, don't talk of Croft, or you'll bring my spring madness
upon me before its time. It seems almost incredible that we
have only been two years and four months away from Croft
and the old open life. I was looking at the picture of the
Mistress of the Kennels just now. Do you remember that
morning? Tara's first litter hadn't long been weaned. My
goodness, the air was sweet in that meadow!"

"Yes, and it was old Tara's third day out, after that awful
illness. Well, well, it's a blessed thing to know that she is
happy and has such a lovely home down in Devonshire, isn't
it?"

"Yes, oh yes; I know it might have been worse, and I'm a
brute to be discontented, but—two and a half years! I know
my idea was that we would not go back till it seemed sure we
really should be able to stay; no more returns to town with
our tails between our legs. But, all the same, when I look out
of that window—if we *really* lived cottage style, you know."

"But should we? Cottages don't have kennels, you know;
not wolfhound kennels, anyhow."

"I know. Oh, of course, it would be quite unjustifiable,
quite mad; but—I thought I felt signs of spring madness
when I looked out of that window this morning."

"Oh, well! Now do you know what I came in for? I came
to tell you that this is the last day of the dog show at the

Agricultural Hall. You remember I have to go over to Mrs. Kenneth's this afternoon, and I think it would be a good plan for you to take an afternoon off and go to the show. If you don't, it will be the third year you have missed it. It will do you good."

"H'm! I should hardly have thought a dog show was a good thing for spring madness; rather dangerous, I should have thought," said the man, with a queer little twisted smile.

"Oh, yes; I think it is all right. You have been working too hard; and besides, it will do you good to meet the people. Do go!"

A little more than an hour later he was on his way to the dog show, at which, in other days, he had been one of the principal exhibitors. A bout of ill health, combined with consequent diminution of earnings and a characteristic habit of doing things on a more generous scale than his income justified, had led to a breakup of his country home, with its big kennels and stabling, and a descent upon London in pursuit of economical living and increased earnings. Parting with the kennels and their inhabitants had been the severest wrench of all; and it is probable that, even in the mean little town flat, room would have been found for Tara, the well-loved mother of Irish wolfhound heroes, except that an excellent home had been offered her in Devonshire. The lady to whom Tara had, after long deliberations, been sold by the Master had been extremely keen about purchasing her, and in addition to offering a splendid home, had promised faithfully that in no circumstances whatever would she think of parting with Tara unless to the Master himself.

He had been very much concerned about other matters and other troubles at the time, but when the actual morning of Tara's departure had arrived, he had begun to feel very bad about it. The household gathered around to bid good-by to the beautiful hound, and her master himself took her to the station. When Tara was in the guard's van, she looked out through a barred window at her friend on the station platform, and he said afterwards that the situation exhausted every ounce of self-control he possessed. He had an overpowering impulse, even when the train was moving, to jump aboard and release Tara.

But glowing reports were received of Tara's happiness in her new home, with its extensive grounds and generous management; and though Tara was never forgotten—one does not forget such a mother of heroes when one has bred her and nursed her through mortal illness—her master had ceased to grieve about her or to feel self-reproachful about having parted with her.

Arrived in the great show building, he wandered up and down between the benches, pausing now and again to speak to an old acquaintance, human or canine, as the case might be. But this was the last day of the show, and the majority of the exhibitors were away. The place had a half-dismantled air about it. The show was virtually over. Presently the Master found himself in a kind of outbuilding, where an auction sale of dogs was being held. There he sat down on a chair at the edge of the ring in which the dogs for sale were being led to and fro by attendants for inspection.

After a while a young Irish wolfhound was led into the ring, and immediately monopolized the Master's attention, for it was a dog of his own breeding, sold by him from his country home, Croft. He handled the dog with a good deal of interest and was expatiating upon its merits to a small group of possible buyers when he felt another dog nuzzling his arm and wrist from behind. But the Master was too much interested in examining the young hound then being offered for sale to pay attention to any other animal. In due course, however, the young wolfhound was sold and led away, and the auctioneer was heard to say:

"And now, ladies and gentlemen, we come to lot number 127. This magnificent bitch, whose show record I will read to you directly, is, as most of you are probably aware, by the famous Champion O'Leary. Come, come, man; let's have that bitch in the ring, please."

The auctioneer spoke sharply to an attendant who stood close to the Master's seat, tugging at a chain. The Master, who had been busy in conversation up till that moment, turned now to respond to the pressingly affectionate advances of the unseen animal, whose cold muzzle he had felt at his wrist for some minutes past.

"Just push her out for me, sir, if you please," said the rebuked attendant sulkily. "I can't get her to budge from your chair. The brute's as strong as a mule."

"Let me have the chain a minute," said the Master, as he rose from his chair "I expect you've frightened the— Why— Tara! Tara—dear—old—lady. Who the devil put this hound in here?"

"Mrs. Forsyth, the owner, put her in," said a groom, who forced his way forward through the crowd.

The Master wasted some moments, but not many, in wondering and disgusted expostulation, while fondling the head of poor Tara, who had stood erect with her forepaws on his shoulders the instant he recognized her, her noble face all alight with gladness and love. Through ten acutely unhappy minutes she had nuzzled her friend's hand and gained never a hint of recognition or response. Then the Master walked up to the auctioneer's rostrum, followed by Tara, who, with no apparent effort, dragged the sulky, puzzled attendant along, paying not the slightest heed to his angry jerks at her collar.

"I'm sorry," said the auctioneer, after a few moments' conversation, "but I cannot possibly postpone the sale, can I? I had my instructions direct from the owner, and she should know. I am told the dog is positively to be sold— No, there is no reserve at all. Yes, certainly, I will take your check as deposit, if you will get it endorsed by the show secretary. But— Very well, sir; no need to blame me about it. I'll give you five minutes."

Five minutes was not much of a respite, but the Master meant to make the most of it. To see Tara put up and sold to a dealer in the ring, he felt he could not. The groom said Mrs. Forsyth was in the tearoom, and there the Master sought her, with anger and anxiety in his eye; sought her unavailingly and in a frenzy of haste. To and fro he hurried through the huge, noisy show building. At one moment of his fruitless search he obtained a card from the show secretary stating that his check might be accepted; but even as he thanked the worried official for his confidence in an old exhibitor, he realized with bitterness that he could not by any stretch of fancy pretend that he was able to afford anything like the sort of price that Tara would bring. Not a sign did he see of Mrs. Forsyth, and at last a kennelman informed him that he had seen Mrs. Forsyth leaving the building some time before. Almost despairing now and conscious that the limit of time given him was passed, he hurried back to the auction-room, caught a glimpse of his beautiful Tara standing sorrowful and stately in the ring, head and tail both carried low, and heard a tall, clean-shaven man in a kennel coat bid forty-eight guineas for her.

"Forty-eight!" echoed the auctioneer. "This magnificent Irish wolfhound bitch, the dam of many winners and two champions, is positively going for forty—"

"Forty-nine!" cried the Master, with a tightening of his lips.

And then he saw the mean, ferrety face of a well-known low-class dealer thrust forward from among the crowd. This dealer was notorious for keeping a large number of big Danes and Newfoundlands in the miserable back yard of a cobbler's shop in the East End of London. He had been ordered out of show rings before that day for malpractices. He had never owned a wolfhound, but he was a shrewd business judge of the values of dogs. He nodded to the auctioneer, and that gentleman nodded responsively before taking up his tale afresh.

"Fifty guineas only is offered for the celebrated Irish wolfhound Tara, by the famous Champion O'Leary. Fifty-one guineas— Thank *you*, sir. Fifty and one guineas is my last bid—"

The auctioneer babbled serenely on, and the Master followed his words, rather pale in the face now, for fifty-one guineas was a great deal more than he could afford to pay.

The ferret-faced dealer raised the price to fifty-three guineas, and the Master bit his lip and made it fifty-four.

"May I say fifty-five for you, sir?" said the auctioneer to the clean-shaven man in the kennel coat.

"If you'll just wait one moment, sir; I must just ask my—" The clean-shaven man was edging his way toward the back of the crowd, where several ladies and gentlemen were seated at a table just out of sight of the ring.

"Time and tide and auctioneers wait for no man, sir," continued the auctioneer. "The hammer is very near to falling, gentlemen. The magnificent Irish wolfhound Tara is going for fifty-four guineas only; for fifty-four guin—and one— Thank *you*, sir"—this to the ferret-faced dealer—"at fifty-five guineas only, this noble animal is going for fif— Why, gentlemen, what has come over us this afternoon? What am I to say for the gentleman who appeared to be recognized by this fine animal? Surely, sir, civility demands a little recognition of such touching devotion!"

"We're not dealing in personalities, sir," snapped the Master. "Sixty guineas!"

And then he turned on his heel, this desperate bid being far more than he could afford. The auctioneer smiled amiably.

"As you say, sir, this is strict business; and all I am offered for this magnificent hound, gentlemen, is sixty guineas! But my instructions are to sell; and sell I must, whatever the figure." He raised his hammer. "At sixty guineas, gent—and one. At sixty-one guineas, gentlemen; lot number 127 is going—a rare bargain for somebody—going! Thank *you*, sir! That's a little better, gentlemen. Seventy guineas I think you said, sir?"—this to the man in the kennel coat, who had returned from his visit to the back of the crowd.

The ferret-faced dealer who had bid sixty-one guineas now turned his back on the ring; and, as he heard the cry of seventy guineas, the Master moved slowly forward among the crowd toward the door of the building. He dared not offer more, and he could not wait to see Tara led out of the ring by some stranger. He paused a moment, without looking up, and heard the auctioneer's "Going, going, gone!" Then he walked to the entrance of the main hall to escape from the scene of so grievous a disappointment.

Outside, in the main building, while moodily filling a pipe, the Master decided that, whatever happened, he must find out who had purchased Tara in order that he might put in a word for his old friend and thereby, it might be, ensure more consideration for her in her new home. There were one or two little whims and peculiarities of hers that he must explain. He looked along the dusty, littered hall and, in the distance, saw an elderly lady leading an Irish wolfhound. A moment later he recognized the hound as Tara and the lady as a good friend of his own, a kindly, wealthy Yorkshire woman who had bought two whelps from him before he left Croft and with whom he had corresponded since. Now she was walking directly toward him, leading Tara, and smiling and nodding to him. Just then the lady leaned forward and unsnapped Tara's chain. In an instant, the great hound bounded forward to greet her well-loved friend, the Master, furiously nuzzling his hands and finally standing erect to reach his face, a paw on either shoulder, her soft eyes glistening, brimming over with canine love and delight. The man's eyes were not altogether dry, either, as he muttered and growled affectionate nonsense in Tara's silky ears. His heart swelled as he felt the tremulous excitement in the great hound's limbs.

"You see, dear old Tara cannot be deceived; she knows her real friends," said the lady from Yorkshire, as she shook hands with the Master. "Please take her chain and never give anyone else the right to handle it. You will allow me this pleasure, I am sure, if only because of the love I bear Tara's son." (One of the whelps this lady had bought from him was a son of Tara.) "I know Mrs. Forsyth quite well—a whimsical, fanciful little person, who takes up a new fad every month and is apt to change her pets as often as her gloves. I could not possibly let a stranger buy the beautiful mother of my Dhulert, and it gives me so much real pleasure to be the means of bringing her to your hands again."

This good woman bowed her silvery head when the Master took her hand in his because she had caught a glimpse of what glistened in his eyes as he tried to give words to the gratitude that filled a heart already swelled by another emotion inspired by Tara.

They walked all the way home, the Master and Tara; and twice they made considerable detours for the sake of spending a few minutes in open spaces, where there was grass—smutty and soiled it is true, but grass—and comparative solitude. In those places they exchanged remarks, and Tara placed a little London mud on each of the Master's shoulders, and he made curious noises in his throat, such as Tara had been wont to associate with early morning scampers in an upland orchard after rabbits.

At last they came to the "mansions" and made a great show of creeping along close to the railing and dodging quickly in at the entrance to avoid being seen from the windows above. As a matter of fact, tenants of the flats in these buildings were not supposed to keep dogs at all, while the idea of an Irish wolfhound thirty-two inches high at the shoulder—! But it was little the Master cared that night. The meeting between Tara and the Mistress of the Kennels was a spectacle that afforded him real joy. The flat seemed ridiculously tiny once Tara was inside it; but like all her race, this mother of heroes was a marvel of deftness and could walk in and out of the Mistress's little drawing room without so much as brushing a chair leg. There was great rejoicing in the little flat that night—and a deal of wonderful planning, too.

And this was how Tara, the mother of heroes, returned to the friends who had watched over her birth and early training and later motherhood with every sort of loving care.

2: IN THE BEGINNING

IT was little that Tara, the wolfhound, cared about lack of space as long as she could stretch her great length along a hearthrug, with her long, bearded muzzle resting on her friend's slippers, and gaze at him, while he sat at his work, through the forest of overhanging eyebrows that screened her soft, brown eyes. And in any case, the next four months of her life, after the happy meeting at the show, which restored her to her old friend, were too full of changing happenings and variety of scene and occupation to leave time for much consideration about the size of quarters.

For one thing, it was within a few days of the show that Tara was taken on a two-day visit to a farm in Oxfordshire, where she renewed her old acquaintance with one of the greatest aristocrats of her race, Champion Dermot Asthore, the father of those great young hounds she had given to the world.

After that, something considerable seemed to happen pretty well every day. The Master spoke laughingly of the spring madness that was as quicksilver to his heels and of great profit to furniture movers. He laughed a good deal and took Tara and the Mistress of the Kennels with him on quite a number of journeys from Victoria railway station. Then there came a day of extraordinary confusion at the little flat, when men with aprons stamped about and turned furniture upside down and made foolish remarks about Tara as she sat beside the writing table gravely watching them. That night Tara slept in a loose box in the stable of a country inn, and in the early morning she went out for a glorious run on the Downs with the Master, who seemed to have grown younger since they'd left London.

Within a very few days Tara and her friends had settled down comfortably in a new home. It was an oddly shaped little house full of unexpected angles and doors, and it had a garden and orchard that straggled up the lower slope of one of the Downs. It had a stable, too, of a modest sort, and rather poky, but the coach house was admirable, light, airy, faced southeast and had a new concrete floor, which the Master helped to lay with his own hands. The back half of this coach house consisted of a slightly raised wooden dais; a very pleasant place for a wolfhound to lie when spring sunshine was flooding the coach house. But Tara did not spend much of her time there, for between the stabling and the house there was a big wooden structure with a tiled roof, large as a good-sized barn, with an entrance like an ordinary house door and comfortably matchboarded inside, like a wooden house. A pleasant old villager who was doing some work in the garden referred to this place as "th' old parish room," but the Master made it his own den and lined one of its sides with books and pictures of dogs and men, fields and kennels. The actual house, for all its rambling shape, was small, and possibly this was why the Master chose to utilize this outside place as his den and to fix a big stove in it for heating. Here, too, at one end, just beyond the big writing desk, was a raised wooden dais or bed like that in the coach house, a good six feet square, with sides to it, perhaps six inches high. Tara watched the making of this dais, saw the master cover its floor with a kind of sawdust that had a strong, pleasant small, and then nail down a tightly stretched piece of old carpet over that, making altogether, as she thought, a very excellent bed. And as such Tara used it by night, but in the daytime she usually preferred to stretch herself beside the writing desk, or on the rug by the door, where the sunshine formed a pool of light and warmth on a fine morning.

Here it was that Tara took her meals, a dish of milk in the morning, with a little bread or biscuit, and the real meal of the day, the dinner, which the Mistress of the Kennels always prepared with her own hands.

As time went on, the great hound tended to become less active. There were any number of rabbits on the Downs beyond the orchard, and at first, in her before-breakfast ramble with the Master, Tara used to enjoy greatly running down one or two of these. But after a little time the Master seemed to make a point of discouraging this, even to the extent of resting a hand lightly upon Tara's collar as she walked beside him; and, gradually, she herself lost inclination for the sport, except where greatly tempted, as by a rabbit's jumping suddenly for its burrow close beside her. In the afternoon, when Tara generally went out with the Mistress of the Kennels for a good long round, she wore a lead on her collar now, so that even sudden inspirations to gallop were checked in the bud, and a sedate gait was maintained always. Without troubling her head to think much about it, Tara had a generally contented feeling that these precautions were wise and good. The same prudent feeling influenced her in the matter of meals now. Though she frequently felt that she would much rather be without her morning milk, she always lapped it up carefully and conscientiously swabbed the dish bright and dry with her great red tongue. She could not have explained, even to herself, just why she did these things; but subconscious understanding and foreknowledge play a large part in a wolfhound's life, and so does subconscious memory and the inherited thing we call instinct.

But it was not alone in such matters as refraining from violent exercise and the taking of food whether inclined for it or not that a sort of prescience guided beautiful Tara at this time in her new home beside the Sussex Downs. There came a morning when, as she strolled about the strip of shrubbery and orchard that lay between the stabling and the house, it occurred to her that it would be a good thing to dig a hole somewhere in the ground; the sort of hole or cave into which a great hound like herself could creep for shelter if need be; a cave in which she could live for a while. Tara did not know that the Master was watching her at this time; but he was, and there was a sympathetic and understanding sort of smile on his face when Tara forced her way in between two large shrubs and began excavating. The earth was soft and moist there, and Tara's powerful forefeet scooped it out in regular shovelfuls for her hind feet to scatter in an earthy rain behind her. She made a cavern as big as herself and then divided the rest of the day between the beautiful big dais in

the coach house, all dry and sweet and clean, and her fra-
grant, carpeted great bed in "th' old parish room." Lying
there at her ease, with one eye on the Master's shoulder,
where it showed around the side of his high-topped writing
desk, Tara wondered vaguely why she had troubled to dig
that hole in the wet earth. But the Master knew all about it,
and he seemed quite satisfied.

On the following day Tara gravely inspected the hole she
had dug and decided that it was not altogether good. So she
went and dug another in a rather more secluded spot, and
then came back and dozed comfortably at the Master's feet
while he wrote. Later on in the day she strolled around the
whole premises and inspected carefully the various places in
which, during the past week or so, she had buried large bones.
The next day found Tara extremely restless and rather unhappy. She had an uncomfortable feeling that she had forgotten some important matter that required attention. In her
effort to recall what the thing could be, she dug two or three
more holes and finally, a thing she had never thought of doing before, took one of the Master's slippers—always a singularly dear and comforting piece of property to Tara—and
buried it about two feet deep in a little ditch. She felt vaguely
ashamed about this, though she had no idea that the Master
had watched her taking the slipper away; but she could not
bring herself to return the slipper because of the hazy need
she felt for laying up treasure.

During the afternoon, Tara's general uneasiness increased.
She felt thoroughly uncomfortable and worried, convinced
that she had forgotten some really important matter, and dis-
inclined either to go out or to stay in. Fifty times the Master
opened and closed doors to suit her changing whims, until
poor Tara felt quite ashamed of herself, though still unable
to settle down. As a sort of savory after dinner, the Master
gave her some silky, warm olive oil; an odd thing to take,

Tara thought, but upon the whole pleasing and comforting. Then, suddenly, as she woke from a doze of about ten seconds' duration, Tara decided that it would be a good thing to tear a hole in the middle of the tight-stretched old carpet on her big bed. She got to work at once, pleased to think that she had remembered this little matter in good time, and was distinctly disappointed when the Master came and sat beside her on the edge of the bed and playfully held her paws, after gently lowering her into a lying position.

While Tara was gradually forgetting her desire to tear the bed covering, a cart stopped outside the house, and a whiff, the hint of an odor, drifted in through the open door of the den and caused the great hound's nose to wrinkle ominously. Next moment she gave a savage bark, deep, threatening, and sonorous, and sprang to her feet. She was not quite sure what ailed her, but she was conscious of an access of great danger, of passionate hostility. After soothing her, the Master carefully locked the door of the den, went around through the gateway leading to the front of the house, and took delivery of a large hamper from the station carrier. Then the Mistress of the Kennels came and sat in the Master's den for perhaps half an hour, while he was busy down at the coach house with the hamper and a lantern and a dish of dog's dinner of a milky, sloppy sort.

That was a strange, eventful night in the den. All the country around was silent as the grave, and the air of the June night was soft and sweet as the petals of wild roses. The Mistress of the Kennels was persuaded into going to bed early, but the Master sat behind his big desk, writing beneath a carefully shaded lamp and rising quietly every now and again to peer over the top of the high desk in the direction of the big bed in the shadow, where Tara lay. Many things happened in the meantime, but it was just after the clock in the tower of the village church had struck the hour of one that the Master was thrilled by a cry from Tara; the fifth he had heard during the past three and a half hours.

He leaned forward on his elbows, waiting and listening. Tara had never heard of duty or self-control. But the moment of that cry of hers was the only moment she allowed for self-consideration or the play of her own inclinations. In the next moment she was busying herself, with the most exquisite delicacy and precision, over the care of her latest offspring; the last late-comer in her new family of five. In that next instant, too, a weak, bleating little cry, a voice that was not at all like Tara's, smote pleasantly upon the ears of the Master where he waited, peering watchfully from beside the deeply shaded lamp on his desk.

It was then, just after the Master heard that little bleating cry that told of new life in the world, that Tara, with infinite care and precaution, lowered her great bulk upon the bed in a curve—she had been standing—the center of which was occupied by four glossy Irish wolfhound puppies, who had arrived respectively at ten, eleven, twelve, and half-past twelve that night. The four, then blindly groveling over the carpeted bed, were now perfectly sheltered in the still heaving hollow of their mother's flank. These pups had not arranged themselves conveniently in a cluster to receive their loving mother's caress. On the contrary, they were all groping in different directions at the moment in which Tara's pain-racked body was lowered to rest and to shelter them. But while yet that great body hung over them in the act of descending, it had twisted and curved into the required lines, and a soft muzzle had thrust this puppy that way and the other another way, the mother's soft, filmy eyes missing nothing before her or behind. One inch of miscalculation and the life would have been crushed out of one of those tiny creatures. But pain brought no miscalculation for Tara.

One quick movement of her head satisfied the mother that her four firstborn were safe and well disposed. Immediately then, with never a thought of rest, her nose thrust the new-comer into position between her forepaws, and she proceeded to administer the life-giving and stimulating tongue-wash. Over and over the little shapeless gray form was turned, cheeping and bleating, until every crevice of its soft anatomy had come under the vivifying sweep of six inches of scarlet tongue, warm and tenderly rough. Then the mother's sensitive nose thrust and coaxed the little creature to its nesting place under her flank, where three sisters and a brother already nosed complainingly among milk-swollen dugs, quite indifferent to the coming of an addition to their number.

Then, and not till then, did the beautiful mother permit herself to draw a long breath of relief and lower her massive head upon her forepaws. A moment later, a desire that overcame weariness impelled Tara to part her hot jaws and glance in the direction of the shaded lamp. Not the least movement of hers escaped the Master, and in the moment of her glance, he came forward with a dish of fresh cold water in his hand. The mother lapped slowly, weakly, gratefully. The man moved very gently and deftly before her, and no anxiety came into her brown eyes when he leaned forward to examine the litter at her flank.

"There, there, pet; all right, my Tara girl," murmured the man, as he stepped back softly to his table, to return a moment later with a dish of warm milk and water, which the slightly rested mother drank with eagerness, though the effort necessary for lapping in that constrained position, and without disturbing the little ones beside her, was far from pleasant.

Ten minutes later the dam very gently changed her position, all idea of rest having left her now, and proceeded

systematically to lick first her own swollen dugs and then the
little featureless faces of her offspring, while the Master stood
in the shadow of his desk, watching and waiting. Within another few minutes the five pups were immersed in the most
important affair of life (from their point of view) and, with
wriggling tails and tiny, heaving flanks, with impatient, outthrust pink forefeet, wet faces, and gaping little jaws, were
nursing in a row like clockwork.

The mother turned a proud, filmy eye in the direction of
her friend, the Master, and allowed her massive head to fall
on its side, her whole great form outstretched to reap the
benefit of a few more minutes of needed repose.

"Good girl!" whispered the Master. "Five's a very good
number. I should have been sorry to see a big litter for Tara.
And, anyhow, that last one, the gray, is about equal to any
two I ever saw."

The Master lay down to sleep presently on the couch; and
before many hours of the June daylight had passed, he had
verified his impressions of that last-born son of Tara's as a
gray-brindle and the biggest whelp of its age that he had ever
seen. For purposes of registration in the books of the Kennel
Club, the late-comer was forthwith christened by the Mistress
of the Kennels, under the name of Finn, in honor of the
memory of the fourth-century warrior Finn, son of Cumall,
lord of three hundred Irish wolfhounds. Finn was chief of
King Cormac's household and master of his hounds, for the
most honored counsellor that the ancient Kings of Ireland
had were always masters of the hounds.

And this was the way of the Irish wolfhound Finn's entry
into the world, at the end of the first hour of a June day, in
the Master's den beside the Sussex Downs. Finn rested easily
in the palm of the Master's right hand when christened by
the Mistress of the Kennels, for he was little bigger than a
week-old kitten. But he was none the less Finn, the lineal

descendant of King Cormac's battlehounds of fifteen hundred years ago; and it was said he had the makings of the biggest wolfhound ever bred.

3: THE FOSTER MOTHER

FINN'S first adventure came to him when he was no more than about thirty-seven hours old and, of course, still blind as any bat. That being so, it may be taken that the gray whelp was not particularly interested. Still, the event was important and probably affected the whole of Finn's afterlife. This was the way of it.

Early on the second morning of his life, Finn was lying snugly asleep between his mother's hind legs on the great bed at the stove end of the outside den. When a litter of puppies are lying with their mother, there is always one place which is snugger and in various ways rather better than any other place. You would have said that the little, more or less shapeless, blind lump of gristle and skin that was Finn at this stage had no more intelligence or reasoning power than a potato; but from the very beginning, this best place had been exclusively occupied by him; and if while he slept, one of his wakeful brothers or sisters crawled over him and momentarily usurped his proud position, then, in the very moment of his awakening, that other puppy would be rolled backward, full of gurgling and futile protestation, and Finn would resume the picked place. Whatever was best in the way of warmth and food and comfort Finn obtained, even at this absurdly rudimentary stage, by superior weight, energy, and vitality.

Finn and the rest were sound asleep, and Tara was dozing

with one brown eye uncovered when the Master came into
the den on that second morning and spoke invitingly to her.
The great bitch rose slowly and with gentle care, and Finn,
with the other sucklings, rolled helplessly on his back, sleep-
ily cheeping a puny remonstrance, though he had no idea
what he wanted. Then, in his ridiculously masterful way,
Finn grovelingly burrowed under the other puppies, so that
he might have the benefit of all their warmth, and was asleep
again. Tara eyed the blind things for a moment with maternal solicitude and then, seeing that all was well with them,
followed the Master out into the bright, fresh sunshine of the
stable yard.

"Come and see the Mistress, old lady; come along and
stretch yourself," said her friend.

And so Tara strolled around the yard twice and then across
to the back-kitchen door, where, inside the house, she had
some warm bread and milk with the Mistress of the Kennels.
Tara lapped steadily and conscientiously but without much
appetite. Suddenly, when the basin was about three quarters
empty, she realized with a start that the Master had left her.
She gave one quick look to right and left, and then, the
mother anxiety shining in her brown eyes, she reached the
outer door in a bound.

"Look out for Tara!" cried the Mistress through the open
window.

"All right! I'm clear now. Let her in, will you?" answered
the Master, from beyond the gate leading to the coach house.

So the Mistress opened the house door, and in three catlike
bounds Tara reached the door of the den and stood erect, her
forepaws against the door, more than six feet above the
ground.

"There, there, pet; your children are all right, you see,"
said the Mistress, as she let Tara into the den.

In a moment, lighter of foot than a terrier, for all that she

weighed as much as an average man, Tara was in the midst
of the big bed, where she saw her puppies bunched snugly
and asleep. She looked up gratefully at the Mistress, as the
roused pups (she had touched them with her nose) came mew-
ing about her feet, and coiled down at once to nurse them,
apparently unconscious of the fact that there were only four
mouths to feed instead of five. One cannot say for certain
whether or not she missed Finn then. She licked the four
assiduously while they nursed; and, in any case, four gaping
little mouths and four wriggling, helpless little bodies represent a considerable claim upon a wolfhound mother's attention and strength; also, it may be that if she did notice that
the big gray whelp was missing, she was too wise and devoted
a mother and nurse to allow herself to injure the remaining
four by fretting and worrying over matters beyond her immediate control.

Having seen Tara comfortably settled down with her family of four, the Mistress hurried back to the house in time to
see the Master unwrapping little Finn from a soft old blanket
and placing him carefully in the midst of three puppies of
perhaps half his size in a hamper near the kitchen stove. Finn
bleated rather languidly for two minutes in his new environment and then, being very full of milk and very warm, forgot
what the trouble was and fell asleep. The Master closed the
lid of the hamper then and said:

"I'll let them have a good two hours together there. Finn
ought to assimilate the smell of the others pretty well by then.
What do you think of the foster?"

"Oh, I like her," said the Mistress of the Kennels. "She
seems a nice, affectionate little beast, and I think she has quite
recovered from the effects of that awful journey. And I think
she will be a good mother. She seems to have any amount of
milk—more than is comfortable for her, poor little thing!"

"Yes; that's exactly what I want. I want her to be uncom-

fortably heavy for the time, and then she will be the less likely
to resent my great big Finn's introduction."

"Then you have decided to put Finn to the foster mother?"

"Yes. You see, poor old Tara—well, she—"

"Yes, I know; she's poor old Tara—spoiled darling!"

The Master chuckled. "Well, perhaps it is partly that.
And, anyway, she deserves it. The old girl has done a good
share of prize-winning and nursing and the rest of it. I think
of her as a lady who has earned repose, particularly after—"

"Yes, I know; the illness, you mean."

"Well, anyhow, I think four pups quite enough for her to
nurse. And, as a matter of fact, I am none too comfortable
about that. You know I have always believed that that awful
bout of mammitis permanently affected her; her heart and—
and other things, too I am not at all sure that we may not
have to take them all from her."

"Yes, I see." The Mistress of the Kennels was thoughtfully
balancing on the tip of her forefinger a big wooden spoon,
used in the mixing of Tara's meals. "But why do you choose
Finn for the foster?"

"Well, now, that's rather a nice point and involves a conviction of mine that I know you'll resent, because you rightly
think Tara the perfection of all that a wolfhound should be.
A mongrel's milk is far stronger, heartier food than the milk
of so highly bred a great lady as Tara. Tara gives the most
aristocratic blood in the world; but when you come to food,
the nourishment that is to build up bone and muscle and
hardy health—that's different. Also, I only mean to give the
foster this one pup, though I dare say she is capable of rearing two or three. Therefore, that one pup ought to do exceedingly well with her. Now Finn, as you see him, is the
biggest pup I ever knew, and I want to give him every chance
of growing into the biggest Irish wolfhound living. That's
why he is going to have this sheep-dog foster all to his little

self, and unless I'm mistaken, you'll find him in a week the
fattest little tub of a pup in all England."

In about one hour from that time, Finn woke among his
strange bedfellows and trampled all over them in a vain and
wrathful search for his mother's dugs. He bleated vigorously
for three minutes; and then the warmth of that snug corner
of the kitchen sent him off to sleep again.

Another hour passed, and when Finn woke this time, one
could tell from the furious lunges he made over the little
bodies of his foster brothers that he had arrived at a serious
determination to let nothing stand any longer between himself and a good square meal. Several times Finn quite thought
he had at length found a teat, and in its infantile, impotent
way, the blind fury he displayed was quite terrible when he
discovered he was merely chewing the muzzle of one of the
other pups. On one of these occasions, Finn spluttered and
swore so vehemently that the effort completely robbed him
of what rudimentary sense of balance he had, and he rolled
over on his back, leaving all his four pink feet wriggling in
the air in a passion of protest.

It was in this undignified position that the Master presently found the gray whelp, and he chuckled as he picked
up Finn, with two of the other pups, and wrapped them together in a warm blanket. The remaining puppy was handed
over to the gardener and seen no more in that place. The
next thing Finn knew was that his gaping mouth, held open
by the Master's thumb and forefinger, was being pressed
against a soft surface from which warm milk trickled. Immediately his little hind legs began to work like pistons and
his forepaws to knead and pound at the soft udder from
which the milk was drawn. Finn, with his two foster brothers,
was at the dugs of the foster mother, a soft-eyed little sheep
dog, then occupying a very comfortable corner of the big bed
in the coach house.

The Master sat watchfully beside the sheep dog. She was very glad to be eased of some of her superabundance of milk and curved her elastic body forward to simplify matters for the pups. Then she began to lick the back and flank of the pup nearest her head; one of her own. The Master leaned forward. The foster's sensitive nose passed over the back of the first pup to the wriggling tail of Finn; and her big eyes hardened and looked queerly straight down her muzzle at the fat gray back of the stranger; a back twice as broad as those of her own pups. No warm tongue curled out over Finn's fat back; instead, a nose made curiously harsh and unsympathetic pushed him clear away from the place he had selected, after spluttering hurried investigation, and out upon the straw of the bed.

Immediately then, and almost before Finn's sticky mouth could open in a bleat of protest, the Master's hand had returned him to the warm dugs. Again came the harsh, suspicious nose of the foster about Finn's tail, and this time a low growl followed the resentful sniff.

But, though Finn instinctively wriggled his hindquarters from under that cold muzzle, his mouth and forefeet vigorously pursued their business; and before the threatened bite came, the Master's hand (a firm one and soothing) had caressingly pressed the foster's head back upon the straw and held it there.

His hand continued to rest on the sheep dog's neck or head till the three pups were comfortably full and the foster herself was comfortably eased of her bounteous milk supply. Then, gently, he removed his hand, and the foster proceeded to lick her own two pups with exemplary diligence. She refrained from taking any active steps against the big gray pup, but she very pointedly ignored him. And when, in due course, Finn came galumphing about her neck, with all the doddering insolence of the full-fed pup, she turned her head in the opposite direction with cool superciliousness and exhaled a long breath through her nose, as though she found the air offensive. But the Master petted her and gave her a little warm bread and milk. Then he took the three puppies away in the warm blanket and handed one of them to someone who waited outside the door of the back kitchen. Finn, with one sleepy foster brother, was replaced in the hamper near the kitchen stove.

A couple of hours later, the foster mother began to worry and to wish that her puppies would come and take another meal. At about the same time Finn and his diminutive companion in the hamper began to worry and to wish that they could have another meal. Ten minutes after that they were carried down to the coach house and put to nurse again. While they fed vigorously, the foster, apparently by accident, touched Finn once or twice with her tongue, in process of licking her own pup; and she did not growl.

"Good!" said the Master, and he sat down on a barrel of disinfectant powder to fill a pipe.

Then both puppies began to grovel and slide about the foster's legs and body, this being the natural order of things for very young puppies: to feed full, to grovel and wriggle, to sleep; and then to begin again at the beginning. But for the complete comfort and well-being of puppies at this age, certain maternal attentions, apart from the provision of nourishment, are requisite. For several minutes the foster mother plied her own offspring with every good office and severely ignored the rotund and would-be playful Finn.

The Master watched closely, but nothing happened, save that the bitch ostentatiously closed her eyes. Then instinct moved again strongly in shapeless little Finn, and he straddled the foster's nose, so that his round stomach pressed on her nostrils. There he wriggled helplessly. Then a curious thing happened while the Master leaned forward, prepared to snatch the pup from danger. The sheep dog emitted a low, angry growl, which filled Finn with uncomprehending fear and toppled him over on his fat back. But even while she growled, maternity asserted its claim strongly in the kindly heart of this soft-eyed sheep dog. Finn did not know in the least what he wanted; but the wise little sheep dog did; and, her growl ended, she rolled Finn into the required position with her nose and give him the licking and tongue-washing his bodily comfort demanded, with quiet, conscientious thoroughness. When this was over, Finn, feeling ever so much more content, sidled back to a place beside the other pup, and in a minute the pair of them were fast asleep in the warm shelter of the foster's flank. Then the Master laid down his pipe and bent forward to stroke and fondle the little sheep dog for two or three minutes, chatting with her and establishing firmly the friendship already begun between them. And then, feeling quite safe in the matter, now that the foster had once licked Finn into comfort, he went away and left the three together while he paid a visit to Tara.

Next morning, while the foster mother was being petted and fed in the garden, someone removed her own little puppy from the bed, and when she returned to the coach house, full of the contentment inspired by a good meal, exercise, and kindly petting, it was to find her bed occupied only by the big gray whelp. But she showed no more than momentary surprise and uneasiness and within the minute was busily engaged in giving Finn his morning tubbing and polishing, after which she disposed herself with great consideration in a position that made nursing an easy delight for Finn and enabled his assiduous foster mother to watch the undulations of his fat back, out of the tail of her left eye, while apparently sleeping.

The sturdy, kindly, plebeian sheep dog proved an admirable foster mother, diligent, thorough, and forgetful of nothing. It was particularly good for Finn that the sheep dog proved so sterling a soul, for though he naturally knew and cared nothing about it all, Finn received less attention during the next few days from the Master and the Mistress than they were wont to give their canine families.

The Master's doubts about Tara's health had been fully justified. Her puppies were thin and inclined to be ailing, and she herself was only just saved, by means of scrupulous care and attention and the use of drugs, from a severe illness. Meantime, another foster was telegraphed for, and an hour after this newcomer's arrival, one of Tara's pups died. The Master had no time to be greatly concerned about this because of his anxiety regarding Tara herself. He felt that another bout of the illness in which she had nearly lost her life in the early days would almost certainly be fatal, and the steps he took to stave this off kept him very busy. In addition, a carpenter had to be set to work in a great hurry to put together a suitable bed for the new foster mother in a shed in the orchard. Fortunately, the weather was very favorable, and the three puppies taken from Tara soon picked up their lost ground when they were established with their foster, an active, cross-bred spaniel-retriever.

But Finn in the coach house knew nothing of all this. Apart from anything else, he was still perfectly blind; also, he had as much of the best kind of nourishment as he was capable of absorbing and was watched over and cared for and ministered to by the loyal little sheep dog quite as scrupulously as a human baby is tended. She had only one whelp to care for, and of that one she hardly ever lost sight, even when sleeping. If the blind, foolish Finn wriggled from her side in the middle of the night, he ran no risk of taking cold, for if the sheep dog did not see him, then her instinct woke her within the minute, and up she got to nose her erring infant back to sleep and warmth and safety.

On the evening of his tenth day in the world, Finn was still perfectly blind. His eyes as yet showed no signs of opening. This rather surprised the Master when he looked in before shutting up for the night. He was quite easy in his mind now about Tara, who was almost well again, to all appearances, and lay contentedly in the den all day, having apparently forgotten not only her illness but also its causes and her puppies. She was rather listless and lackadaisical but seemed to be well content if she could lie within sight of the Master and dream. And now the Master was chatting with the sheepdog foster, after having had a good look at Finn and before shutting up for the night.

"But perhaps it is well he is still blind, for your sake, old lady," said he to the foster. "He will be a bit of a handful for you before you've done with him, I fancy. Never mind, little bitch; you must do your best for Finn, for he's a great pup."

And a great little pup he assuredly was to be sprawling across that little sheep dog's sandy flank. He covered pretty nearly as much space as a whole litter of her own kind would have occupied. His pink pads looked monstrous now; his timbers were twice the thickness you would have expected; and his shapeless, abundantly nourished body was very nearly as broad at the haunch as it was long from neck to tail. His flat black nose was remarkably broad in spite of the unusual length of the black-marked muzzle, and the Master, who had studied wolfhound puppies very closely, seemed particularly pleased about this. Finn's corners, so to say, were practically black. His body, as a whole, was of a steely, brindle gray, but the center of the back of his tail and its tip were almost black, and so were his little podgy hocks, knees, muzzle, brows (if he could be said to have any), and the hair over his gristly shoulder bones.

The light of Finn's twelfth day on earth had already filled the coach house through its back windows when the sheep dog

stirred next morning and yawned. The slight sound and
movement woke Finn, and automatically he burrowed vigorously after his breakfast without an instant's hestitation. Presently he emerged with milky nose from the foster's flanks and
meandered forth to be licked and made comfortable. The
licking ended, the foster rose and stepped off the bed to
stretch her limbs. Finn rolled rollickingly over on his back
and then staggered up and onto his absurdly large and
spreading feet. Then he backed sideways among the straw,
like a crab. Then he tried to rub one eye with one of his
mushroom-like forefeet and, failing abjectly in that, fell
plump on his nose. Staggering to his feet again, Finn turned
his face once toward the broad sunbeam that divided the
coach house in two parts from the side window; and then,
as though tried beyond endurance, he opened wide his jaws
and bleated forth his fright and distress to the world, so that
the patient little foster mother was obliged to cut her con-
stitutional short and hop back to bed, lolling a solicitous
tongue and making queer comforting noises in her throat.

But for some several minutes the puppy absolutely refused
to be comforted; and when the Master came in an hour or so
later, he understood at a glance what Finn's trouble was,
though the casual observer might well have thought there
was no particular change in his circumstances. The fact was
Finn had sustained a real shock, and his perturbation about
it lasted for nearly half an hour, after which it retired, overcome by youthful curiosity. Finn had suddenly awakened to
the fact that he was no longer blind; he had stepped, at one
uncertain stride, into a seeing life.

He spent practically the whole of that day testing this new
sense, which had come to him with so great a shock. For instance, he found that if he crawled a certain distance from
the foster in one direction, the air before him became whiter
and whiter, until at last he stubbed his toes and his nose

against it. And that was his first acquaintance with walls. Then, when he crawled in another direction, he came presently to a ledge several inches in height, and when, as the result of really herculean efforts, he had raised his fat body upon that ledge, the floor beyond jumped up and hit him very hard and left him helpless as a turtle on its back, till the foster came and lifted him back to bed in her jaws. That was how he learned that it was not wise for very small pups to climb over the edges of beds.

From this point onward, Finn's progress was rapid. Whereas till now he had seemed little more than an appendage of the sheep-dog foster mother, he now rapidly developed a personality, and a very masterful one, of his own. His eyes were idle only when he slept; and the same might have been said of every part of him. He groveled most industriously during all his waking hours until his podgy legs had hardened sufficiently to bear his weight—with many falls, of course—and then he began to scurry about on his feet. His usual style of progression at this period was to take from two to four abrupt, jerky strides, rather with the air of a fussy and corpulent old gentleman who had to catch a train, and then to subside in a confused lump, on chest and nose, with tail waggling angrily in mid-air. This was not so annoying to the gray pup as one might suppose because, though generally in a hurry, he always forgot his intended destination by the time he had taken three steps toward it, and therefore a sudden halt at the fourth seemed reasonable enough and quite an agreeable diversion.

During the third week of his life, the weather being very fine, Finn, with the other pups, was treated to long sun baths in a little fenced-in square of gravel that was covered with deodorized sawdust. These sun baths were extremely good for the pups and provided pleasant periods of rest and relaxation for the foster mothers, who, though never allowed to see each other, were each within smelling distance of the pups, one upon one side and one on the other.

On Finn's twenty-first morning he spent the better part of half an hour in the lap of the Mistress of the Kennels, learning to lap warm milk and water. First of all, he learned to suck the milky tip of the Mistress's little finger. Then, gradually, his nose was made to follow the little finger-tip into the milk; and, one way and another, he consumed during that first lesson about a tablespoonful of milk. In the afternoon he was kept for perhaps two and a half hours from the foster mother, and then he, with the other pups, made great progress in the art of lapping, though they were all glad to approach the feeding question in a more serious and practical manner on being returned to their foster mothers. Still, they had learned something, and the succeeding lessons of each following day brought quick familiarity and facility. In fact, the trouble with Finn, after two or three days, was that, in his lusty eagerness for nourishment, he generally risked the suicide's end by stumbling forward and plunging his whole face in the milk.

Toward the end of the fourth week these lessons in lapping became real meals, and the milk so consumed was always fortified with a thickening of some cereal rich in phosphates, besides minute doses of precipitated phosphate of lime, intended to stiffen the gristly leg bones of these heavy pups and increase bone development. The foster mothers had been taking this and communicating it in their milk all along.

On the morning that ended Finn's fifth week in the world, all the pups were solemnly weighed in the kitchen scales, which were brought into the coach house for that purpose. The Master stood by with a notebook, and these are the weights he recorded:

Fawn bitch .	.	10¾ pounds
Gray bitch		11¼ pounds
Fawn dog		12 pounds 3 ounces
Finn	...	14 pounds 4 ounces

In other words, at the age of five weeks and while still a suckling pup, Finn weighed as much as some full-grown prize-winning fox terriers and was similar to that breed when fully developed, in point of size, though not, of course, shapely or set. After corresponding with other breeders, the Master was confirmed in his already expressed conviction that, thus far, Finn was a maker and breaker of records.

During the week following this weighing, Finn was only allowed to visit his foster mother once each day, for half an hour or so. But the meals he lapped from a dish, in his own blundering way, included broth now, as well as milky foods, and he still slept with the foster at night. During the next week—in fine, dry July weather—all four puppies were gamboling together in the orchard, from six in the morning till six at night.

A twig, a leaf, or a stone would be endowed with the attributes of some cunning and fierce quarry, to be stalked, run down, and finally torn in sunder with marvelous heroism. The sun shone warm and sweetly over all, there beside the immemorial Sussex Downs; life and the dry old earth were very, very good—if only one's breath did not give out so soon and one's forelegs had not so annoying a trick of doubling up; and then— What was that rascally fawn pup rushing for? The Mistress with the four little dishes and the big basin? Another meal? Here goes! Bother! I should certainly have reached her first, if I hadn't turned that somersault over the fawn pup!

That was how it seemed to Finn, whose life was one long, happy play and swagger at this time. But there were moments

of a kind of seriousness, too, in which Finn had glimpses of
real life. That very night, or rather late afternoon, Finn discovered that he could bark, more or less as grown-up dogs
bark. True, his first, second, and third barks proved too
much for his unstable equilibrium, and he rolled over on his
side in emitting the noble sounds. But the fourth time he
leaned against the table leg under the oak tree and on that
occasion was able to stand proudly to observe the paralyzing
effect of his performance upon the others of his family, who
sat around him on their podgy haunches in a respectfully
wide circle and marveled fearfully at his robust prowess.
They had all yapped before, but this deep, resonant bark—
fully one in three had no crack in it—this was an achieve-
ment indeed. After a while the gray bitch pup came and
tentatively chewed Finn's backbone, with a vague idea that
the sound came from there.

When Finn was escorted—prancing drunkenly—to the coach
house that evening after his supper, the little sheep dog
within was just finishing her supper. Finn conceived the notion of showing his foster mother what he could do, and
accordingly he swaggered unsteadily into the coach house,
delivering loud barks, all up and down the scale, as he advanced. The little sheep dog (less than twice Finn's size now)
raised her nose from the dish and barked angrily in good
earnest. Finn rolled forward and sniffed in casual fashion at
her dish. Whereupon the foster growled at him quite ferociously and shouldered the great whelp out of her way. The
Master, who was looking on, nodded his head once or twice
thoughtfully.

"Yes," he said, as Finn sidled off to the bed rather crest-
fallen, "I think you may take that as your notice to quit,
my son; that's weaning. You've been a good deal on your
own lately, you know. Well, I had meant this for your last
night as a baby, anyhow."

And that was the last Finn saw of any foster mother. That was the end of babyhood and the beginning of childhood for Finn.

4: YOUTH BESIDE THE DOWNS

FINN did not have more than one solitary night for the present. His great bed in the coach house, which was twelve feet long by six feet broad, was shared the next night by the other three puppies, who had seen the last of their foster mother that morning. They whimpered a little after the last night meal, when they found themselves bereft of maternal attention, and this gave Finn an opportunity for indulging in a certain amount of swagger on the strength of his previous night's experience. He had already adopted the air of a dog accustomed to go his own way and to sleep alone. Thus from the very outset, here as elsewhere, he gave his comrades to understand that he was master and that no one must presume to trespass upon any quarter he took up as his own. All day long the four puppies had the run of the shed in the orchard, which was kept wide open. If a shower of rain came, they were bustled into this place by the Mistress of the Kennels, and there most of their meals were served to them.

At the age of five weeks Finn weighed just over fourteen pounds. Sixteen days later he weighed 22 pounds 2 ounces. Growth at the rate of just half a pound per day requires a good deal of wise feeding and care. At the age of twenty weeks Finn weighed ninety-one and a quarter pounds. Puppies' legs are easily bowed and rarely straightened. Finn and his brother and sisters were never allowed on damp ground at this period. It was rarely that they were out of the sight of either the Master or the Mistress of the Kennels for more than half an hour at a time. As the Master said, breeding champion Irish wolfhounds is no light undertaking.

But of these things Finn and his companions knew nothing. To them life was the most delightfully haphazard affair, made up exclusively of playing, sleeping, and eating, with a little occasional fighting and mock fighting (over the huge bones that were placed at their disposal to serve the purpose of toothbrushes and tooth sharpeners) by way of diversion and excitement. Their play was not at all unlike that of human children. They loved to dig holes in the ground; to hide behind tree trunks and spring out upon one another with terrifying cries and pretended fierceness. All kinds of make-believe appealed to them greatly, and to none of them more keenly than to Finn, who liked to come galloping down from the other end of the orchard to the old oak tree, making believe that he was pursued by a savage and remorseless enemy.

One morning, very much to the amazement of the pups, the Master came strolling into the orchard, followed by a huge creature of their own species, who walked with the slow and gracious dignity of a great queen. None of them guessed that this was Tara, their own mother, and Tara herself gave no sign of being aware that these were her own children. After some minutes of embarrassed, watchful uncertainty, Finn, greatly daring, ventured to step out from among his companions and approach Tara closely enough to sniff warily at her legs and tail, his own tail hanging meekly on the ground the while. Tara sniffed at him once with amiable indifference and then turned her head the other way. Two minutes later Finn had discovered that this great hound was perfectly well meaning and kindly disposed, and his habit and nature being what they were, he then placed himself at once upon terms of highly presumptuous familiarity. Having

watched their daring brother from a distance so far, the other
pups now took heart and were soon sniffing respectfully about
Tara's legs. For a moment the mother of heroes felt, or pretended to feel, mere boredom; but as the Master turned away
to look at some distant object—a diplomatic move upon his
part—Tara seemed to smile, stretched out her forelegs on the
ground, exactly as a cat will when about to play, and, again
in catlike fashion, began to spring about, around, and over
the half-fearful but wholly delighted puppies. When the
Master turned around again, the five of them, mother and
four children, were in the midst of the wildest sort of frolic,
and impudent Finn had actually reached the stage of growling at his mother with theatrical savagery and leaping at the
loose skin about her throat with widely distended eyes and
gaping jaws.

After this Tara spent most of her days in the orchard with
the pups. When tired of their frivolity, she would retire to
the roots of the oak tree and give them to understand that
they were not to bother her further, or she would leap the
gate leading into the garden, leaving her offspring gaping
admiringly upon its orchard side, and stroll into the Master's
den for an hour or so. On one occasion she opened a new
vista of life before Finn and the others. At the higher end of
the orchard, nearest to the open downs, there were a number
of rabbit earths, and one morning, when the four pups were
frolicsomely following Tara in that direction, an unwary
rabbit allowed the dogs to get between himself and the
earths. Too late the rabbit started up from the leaf he had
been nibbling and headed for his burrow. Tara bounded forward and cut off his retreat. Wheeling then at a tangent, the
rabbit flew toward the far end of the orchard, where there
was a gap in the fence. Tara was after him like the wind, her
puppies excitedly galloping in her wake, yapping with de-

light. Halfway across the orchard Tara overtook the rabbit, and her great jaws closed upon the middle of its body, smashing the spinal column and killing it instantaneously. A moment later, Finn was on the scene in a frenzy of excitement. Tara drew back, eying the dead rabbit with lofty unconcern. Finn, on the other hand, endowed the poor dead little beast with the dangerous ferocity of a live tiger and sprang upon it, snarling and growling desperately. Round and round his head he whirled the rabbit till his throat was half choked with fur, and by that time the other puppies butted in, each snatching a hold where it could and tugging valorously. Then it was that the Master arrived, attracted by the noise of the youngsters' yapping, and the pups saw no more of their victim.

But this brought a new interest into Finn's life, and much of his time now was spent in the neighborhood of the rabbit earths. Many glorious runs Finn had after venturesome rabbits in that corner of the orchard, but he was not fleet enough as yet to catch them, and possibly his jaws could hardly have managed the killing in any case. But even so, he experienced great joy in stalking, hunting, and lying in wait.

On a glorious mellow afternoon in September, when the four pups, captained as usual by Finn, were having great fun with a hammock chair, from which they had managed to tear the canvas, they looked up suddenly, and not without some sense of shame, to see three people strolling into the orchard from the garden with Tara. There was the Master and the Mistress of the Kennels and a stately white-haired lady, who fondled Tara's beautiful head as she walked. Tara was walking with great care and delicacy to make the fondling easy. She had no idea who the lady might be but yet remembered having met her before upon more than one occasion. This was the lady from Yorkshire who had been the generous means of restoring Tara to the Master. She was staying now in Sussex for a few days and had been asked to come to the house beside the downs to see Tara's children.

"You have not disposed of any of them yet, then?" said the lady to the Master.

"Oh, no; I should not have thought of doing that until you had an opportunity of making your choice," he replied. "That is a small return for your gift of Tara herself; but I should like to think of your having one of this family, and it would make me unhappy if you were to deny me the oppor-tunity of giving you your real choice. That was why I asked you to come today."

The three were seated now, so that they might observe and admire the family at leisure.

"That gray dog there is Finn When he was weighed yester-day, he scaled nine pounds more than the biggest of the other three, and they are as big as any whelps of their age I have seen. That gray dog is going to be the biggest Irish wolf-hound bred in our time, in my opinion; and if you choose him, he will do you credit. He should be a great champion one day."

"It is very, very good of you, and I shall be delighted to have one of Tara's children."

And then the visitor stopped, gazed thoughtfully at the puppies. Her kind heart was a good deal moved, and she guessed—more than the Master gave her credit for guessing—how much hope and pride he had centered on the rearing of Finn. When the visitor spoke again, it was to say slowly:

"Finn is quite splendid—there is not a doubt of that—and I can easily believe he will do all that you expect of him. But if I may be quite frank, what I should really like most would be to have a female. I should then feel that I not only had one of Tara's children of this family but also that I had a possible future mother of heroes. But—perhaps you want to keep both females or to dispose of them otherwise?"

It was with an undeniable thrill of pleasure that the Master hailed the unexpected chance of being able to keep Finn. He had made up his mind that Finn would be chosen and was quite prepared and glad to make the sacrifice; but it was a notable sacrifice, and if the same end could be served without losing Finn, why that was blithe news. But honesty and real gratitude made him point out to the visitor that she might never again have the opportunity of obtaining the kind of hound that Finn would make. However, she stuck to her preference for a daughter, and so it was decided.

A week later another visitor came, this time from Somerset, and his choice fell upon the fawn dog after half an hour spent in trying to tempt the Master to part with Finn.

So the fawn dog whelp went, and Finn stayed with the gray bitch pup, and Tara's family was thus reduced to two. The Master said that as he had sold only one puppy of the family so far, he really could not afford to keep Finn's sister; but however that might be, he kept her for the present, and now that there were only two of the youngsters, they began to live more like grown hounds. As autumn advanced, the pair were gradually given more and more in the way of grown-up privileges. They learned to come into the den with Tara and to behave themselves with discretion when there. They never saw such a thing as a whip, but the Master spoke to them with all the sharp emphasis of a growl when original canine sin tempted them to the chewing of newspapers or the attempt to tear rugs. Also, they learned much from Tara of the deportment and dignity that becomes a wolfhound. In the latter part of November, their meals were reduced in number from four to three a day, and they were presented with green leather collars with the Master's name engraved in brass. These were for outdoor wear only, outside the doors of the home premises, that is, and with them came lessons in leading, which required a good deal of patience on the part of the Mistress of the Kennels, for after the first two lessons, which were given by the Master, much of the teaching work fell to her.

Early in the morning, as a general thing, the Master took Tara and the two youngsters out on the Downs, and these were altogether delightful experiences for Finn and his sister. It was on one of these occasions, and just after entering his sixth month, that Finn tasted the joy and pride of his first kill. He had started with Tara after a rabbit, which had scurried out from behind a little hillock no more than ten paces distant. The rabbit wheeled at a tangent from under Tara's nose and, as it headed down the slope, was bound to cross Finn's course. The gray whelp's heart swelled within him; his jaws dripped as he galloped. The fateful moment came, and the whelp seized his prey precisely as Tara would have seized it, a little behind the shoulders. It was bad for the rabbit, because Finn was neither practiced nor powerful enough to kill instantaneously as his mother would have done. But his vehemence in shaking was such that before Tara reached his side, the quarry was dead. Tara sniffed at the dead rabbit with the air of an official inspector of such matters and then sat up on her haunches to indicate that she had no wish to interfere with her son's prize. As for Finn, he was uncertain what course to adopt. The rabbit was very thoroughly killed; killed with a thoroughness that would have sufficed for half a dozen rabbits. A number of obscure instincts were at work in Finn's mind as he jerkily licked, withdrew from, and nosed again at his first kill. In the main his instincts said, "Tear and eat!" But he was not hungry. The Master believed in giving the dogs a snack before the morning run and breakfast after it, because this prevents a dog being anxious to pick up any more or less edible trifle of an undesirable kind that he may meet. And, then, there were other instincts. It was long, very long, since Finn's kind had been killers for eating purposes. Finn was undecided in the matter. He certainly would have allowed no dog to take his quarry from him; but the matter was decided for him when the Master arrived on the scene and picked up the rabbit by its hind legs. Finn jumped to catch it in his jaws; but the Master spoke with unmistakable decision when he bade Finn drop it, and there the matter ended, except as a proud and inspiring memory and ground for added swagger on Finn's part.

In the quiet corner of Sussex, where Finn was born, it was the rarest thing for the wolfhounds to meet another dog; but it did occur at times, and then it was odd to see how strong the instinct of their race was in the whelps. They seemed to take it as a matter of course that other dogs must be lesser creatures and that, as such, they were to be treated with every sort of courtesy, patience, and good humor. Finn and his sister never made advances, but they would stand politely still while the stranger sniffed all around them. For pups in their first half-year, they were extraordinarily dignified. The notion of snapping or snarling at a stranger, human or brute, simply never occurred to either of them, never for an instant. That there were certain creatures whose part it was to be chased and killed seemed evident to Finn, but that there was any created thing in the world to be feared, mistrusted, hated, or snapped at, he did not believe.

5: THE ORDEAL OF THE RING

FINN'S first winter was a mild one, and it passed without his noticing anything remarkable in climatic conditions. But spring asserted itself notably in his veins and appeared to enter into a partnership with his lusty youth and wholesome, generous scale of living to speed the young wolfhound's growth in wonderful style. Long, slow trots along the Sussex highways and byways, behind the bicycle of the Master or the Mistress, hardened Finn's round feet without ever overstraining his young legs, for the reason that the pace was always set with special reference to his capabilities.

On the morning of his first birthday, Finn, with his sister Kathleen and Tara and the Master, walked down to the little local railway station and was weighed. He weighed one hundred and nineteen pounds, exactly twenty-six and one-half pounds more than his sister and thirteen pounds less than his mother. With the standard pressed down upon his shoulder bones, he stood within an eighth of an inch of thirty-five inches in height (The height of wolfhounds is measured from the shoulder to the ground, not from the head.) It must be remembered that although some dogs reach their full development in one year from birth, Irish wolfhounds are not really fully developed before the end of the second year, though they may be said to attain their full height, and probably their full length, in about eighteen months. But he was a noble-looking young hound, even on this day that, technically, saw the end of his whelphood.

And then came three more months of Sussex downland summer, the hunting of innumerable rabbits, out-of-door days that were fifteen hours long, and a steadily increasing amount of slow road exercise, for which Finn was still forti-

fied by three good meals a day. In early October the Master
devised a new game, tolerably amusing in its way but rather
lacking in point and excitement, Finn thought. A ring was
marked out in the orchard by means of a few faggots being
stuck into the ground at intervals, and in the center of this
ring the Mistress of the Kennels would take up her stand as
a sort of director of ceremonies. Then, sometimes with the
assistance of the maidservant and the gardener, and sometimes a couple of village lads, Tara and Kathleen and Finn
would be led gravely around and around, and to and fro, by
the Master, while all their movements were closely watched
from the center of the ring. At first Finn found this a good
deal of a nuisance, because he disliked having a lead attached
to his collar; his inclination was to pull against it sideways.
Before him always, however, he had the gracious example of
his beautiful mother, who never did more than keep the lead
nicely tight while she marched around, with her head well
up, her tail hanging in a graceful, sweeping curve, and her
whole body radiantly expressive of alertness. Gradually it was
borne in upon Finn that these were matters that touched his
reputation, his pride, his belief in himself; that he, Finn, was
being observed and judged with regard to his appearance and
deportment. At the end of a week he could march as sedately
as Tara herself, bound forward with the springy elasticity of a
tiger cat at a touch of his flank from the Master's hand, stand
erect on his hind feet, with one forepaw on the Master's forefinger raised shoulder high, or fall to attention with hindquarters well set out, forefeet even and forward, head up, and
tail correctly curved, in the position of a thoroughbred hack-
ney at rest. It was great fun to find how easily commendation
could be earned from the Master in this simple manner, for
Finn never realized that quite a number of hours of patient
instruction and practice had been devoted to the attainment
of this end.

Then there came a mid-October morning when, in place of the early scamper on the Downs, Finn and Kathleen were given a light breakfast a little before daylight arrived and after that were treated to an unusually elaborate grooming. Finn had an exciting sense of impending change and adventure, and even Tara seemed moved to a stately kind of restlessness, which kept her pacing the den as though performing a minuet instead of sitting or lying at her ease. Tara seemed to be a good deal moved and excited when two bright nickel chains, with queer little tin medals attached to them, were produced and fitted on two new green collars for Finn and Kathleen. (Finn and Kathleen had never seen dog chains before and paid very little heed to them now.)

Tara watched them wistfully as they all filed out of the stable-yard gateway to the road and then, with the philosophy born of honored age and matronhood, returned to the den and lay down with her muzzle on the Master's slippers.

Finn was weighed on the station platform that morning and turned the scale at one hundred and thirty-nine pounds, with nine months still before him for "furnishing."

And then a train came roaring into the station, and Finn and Kathleen, who up till now had only occasionally seen trains from a distance, lowered their tails and pulled back a little on their chains. The Master had a pleasant way with people like railway guards, and this particular train had not very many people in it. Accordingly the two young hounds presently found themselves in a passenger compartment, the door of which was locked. So chains were removed, and while Finn stood with his nose against the glass of one window, Kathleen, facing the other way, had her nose against the opposite window. When the train started with a jerk, Finn had his first abrupt sensation of travel, and he did not like it at all. It seemed to him that the ground was suddenly snatched from under him, and then he saw trees and posts and houses flying bodily past him. He barked loudly at one little flying house, which seemed almost to brush the window against which his nose rested, and the Mistress of the Kennels laughed at him as she placed a hand caressingly on his neck. Finn did not again bark at a flying house or tree; but though the whole experience interested him very much, he was greatly puzzled by some of the phenomena connected with this railway journey.

In due course, but not before Finn had become comparatively blasé as a traveler and more than a little weary of the whole thing, the chains were put on again, and the hounds were led out from the train into the midst of a crowd of strange people. Finn had no idea that there were so many people in the world as he found pressing about him now. Many of them were leading dogs on chains. Finn's attitude toward these strange dogs was one of considerable reserve. He was very self-conscious; rather like a young man from the country who suddenly and unexpectedly found himself in the midst of some fashionable crush in London.

New experiences were crowding thick and fast upon Finn and Kathleen just now. After rubbing shoulders with this astonishing crowd for some minutes, they found themselves face to face for the first time in their lives with a flight of steps. True, they each felt a soothing hand on their shoulders, a hand they knew and loved, but the thing was disconcerting nonetheless. At first glance these steps obviously called for small leaps and bounds as a mode of progression. And yet, when one took ever so small a leap, one's nose inevitably came into sharp contact with the legs of strange humans who climbed in front; a distinctly unpleasant experience, because undignified, and implying a desire for familiarity that Finn by no means felt.

However, an end came to the steps at length, and then, after walking some distance in the open road and being al-

lowed to run loose for a few minutes in a quiet street, full of
strange, strong smells and a curious absence of air, Finn and
Kathleen were led into a large building, bigger than the
orchard at home and containing, besides countless humans,
all the dogs that ever were in all the world, all talking in-
coherently and together. At least, that was how it struck Finn
and Kathleen. As a matter of fact, there were some thousands
of dogs in the Crystal Palace that day, for it was the opening
day of the great annual Kennel Club Show, the biggest society
event of the year among dogs.

It is difficult to conceive precisely how great an ordeal it
was for Finn and Kathleen to face when they were led down
the length of this great building to their own particular
bench among the other Irish wolfhounds, of whom there were
some thirty or forty present. For fifty yards or more they
walked down an aisle between double rows of benches, every
yard of which was occupied by terriers of one sort and another, all yapping and barking at the top of their respective
registers. Finn and Kathleen, up till that morning, had never
been at close quarters with more than one dog at a time and
had never seen more than about a dozen dogs altogether outside their own breed. The noise of barking, the pungency and
variety of smells, and the crowded multiplicity of doggy personalities were at first overpowering, and Finn and his sister
walked with lowered tails, quick-shifting eyes, raised hackles,
and twitching skin. But pride of race and the self-confidence
that goes with exceptional strength soon came to Finn's aid,
and by the time he reached his own bench, his tail was carried
high and muzzle also, though he walked with unusual rigidity
and at heart was far from comfortable.

Though the benches were continuous, the space allotted to
each dog was divided from that of the next dog by a strong
galvanized iron network, and each dog's chain was fastened
to the back of his bench. Finn had his sister upon his right

and (though he never suspected it) his redoubtable sire, the great Champion Dermot Asthore, on his left.

Heavy-coated, massive old Dermot Asthore took no more notice of Finn than of the rest of the show. He was supremely bored, and since he was perfectly aware that the show lasted three days, his immediate prospect disgusted him. But Finn was not otherwise neglected. The Mistress of the Kennels had a little campstool, and on this she sat midway between Finn and Kathleen. Finn also had the Master's bag in his section of the bench; and that was rather nice and companionable Also, the Master himself seemed seldom to be far away. He flitted to and fro, generally in conversation with somebody, and was always followed, for so long as he was in sight, by the eyes of Finn and Kathleen. In his hand he carried a yellow book, which told him the names of every dog in all that vast assemblage.

The Mistress of the Kennels was studying a similar book, and if Finn, whose muzzle at this time was just above her shoulder, could have read, he would have seen that she was busy with the Irish wolfhound section of the catalogue. This showed her that there were three separate classes for Irish wolfhound dogs and three for bitches of the same breed—Open, Limit, and Novice; with first, second, and third prizes to be won in each class. The Open classes were for all and any Irish wolfhounds of each sex; the Limit classes were for such as had not previously won more than six first prizes; and the Novice classes were for hounds that had never won a first prize in any show. There was also a Junior class for hounds of both sexes under the age of eighteen months. In the Open dog class there appeared the names of no fewer than two fully fledged champions and two other fully developed hounds that were already within measurable reach of championship honors; besides several other wolfhounds of high repute and proved prowess as prize winners at shows.

In the Open bitch class there was one champion entered and four or five others of whom great things had been predicted. In the other classes it was evident that competition would be brisk. In the Limit class, for example, were several hounds well past maturity who had already won at other shows as many as four and five first prizes. The Novice classes included the names of some extremely promising hounds, several of whom had already won second and third prizes elsewhere. In the Junior class there were four other entries, besides those of Finn and Kathleen. But Finn and Kathleen had been boldly entered right through in all classes for which they were eligible. Old breeders who had not seen them smiled over the breeder's enthusiasm in entering fifteen-month-old youngsters in Open classes, where they would meet old champions, whose very names carried great weight, both with the judges and the public.

Now and again, however, an old breeder, passing leisurely along the benches, would pause when he had passed Kathleen and, after a quick glance back, return to Finn's place, looking up his number in the catalogue and gazing at the young hound with a gravely calculating eye. "Fifteen months old!" muttered one of these, glancing to and fro between his catalogue and Finn. "H'm! By old Dermot—Tara. Yes. Finn. Ah!" And so on down the benches. Finn had a notion that these men knew a good deal; they had a knowledgeable way with them. Finn would have obeyed them readily. That was how their manner impressed him.

By the time Finn had to some extent exhausted the first novelty of his surroundings and was contemplating the desirability of sleeping off some of its effects, the Master came along with something of a rush, chains were unsnapped, and Finn and his sister were taken down from the bench. A number of other wolfhounds were leaving the bench at the same time and being led in the direction of a fenced-in judging ring (square in shape, by the way) at one end of the building. The dog classes for Irish wolfhounds were about to be judged, and the Mistress of the Kennels brought Kathleen along, though her sex was not to be judged for some time, because she knew the youngster would be unhappy if left alone on the bench. The Master was leading Finn, and before they entered the ring, he passed his hand solicitously over the dog's immature brows and beard once or twice. The Mistress found a place for herself beside the ring with Kathleen, which not only gave her a good view of the judging but also showed her plainly to all in the ring. This was for Finn's special benefit. And then the Master walked into the ring with Finn and took up his place next to the lady who led the grand old hound who had sired Finn—Champion Dermot.

In the center of the ring, accompanied by a busy steward with a sheaf of notes in his hand, stood the judge of Irish wolfhounds, a man grown gray, white-haired indeed, in the study of dogs. No man living could claim to know more of Irish wolfhounds than this white-haired judge, who stood in the center of a ring formed by all the greatest aristocrats of the historic breed.

"Move them around, please," he said quietly. "Keep them moving as freely as possible."

Finn was the only hound in that ring under two and a half years of age, and Finn was just fifteen months old, a child among the acknowledged leaders and chieftains of his race. One noticed it in the comparative angularity and legginess of his build. He carried less flesh than the others, was far less set; in a word, they had "furnished" and Finn had not. The Mistress of the Kennels, from her place beside the ring, noticed these things and sighed for the soaring ambition that had led to the entering of this tyro in Open class.

"Finn, boy!" said she, in an impressive, long-drawn whisper, as Finn passed her place. The youngster's ears lifted, and his fine neck curved superbly as he looked around at the Mistress. And just then the Master bent over him, whispering close beside his ear.

"Chu, chu, chu-u-u, Finn!" whispered the Master. And that was a nonsense word connected with two things only: the unexpected rising of a rabbit ahead and the game in which Finn had been led around a ring in the orchard at home. And, to be sure, there was the Mistress of the Kennels looking on all the time, and Finn and the Master walking around, and—

And it was thus that Finn passed a judge at a dog show for the first time. It was thus that he realized that it was a show; that he, Finn, was being judged, compared with others of his kind. From that moment Finn showed the best that was in him to show, with an air as kingly as that of any of his warrior ancestors in the ancient days when they were the friends and defenders of kings, the companions in sport of great chieftains When next Finn approached the judge in the march around, the Master touched his flank, and he rose up to his full, towering height, his forepaws higher than a man's head, and the Master pretended to rebuke him with, "Down, Finn! Down, you rascal!" But Finn knew well, by his tone, that all was well and his own appearance most imposing. The judge, in the center of the ring, chewed the end of his pencil reflectively, and now and again he said, "That will do, thank you!" to some exhibitor, and that exhibitor withdrew from the ring with his hound, wearing an elaborately assumed air of indifference or relief and feeling much real chagrin. Occasionally the judge would merely wave his hand for the same purpose, with a nod to some particular exhibitor.

During about the fifth or sixth march around, the judge

waved his hand and nodded to the Master with a murmured remark. The Master's face fell, and as he drew abreast of the opening in the side of the ring, he moved out slowly with Finn. To him then came a steward, fussily official. He was not to withdraw from the ring, it appeared, but only to take up his stand in one corner of it with Champion Dermot Asthore, Champion Munster, and a magnificent hound named Cormac. The judge was making notes on slips of paper now, and in another minute or so the ring was empty, save for the three hounds mentioned and Finn.

And now there came the most searching sort of examination of these four wolfhounds, who were drawn up in a row before the judge. Teeth, eyes, claws, all were in turn closely scrutinized by the man who had weighed and studied such matters for half a century. Muscles and joints were carefully felt, and all in a manner which no self-respecting hound could take exception to. Then the four hounds must walk around once more in single file. Then they must run to and fro, singly. And, lastly, they must stand together to have the measuring standard applied to their shoulders. Young Finn was the last to come under the standard; and the judge measured him four times over before he would admit himself correct in pronouncing Finn a full thirty-five and a half inches at the shoulder. "And I may say, sir, the biggest hound I ever measured. Fifteen and a half months, you say? Remarkable, sir." And this judge knew more about Irish wolfhounds than any other man living.

Cormac's master was told that he could stand aside, and a murmur went around the ring of spectators to the effect that Cormac was the winner. Then Champion Munster was told to stand aside, and the crowd placed him second. And then the judge spent five reflective minutes in pondering over Champion Dermot Asthore, the most famous Irish wolfhound

of his day, and young Finn, his son, and the son of beautiful
Tara. The crowd wondered which of these two was to have
third prize, the celebrated old champion or the tyro.

At last the judge drew back, saying, "That will do, thank
you!"

The crowd surged around the notice board. Excitement
ran high now, for this was the most important wolfhound
class of the whole show, and the stewards were approaching
the board to pin up the winning numbers. The Master
glanced across at the Mistress of the Kennels and stooped
then to fondle Finn's ears and murmur nonsense words to
him. Then he, too, pressed forward to the notice board and
read the awards thus:

1st	No. 247
2nd	No. 248
3rd	No. 261
V.H.C.	No. 256
H.C.	No. 259

Not daring to be quite certain, the Master drew out the
little medal from beside Finn's collar and read again on it
Finn's number: 247. By this single judgment, then, Finn was
declared winner of the Open class for Irish wolfhound dogs,
and that meant that, unless a bitch could be found to beat
him, Finn also had won the Challenge Shield for best Irish
wolfhound in the show. Champion Dermot Asthore, his sire,
came second, Champion Munster third, Cormac very highly
commended, and a dog called Patrick highly commended.

A moment later the Mistress of the Kennels was in possession of the great news, and her arms were about Finn's
neck, while Finn nosed the momentarily neglected Kathleen's muzzle.

"You great, beautiful Finn, do you know you are first? Do

you know you've beaten all the champions?" she said. And
Finn nuzzled her shoulder and wondered why she was in
any doubt about his recognition of a thing so obvious. But
it was a very great triumph all the same; the greatest triumph
that had ever fallen to a breeder of Irish wolfhounds, as some
of those who hastened to congratulate the Master now were
careful to point out.

"For a fifteen months' novice, you know, against two champions and a hound like Cormac—wonderful!" they said. But
all were agreed that Finn justified the award. "He's the tallest
hound in the breed, now," said the judge, as he passed that
way and lingered to pass his hand over Finn's shoulder, "and
he will be the biggest and finest if he lives; distinctly the
finest Irish wolfhound I have ever handled, and—I've handled
most of them." Higher tribute from such a judge no dog
could earn.

In the Limit and Novice classes Finn was awarded first
place as a matter of course. There was nothing there to beat
him. And then came the judging of the bitch classes, in which
Kathleen did extraordinarily well for so young a hound. She
won third prize in the Open class, second in the Limit, and
first in the Novice. And then four other young hounds filed
into the ring with Finn and Kathleen to be judged in the
Junior class. The other four young hounds were of a very
good sort, but they had not the development, the bone,
muscle, and stature of Finn and Kathleen, and there was not
much hesitation in the decision that placed Finn first, Kathleen second, and a youngster called Connemara third.

And then Finn had to be judged beside the winner in the
Open class for bitches, to decide who should be given the
Challenge Shield for the best Irish wolfhound in the show.
And this was a task that tried the white-haired judge's pa-
tience for a long time. The female was Champion Lady Iseult
of Leinster, and one of the most beautiful hounds of her sex

ever seen. She was fully matured, and her reputation was world-wide. Judged on "points," as breeders say, she was very near to perfection. Technically, it was difficult to find fault in her, unless that she was a shade too straight in her hocks, a fault that often goes with great stature in a hound. Finn's hocks were curved like an Arab stallion's, springy as a cat's. The judge tested the two hounds side by side, again and again, and in every way he could think of, but without coming to a decision between them. At last, after passing his hand down the hocks of the Lady Iseult, he asked that they might both be run, as quickly as possible, while led. That seemed to guide him a good deal. But it was clear that the conscientious old judge and breeder was not yet fully satisfied. Finally, he had the opening to the rings closed and a hurdle brought in. Then the Lady Iseult was invited to run at and leap the hurdle. She did so, and with a good grace, returning docilely enough to her master. Then the Master loosed Finn, and the Mistress of the Kennels called him from the far side of the ring. Finn bounded forward with the elasticity of a cat and cleared the hurdle with a perfect spring and fully two feet to spare. The judge stroked his beard, laid a hand on the shoulders of both hounds, and said:

"The young dog has it—the finest hound I ever saw!"

6: REVELATIONS

It is the custom at dog shows for the authorities to distribute certificates on colored cardboard of all the awards made by the judges. At this show of Finn's great triumph, first prize cards were all blue, second prize cards red, and third prize cards yellow. So it fell out that soon after the judging of wolfhounds was over, two red cards and two blue cards were fixed over Kathleen's bench, and the Mistress of the Kennels lavished considerable attention upon her, lest she should be moved to jealousy of Finn. The decoration of the wirework over Finn's bench was most striking.

First, there were four blue first prize cards, for his sensational win in Open, Limit, Novice, and Junior classes. Then there was a very handsome card with ribbons attached, signifying that Finn had won the Challenge Shield for the best Irish wolfhound in the show. And then there were two other blue cards telling that Finn had won two special prizes: one, a medal offered by a member of the Irish Wolfhound Club for the best hound at the show bred by its exhibitor; and another, of two guineas, offered by a well-known Irish sportsman for the biggest Irish wolfhound in the show. And so Finn sat in state beneath a sort of dome consisting of no fewer than seven trophies.

His numerous trophies won him much attention, even from the large majority who were ignorant of his great technical claims to fame. There was always a little group in front of Finn's bench, and those of his admirers who had claims upon the Master—besides many who had none—were continually begging that he should be taken down from the bench, so that they might admire his full stature. Then there were newspaper men with cameras and notebooks; and there were dealers with checkbooks. But these were given no sort of encouragement by the Master. Finn received as much attention in the evening papers that day as any leader of human society. He was conscious of more of this than you might suppose, even though he could not read newspapers; but the thing he was most keenly conscious of was the fact that he had managed greatly to please the Master and the Mistress of the Kennels. Finn felt happy and proud about this, but although he was taken down from the bench several times and led into

out-of-the-way corners where his chain could be removed and
he was able to stretch his limbs, still he became pretty thoroughly tired of the publicity and racket of the dog show before he was led out of the building at ten o'clock that night,
with Kathleen, by the Master. The Mistress had gone home
to Tara early in the evening; but the Master was sleeping
in lodgings near the Palace, which he had engaged on the
clear understanding that he was allowed to bring the wolfhounds there with him. Finn had not realized as yet that one
of the penalties of the fame that he had won lay in the fact
that he was obliged to spend another two whole days in the
show building.

On the evening of the second day of the show, while the
Master was engaged in conversation at some distance from
Finn's bench, the young hounds from the cottage by the
Downs received a visit from a man who showed the utmost
admiration for them, and particularly, of course, for Finn.
This man, whose appearance rather reminded Finn of one
whom he had heard referred to as the gamekeeper down in
Sussex, looked up Finn's name and ancestry in the show
catalogue and gave particular heed to the fine display of prize
cards over his head. He fondled Finn for several minutes,
and Finn knew by the various smells that hung about the
man that he was accustomed to mixing a good deal with dog
folk. Before turning away, this friendly and admiring man
presented Finn with a small piece of meat, which he took
from a paper bag in one of his pockets; and of all the meat
that Finn had ever tasted, this piece had the most fascinating
smell and the most exciting and pleasing flavor. He medi-
tated over this piece of meat for quite a long time, and when,
during the last afternoon of the show, the friendly stranger appeared before him again, Finn welcomed the man effusively
and, with nose and paw, plainly asked for some more of that
fascinating meat. The man chuckled and rubbed the backs

of Finn's ears in an affectionate manner for several minutes. What Finn found more to the point was that, before leaving, the man did present him with another small section of this delicious meat with the fascinating smell.

By payment of a small fee the Master was enabled to take Finn and Kathleen away from the show much earlier on that evening than before, and a few hours later they were all three being welcomed at home by the Mistress of the Kennels and Tara. The three hounds dined sumptuously and in a row, while the Master and the Mistress sat before them fighting their battles over again and discussing their triumph in the show ring. Then, the night being fine, the three were allowed to wander out into the orchard for a quarter of an hour or so before going to bed. The Master remained in his den talking.

Directly Tara reached the orchard she barked out loud, "Who's there?"—an unmistakable sort of bark one would have thought. But the Master was pretty thoroughly tired, and, perhaps, the fact that he was chatting with the Mistress prevented his understanding Tara's bark. At all events, he paid no heed to it. Tara promptly trotted across to the gate between the orchard and the open down, followed closely by Finn and Kathleen. There, much to Finn's delight, they found the friendly stranger of the show. Tara eyed the man with hauteur, as one whose acquaintance she had not made. Finn, with lively recollections of the peculiarly savory meat the stranger dealt in, placed his forepaws on the top of the gate and lolled his tongue at the man in friendly greeting. The man gave Finn a provokingly tiny fragment of the meat and rubbed the young hound's ears in the coaxing way he had. Then he stepped back a pace or two and produced a large piece of the meat.

"Here, boy! Here, Finn! Jump, then, Finn!" The gate was less than five feet high, and the seductive odor of this peculiar

meat floated just beyond it in the still night air. Finn drew
back a pace or two, and then, with a beautiful spring, cleared
the gate easily. While giving Finn the piece of meat he had
been holding, the man slipped a swivel onto the ring of the
handsome green collar, and attached to the swivel there was
a strong leather lead. The man moved on slowly, with another piece of meat in his hand, and Finn paced with him
willingly enough. When Finn had finished the next piece of
meat, he was a hundred yards away from the orchard. He
looked back then, and an uncomfortable thrill passed through
his young heart; it was a vague thrill, conveying no definite
fear or impression to his mind. Still, it was uncomfortable.
He had half a mind to go back and rejoin Tara and Kathleen, and so, tentatively, he halted. If the friendly stranger
had tried to force Finn then, there would have been trouble.
But he did not. Instead, he bent down and played with Finn's
ears and then brought another piece of meat out of his pocket.
Holding this, he moved on again; and the dog followed, forgetful now of his momentary thrill of discomfort. After all,
he thought vaguely, very likely this unaccustomed night walk
was all part of the show and its many novel experiences.
There had been night walks at the end of each show day.
When Finn had had another morsel of the meat, the friendly
stranger put another collar on his neck and removed the
green one. Then he began to trot, and Finn trotted with him
quite contentedly. Finn was always glad to run.

So the two trotted for miles through the mild still October
night, the man breathing heavily. Once something made
Finn pause suddenly; and the pause let him into a secret. The
collar he was wearing now was different from any other he
had known in his short life. If you pulled against it, it slipped
around your throat so tightly as to stop your breathing instantly and absolutely. The only thing to do was to go the
way the collar and lead pulled; then, immediately, the pres-

sure relaxed. It was a collar that had to be obeyed; that was evident.

After a time, Finn and the stranger came to a little town and walked into the yard of an inn. There another man met them, to whom Finn's friend said hurriedly, "I'll walk on. You drive with the cart after me. Don't stop till you're clear of the village."

And then Finn followed his leader out of the yard and through the quiet little village to the open country beyond. But by this time Finn was beginning to feel that the night walk had been prolonged far enough. There was no sign of any more of the aromatic meat coming his way, and he had given up asking for it and nosing the man's pocket. He thought he would like to turn now and get back to Kathleen and Tara and the Master.

Accordingly, Finn asked his leader to stop, and finding that the man took no notice, he asked again, through his nose and urgently. The man paid not the slightest heed to this, and that rather angered Finn, who was not accustomed to being ignored; so he planted his forefeet firmly and stopped dead. As the lead tightened, the slip collar pressed painfully on Finn's throat; but he felt that the time had arrived to bring this excursion to an end and so steeled himself to ignore this pressure.

The man now gave a powerful tug at the leather lead, and at that the pressure of the slip collar forced Finn's tongue out between his teeth. This was really painful, but it was clear in Finn's mind that he must go home, so he remained straining backward.

"Come on 'ere, ye brute!" growled the man savagely, and with a vicious jerk at the lead, he took a step to one side and then kicked Finn on the hindquarters as hard as he could. That was the first real blow Finn had ever received, and it taught him quite a lot. Up till this point it had not occurred to him for a moment that the man entertained any other than kindly, friendly feelings for him. He had never experienced any other sort of attitude. But this savage kick was a revelation to him. Also, it hurt. Finn turned in his tracks and plunged forward in the direction from which they had come with such sudden strength that he almost dragged the lead from the man's strong hand, and would undoubtedly have freed himself but for the slip collar. As it was, the sudden jerk nearly throttled Finn and brought him rolling on his back with all four feet in the air. Before he could rise again, the man had planted two ferocious kicks on his ribs; and Finn was thankful then to draw a free breath by moving toward his persecutor so as to slacken the pressure on the lead.

Just then the dim, smoky lights of a cart appeared at the bend in the road, twenty yards away, in the direction of the village.

"That you, Bill?" cried the man who held Finn, and an affirmative answer reached him from the cart. "Come on, then, and let's get this stubborn beast into the cart." He gave a savage jerk at Finn's slip collar as he spoke, and once more his nailed boot crashed against the bewildered wolfhound's ribs. The man had an itch of anger and brutality upon him by this time. Finn leaped sideways with a quick gasp as the man's boot struck him and the cruel collar tightened; and at this sharp movement of his great body, there in the middle of the road, the pony shied violently, just as it was being drawn in to a standstill; the cart swerved sharply into the hedge, and a cracking sound betrayed the breaking of a shaft.

This was the finishing touch required to round off the naturally vicious temper of the man who held Finn into a passion of sullen, brutal anger. He cursed unceasingly while the man in the cart made the necessary repairs with cord and a couple of sticks from the hedge; and with every curse there was a kick or a vicious blow or a savage jerk at the torturing slip collar, and sometimes all three together. Finn could have killed the man with ease; but so far, the thought of even biting him never occurred to the wolfhound. Every hour that he had spent in the world had taught him that humans were his friends, his very kindly protectors, his guardians and governors, so to say.

The man who held Finn instinctively recognized this, and the knowledge whetted the savagery of his temper and withdrew all restraint from its cruel indulgence. He had no conscious wish to injure the hound; quite the contrary, since Finn represented money to him, and the money was what he desired more than anything else; but he was tired, things seemed to be going ill with him, his temper was thoroughly roused, and the innocent cause of all this, a sensitive, living creature, was tethered and helpless beside him.

When the shaft was mended, the tailboard of the little cart was let down, and, with a savage kick at Finn's hindquarters, the man bade him "Get up, ye brute!" Another kick. Poor Finn tried to squirm forward under the cart to escape the heavy boot of his persecutor. Then he was furiously jerked backward and half throttled.

The other man was used to his friend's temper and said nothing; but he hated to see a valuable animal knocked about, just as he would have hated to see money thrown in the gutter instead of into a publican's till; so he stooped down and lifted Finn's forefeet from the ground and placed them on the floor of the cart.

"My oath!" he said, "but 'e's a tidy weight, ain't he? Up ye go, my bully boy!" And up Finn went, on the spur of another violent kick, which broke the skin across one of his hocks. The lead was now fastened close down to a staple in the floor of the cart, Finn being forced down on his side by the simple process of being knelt upon by his persecutor.

The memory of that night's drive burnt itself deep into

Finn's young mind. He never really forgot it; that is to say, its effect upon his attitude toward men and life was never completely lost. His skin was broken in three or four places; every bone in his body ached from the heavy kicks he had received; an intolerable thirst kept him gasping for every breath he drew; and his muzzle was held hard down against the grimy floorboards of the cart, while his mind was full of a black despairing fear of he knew not what. It was a severe ordeal for one who, up till then, had never even known what it meant to receive a severe verbal scolding, for one who had never seen a man's hand lifted in anger.

An end came at last to this horrible drive.

"Thank Gawd, 'ere's 'orley!" said the man who drove; and after another minute or two the little cart came to a standstill in a walled-in yard. The pony was taken out and stabled, and then the man addressed as "Matey," still sullen and sour, let down the tailboard of the cart with a jerk and dragged Finn out by the collar, allowing him to fall with a thud from the cart to the ground.

Cramped and sore beyond belief, Finn staggered to his feet. A door was opened, and Finn was jerked and dragged into a perfectly dark, evil-smelling hole, about four feet square, with an earthen floor, from which horrible odors rose. The ground in this place was filthy. It had no drainage and no ventilation, except for a few round holes in the door, which was now slammed to and locked on the outside.

"Ain't ye goin' to give 'im a drink, Matey?" asked Bill, outside.

"Drink be blowed! Let 'im wait till mornin'. I'm blessed glad this night's job's done; an' if I can't make fifty quid out 'v it, I shall want to know the reason why, I can tell yer. Big, ugly brute, ain't 'e! Strong as a mule, too. *I'd* want to be paid pretty 'andsome fer the keepin' o' such a brute; but the gent's

red 'ot ter get 'im, I can tell yer. Biggest ever bred, they tell
me."

Their very voices were a misery to the shrinking, aching,
choking Finn, who stood shuddering in his fetid den, his
sensitive nose wrinkling with horror and disgust. His need of
water was the thing that hurt him the most cruelly; but the
nature of his prison was a good deal of a torture, too. This
was a sad plight for the hero of the Kennel Club Show and
the finest living descendant of a fifteen-hundred-year-old line
of princes among dogs.

7: FINN WALKS ALONE

For a long while after the men had left the scene of Finn's
miserable captivity, he remained standing and occupying as
small a space as possible in his prison. The fastidiousness bred
in him by careful rearing told severely against Finn just now.
He had never, until this night, been without water to slake
his thirst; and never, never had he smelt anything so horrible as the earth of the little den in which he was now confined. Finn could not bring himself to move in it. He stood
shrinking by the door, with his nose near a crack beside its
hinges. For long he reflected upon the events of that night
without moving. Then, gradually, thoughts of Kathleen and
Tara, and the sweet cleanliness and freedom of his home beside the Downs, came swimming into Finn's mind, and these
thoughts seemed to add intolerably to the aching of his
bruised bones and muscles, to the soreness of those spots in
which his skin had been broken, and to the misery of the
thirst that kept his tongue protruding at one side of his jaws.

Unable to bear these things any longer, Finn turned cautiously toward the middle of his loathsome prison, and though his feet shrank from the task, scraped a hollow place in its midst of about the bigness of a washbasin. Then, treading as though upon hot bricks, he squirmed his great body around to avoid touching the walls of his prison and sat on his haunches in the hollow he had made. He was now filled with a desire to inform Tara and the Master, and, it may be, the rest of the world, about his sorry plight. And so, seated there in what he had endeavored to make the one approachably clean spot available, Finn pointed his long muzzle toward the stars he could not see and, opening his jaws wide, expelled from them the true Irish wolfhound howl, which seemed to tear its way outward and upward from the very center of the hound's grief-smitten heart, to wind slowly through his lungs and throat and to reach the outer air with very much the effect of a big steamship's siren in a dense fog. It is a sound that carries a very long way. Above all, it is a strange, mysterious, uncanny cry, and not a sound that can be ignored.

Finn was beginning the bass rumble of his sixth howl when the door of his prison was flung suddenly open, and he saw Matey, armed with a hurricane lamp and a short, heavy stick. He was still so new to the ways of Matey's kind of human that he thought his howls had brought him release, and for an instant, he even had a vision of a deep basin of cold water, a meal, and a sweet, clean bed, which his innocent fancy told him Matey might have been engaged in preparing for him. If he had not been so loath to risk touching the walls of his prison, his powerful tail would have wagged as the door opened and the clean night air came in to him. As it was, he leaned forward to express his gratitude for the opening of the door. And as he moved forward delicately, Matey's stick descended on his nose with all the weight of Matey's arm and

Matey's savage anger behind it. There was no more sensitive or vulnerable spot in the whole of Finn's anatomy. The blow was hideously painful, hideously unexpected, hideously demoralizing. It robbed Finn of sight and sense and self-respect and forced a bewildered cry from him. It planted fear and horror in a single instant in a creature who had lived in the world for fifteen months with no consciousness of either. In a few seconds of time the proudest of princes in the dog world was reduced to a shuddering, cringing object, cowering in one corner of a filthy cupboard.

Matey was not only furiously angry, he was also a good deal afraid; and that added cruelty to his anger. He had heard a number of bedroom windows raised as he crossed the walled-in yard; he wanted no inquiries about the source and reason of the weird, siren-like howls that had brought him out in his shirt and trousers. It was his business to see that there were no more howls; and the only means that occurred to his brutal mind were those he now proceeded to put into operation. He closed the door of the den behind him, and he rained down blows upon Finn's shrinking body till his arm ached, and the dog's cries subsided into a low, continuous whimper, the very essence of shame, anguish, fear, and distress. Then when his arm was thoroughly tired, he flung the stick viciously into Finn's face, went out, and locked the door.

For a long time Finn was conscious of nothing but fear and pain and misery. He really had been very badly handled, and though he knew it not, one of his ribs was broken. After an hour or two, he became perfectly silent and began, tentatively and in a half-hearted way, to lick some of his bruises and abrasions. Then, before this task was half accomplished, the exhausted wolfhound fell into a fitful sleep just before daybreak. When he woke, fully a couple of hours later, much of his pain and misery remained with him; but the fear had given place to other feelings, chief among them being the

determination to escape from Matey's dominion. His own
short experience of life gave Finn nothing to draw upon in
coping with the situation in which he now found himself.
He was drawing now, not upon teaching or experience, but
upon instinct. He was acutely conscious of the determination
with which instinct supplied him to seize the very first opportunity of getting clear away from his present environment
and from Matey. This was only the surface of the lesson instinct taught him. There was a lot more in the lesson that
would permanently affect Finn's attitude toward humans and
toward life itself. But the surface was the immediate thing. to
win freedom and never to trust Matey again.

The first result of Finn's lesson was that he examined the
whole of his prison very carefully by the aid chiefly of his
sense of smell and touch. There was hardly any light in the
place. His nose was very sore because Matey's stick had
knocked a large piece of skin from it and bruised it badly.
Also, the smell of every part of Finn's prison was revolting
to him. But, though with sensitively wrinkled nostrils, Finn
made his examination very thoroughly. And in the end he
decided that he could do nothing for the present. Three sides
of his prison were brickwork, and the fourth, the door, presented no edge or corner that his teeth could touch. So Finn
sat still, waiting, listening, and watching, with his tongue
hanging out a little on one side of his mouth by reason of the
horrid dryness that afflicted his throat. And every hour that
he waited brought greater strength to his determination, besides teaching him something in the way of patience and
caution.

Presently, the waiting Finn heard heavy footsteps in the
yard outside, and the muscles of his body gathered themselves
together for action. The door opened, and Finn saw Matey
standing there with a stick and a chain in his hand. Instinct
told Finn on the instant that he must at all hazards avoid

both the stick and the chain; but, more than anything else, the chain.

"Come 'ere!" said Matey. And Finn came But whereas Matey had reckoned on a slow movement, in the course of which his hand would have fallen on Finn's slip collar preparatory to fixing the chain on that, the movement was actually very swift and low to the ground and resulted in Finn's passing out scathless into the walled-in yard.

The yard was quite safe. Matey was not perturbed, and moreover, having slept soundly and breakfasted copiously, he was, for him, in an amiable mood Still, he had no wish to waste time, and he wanted to overhaul his plunder and groom Finn a little before the prospective purchaser arrived. So Matey turned around, leaned forward with a hand resting on one knee, and tried to twist his features into an ingratiating expression as he said:

"Here, then, good dog! Come on, Finn! Here, boy!"

But instinct made Finn's intelligence upon the whole superior to Matey's in this matter, and having already satisfied himself by means of hurried investigation that at present he could not escape from the walled-in yard, the wolfhound stood half a dozen paces distant from the man, waiting, with every nerve and muscle at concert pitch. The man moved forward, with hand outstretched invitingly. The wolfhound moved backward, with hackles slightly raised. Thus they followed each other around the little yard perhaps six times, the distance between them being maintained with nicety and precision by Finn. Then Matey's mental inferiority appeared. He was expecting very shortly now the man from whom he hoped to receive his reward—the price of Finn. His intelligence, such as it was, told him that strategy would now be necessary to enable him to lay hands on the wolfhound; but even while recognizing that, he could not refrain from angrily flinging his chain in Finn's face, after his sixth promenade

of the yard, and cursing the dog savagely before retiring into
the house to prepare a stratagem.

Finn did not snarl as the chain struck him. Instinct had
not carried him so far from education. But he barked angrily
and bounded to one side. While the man was away, Finn examined the gate of the yard through which he had been
driven on the previous night, and though it rattled hopefully
when he plunged against it with his forepaws, raised high
above its fastening, it remained solidly closed.

As Finn turned away from the doors of the yard, Matey
appeared from the house, holding in one outstretched hand a
piece of the same kind of meat with which he had seduced
Finn into accompanying him on the previous evening and
calling the hound to him in a friendly tone. But Finn had
learned a good deal since his first taste of that savory meat—a
good deal more than the man who offered the meat had
learned in the same time. Taking the middle of the yard in
order to leave himself ample space for retreat, he remained
watchfully regarding Matey and refused to advance a step.

Matey cursed the wolfhound angrily, but that did not in-
cline Finn to trust him any the more. Then the man advanced a little in his strategy and tossed a piece of the meat
onto the ground before Finn to inspire confidence. But Finn's
mistrust was too profound to admit of his stooping to pick
this up. He was not very hungry, in any case; and if Matey
had been an observant creature, or even one who used his
memory wisely, he would have known that the offer of drinking water would have been infinitely more tempting to Finn
than any quantity of savory meat.

Then, his petty strategy exhausted and his paltry measure
of self-control with it, Matey started to chase Finn with a
stick. Now and again he succeeded in getting a blow home
as Finn wheeled and leaped before him within the narrow
limits of the yard; and every time the stick touched him Finn

barked angrily. This performance was extremely bad for
Finn. It was calculated to break down some of the most valuable among his acquired qualities, the characteristics that he
acquired with his blood through many generations of wisely
bred and humanely reared hounds. In one sense, it was more
harmful than the merciless and unreasonable punishment
of the previous night because there was no faintest hint of
punishment about it, not even of the sort of punishment that
had followed his howling. That had had the bad qualities of
cruelty and unreasonableness, unjustifiableness. This was not
punishment at all; it was sheer savagery, the savagery of a
running fight in which the man, though he might hurt occasionally, could not conquer. And that is a most demoralizing
sort of happening between dog and man.

Matey was rapidly becoming exhausted and in another moment or two would probably have flung his stick at Finn and
given up his senseless pursuit when, just as the wolfhound
bounded forward from under his stick at the house end of
the yard, the gate leading into that yard opened and Bill appeared. In an instant Finn had sprung for the opening. Bill's
legs were thrust from under him, and as he stumbled, with
one hand on the ground and an oath on his lips, Finn reached
the open road outside. Behind him, for a moment, Finn
heard a hurried scrambling and a deal of broken, breathless
whistling and calling aloud of his name. And then he heard
no more from the place of his captivity and anguish, for he
was already nearing the limits of the little town and galloping hard for the open country, over the road by which he
had traveled some ten hours earlier in Matey's cart.

Finn galloped for about three miles, his heart swelling
within him for joy in his freedom. Then, gradually, his gait
slackened to a canter and then to a trot, and finally the sight
of a wayside pond brought him to a standstill. After a
mechanical look behind him, he walked into the water and

drank and drank and drank till he could drink no more. Finn
emerged from the pond with heaving flanks and dripping
muzzle, conscious now of some of his hurts and bruises but
licking his wet chops with satisfaction, and supremely glad
of his freedom He lay down on the grass near the pond and
proceeded to lick those of his wounds and bruises that were
within licking reach and to pity himself regarding the sharp
pain in his side that his broken rib was causing. With renewed confidence, the young hound stretched himself out
and presently began to doze.

While Finn dozed, a cart approached him from the town he
had left behind, and in this cart were two extremely angry
men. Bill wanted his share of Finn's price; Matey wanted his
larger share of that price, and he also wanted badly to have
Finn securely tied up in a convenient position for being
soundly beaten. His heavy mouth twitched viciously as Matey
thought about it. Suddenly Bill pulled the pony onto its
haunches with a jerk.

"I'm jiggered if that ain't 'im a-waitin' for us!" exclaimed
Bill in a hoarse whisper.

Matey was out of the trap in an instant and, with meat in
his hand, was already beginning a whining call, which was
meant to be extremely ingratiating. But Finn sprang to his
feet at the sound of the cart coming to a standstill and, after
one glance at Matey, was off like a wolf down the empty
country road.

This was yet another lesson learned Finn would not be in
a hurry to rest by the wayside again. After two miles of galloping at the rate of nearly twenty miles an hour, Finn
steadied down to a fast loping gait, which would have kept
him abreast of any other road vehicle except a car, and maintained this for quite a long while. Then, because of the pain
in his side and other pains, he decided to stop. But with his

last-learned lesson fresh in his mind, he had no intention of resting by the roadside. With a twist of pain that cut into his side like a knife, he leapt a field gate and crept along the inner side of the hedge for some distance before finally curling up in a dry hollow beside a hayrick. Here, sheltered by the rick and half buried in dry hay and straw, Finn courted the sleep he needed, so that it came to him swiftly. In his sleep the young wolfhound whimpered occasionally, and once or twice his whole great body shook to the sound of a growling bark, causing two bloodshot eyes to be half opened and then mechanically closed again, with a small grunt, as Finn's muzzle drove a little deeper into the dry hay under his hocks, and he allowed sleep to strengthen its healing hold upon him.

When Finn finally woke, he gaped right in the eye of the setting sun, and all about him was the solemn silence of a fine October twilight. He yawned cavernously and, raising his haunches, stretched his huge trunk from forepaws placed far out. But, in the midst of the stretch, he gave a little smothered yelp of pain and came to earth again, solicitously licking at the ribs of his right side. Matey's heavy boot had done great execution there Slowly, then, Finn rose, and walked out into the darkening twilight of the field. Before he had covered one hundred yards, a rabbit started up from behind a bush and scurried hedgewards for its life. But the distance was too great by three yards, and Finn's jaws snapped its backbone asunder within six feet of its own burrow. This was hard on the rabbit; but it was no more than one tiny instance of the outworking of Nature's most inexorable law. Finn had killed many rabbits before this evening; but in the past he had merely obeyed his hunting and killing instinct. Now this instinct in him was sharpened by hunger, by having slept on the open earth, and by being conscious of no human control or protection. Finn proceeded to eat this particular rabbit, and that was distinctly a new experience for him and one that left him upon the whole pleased with himself.

After his meal Finn strolled along the side of the hedge till he came to a gap and then slipped through to the road. For a mile or two he trotted along the silent road with no particular object in view and then, coming to a grassy lane, turned into that and trotted for another mile or two, leaping a gate and a stile that barred his way at intervals and coming presently to a group of three large ricks. His side was aching dully, and Finn was rather unhappy over finding no sign of the home beside the Downs where his friends were and his own comfortable bed. Having allowed his mind to dwell upon this for several minutes, he sat down on his haunches near one of the ricks and howled to the stars about it all for quite a while.

It was not active unhappiness, let alone misery like that of the previous night, that moved Finn to this vocal display, but only a kind of gentle melancholy such as we call homesickness; and after five minutes of it, he curled up beside one of the ricks, after scratching and turning around and around sufficiently to make a kind of burrow for himself, and was fast asleep in about two minutes.

In the morning, long before the dew was off the grass, Finn set out to do what he had never done before: he set out deliberately to hunt and kill some creature for his breakfast. He very nearly caught an unwary partridge, though the bird did not tempt him nearly so strongly as a thing that ran upon the earth and ran fast. In the end his menu was that of the previous evening, and as he eyed its still warm and furry remains, Finn felt that life was really a very good thing, even when one had a pain in one's side and a large assortment of bruises and sore places in various other parts of one's body.

Toward midday Finn lounged into a rather large village

and did not like it at all. It stirred up in him the recollection
of Matey and his horrible environment, and he began to
hurry, impelled by a nervous dread of some kind of treachery.
Toward the end of the village he passed a pretty creeper-
grown cottage, from the door of which a policeman issued.
The policeman stared at Finn and smacked his own leg. Then
he bent his body in an insinuating manner and called to the
wolfhound, "Here, boy! Here, good dog! Come along!" But
Finn only lengthened his stride and presently broke into a
gallop. He was no longer the guileless, trustful Finn of a
week ago. The rural constable sighed as he resumed an erect
position and watched Finn's disappearing form.

"He must be the dog that's wanted, all right; reg'lar
monster, I'm blessed if he isn't. But takin' one thing with
another, I'd just as soon they catched him somewhere else
than here. Why, I reckon my missis 'ud have a fit. I don't call
it hardly right myself; not 'avin' 'em that size."

Half an hour later, to his great delight, Finn found himself
clear of roads and houses and on the warm, chalky slopes of
the Sussex Downs. These great, smooth, immemorial hills,
with their blunt crests and close-cropped, springy turf,
brought a rush of home feeling into Finn's heart, which made
his eyes misty, so that he had to sit down and give vent to
two or three long-drawn howls by way of expressing his gentle
melancholy. But Finn's nose told him plainly that he had
never before been on these particular Downs.

Toward evening he coursed and killed another rabbit, eating half of it and providing, in the other half that he left, a
substantial repast for a prowling weasel who followed in his
trail.

Something—it may have been merely the fact that the day
had not been in any way exhausting like its predecessors—
prevented Finn from being inclined to curl down and sleep
when he passed a convenient wheat rick in a valley an hour

after his supper. The night was fine and clear, and night life
in the open, with its many mysterious rustlings, bird and
animal calls, and other enticing sounds and smells, was beginning to present considerable attractions to Finn. Later on,
however, the young wolfhound began to tire of the freedom
of the night, and homesick longings rose in his heart as he
thought of the coach house and of Kathleen. It was at about
this time that Finn fell to walking along a narrow white sheep
walk, on the side of a big, billowy down, which seemed to
him pleasanter and more homely than any of the hills he had
traversed that evening Gradually the track in the chalk deep-
ened and widened a little, until it became a path sunk in the
hillside to a depth of fifteen or twenty feet, and ended in a
five-barred gate beside a road. Finn leaped the gate with a
strange feeling of exultation in his heart, which made him
careless of the sharp pain the leap brought to his side. His
nose drooped eagerly to the surface of the road, and he whimpered softly as he ran with tail swaying from side to side
and a great tenderness welling up within him.

Two minutes later he came to a white gate leading to a
shrub-sheltered garden before a small, low rambling little
house. He leaped the little gate and turned sharply to the
right in the garden. But then his way was blocked by high
doors, set in masonry, which could not possibly be climbed
or jumped. Before these gates, which evidently led to the
stables and rear of the house, Finn sat down on his haunches.
Then he lifted his long muzzle heavenward and howled
lugubriously. He continued his howling steadily for about
one minute and a half, and at the end of that time a door
opened behind him in the front of the house and a man clad
in pajamas rushed out into the garden. Finn had studiously
avoided men for these two days past now; but far from avoid-
ing this man, he rose on his hind legs to give greeting and
could hardly be induced to lower his front paws, even when

the man in pajamas had removed his caressing arms from about the wolfhound's shoulders. The man, you see, was the Master, and three minutes afterwards he was joined by the Mistress of the Kennels.

8: THE HEART OF TARA

THE Mistress of the Kennels held on to one of Finn's fore-paws as though she feared he might be spirited away from the den, even while he was being welcomed home there. The fatted calf took the form of a dish of new milk and some sardines on toast, which had been prepared for the next morning's breakfast. But this came later and was polished off by Finn more by reason of its rare daintiness and his desire to live up to what the occasion seemed to demand of him than because he was hungry. At an early stage in proceedings the Master noticed and removed the slip collar.

"Well, that disposes of the theory that Finn wandered away of his own accord," said the Master. "If the police know their business, this ought to help them." Then he turned to Finn again. "You didn't know there was a twenty-five-pound reward out for you, my son, did you? It was to have been made fifty pounds in another day or two; though if you did but know it, our solvency demands rather that you should be sold than paid for in that fashion."

While these remarks were being made, the Master was care-fully examining Finn all over, parting the wolfhound's dense hard hair over places in which the skin beneath had been broken and pressing his fingers along the lines of different bones and muscles solicitously. There was a half-spoken oath

on the Master's lips when Finn winced from him as his hand
passed down the ribs of the hound's right side.

"There is a rib broken here," he said to the Mistress, "unless I am much mistaken. When the post office opens in the
morning, we must wire for Turle, the vet. Thieving's bad
enough, but—there are some stupid brutes in this world! Finn
has been handled more roughly than an understanding man
would handle a tiger. And look at his face. Look into his eyes.
Notice his keenly watchful air, even while I am handling
him. Well, Finn, my son, you have said good-by to puppyhood
with a vengeance now. Unless I am much mistaken, he has
crowded more into the last three days than all the rest of his
life till now has taught him. The youth has gone; there is a
certain new hardness. Watch his eye now as I lift my hand!"

The Master lifted his hand with a sudden jerk, and the two
who were watching Finn's eyes saw something in them that
they had never seen in Kathleen's, nor yet even in Tara's
eyes; for neither Tara nor her daughter had ever pitted her
agility against man's brutality. They had never been clubbed
or kicked; they had never seen as far into the ugly places of
human nature as Finn; and you might brandish your arms in
any way you chose before old Tara or Kathleen, and while
the one would have blinked at you with courteous tolerance
of your foolishness, the other would have suspected you of
inventing a new game and gamboled before you like a huge
kitten.

It was not, of course, that Finn was foolish enough to dis-
trust the Master or suspect him of any hostile intention. But
certain instincts had been awakened in the young wolfhound,
and for a long time, at all events, and probably for the rest of
his life, those instincts would not again become dormant. In
some respects he may have been the better off; certainly he
was better equipped to face the world; but the Master, naturally enough, could not withhold a sigh for the old utter trust-

fulness that had held even the instincts of self-preservation in abeyance.

To a great extent, however, the Master's sympathetic anger over Finn's wounds and twinges of regret regarding the subtle changes he recognized in the hound were outbalanced by the joy he felt at seeing Finn safe in his den again. The loss of Finn had been hard to bear, and not the less hard because it came immediately after the great triumph of the show. There were the seven prize cards adorning the wall over Tara's great bed in the den; but their presence had been something of a mockery in the absence of their winner. When the Master and the Mistress finally bade Finn good night, after making him thoroughly comfortable in his own clean, big bed, the coach-house door was carefully padlocked.

It could not have been said a month later that Finn was physically the worse for his adventure in the hands of Matey. His ribs were sound once more, and all his wounds and bruises were healed, though a light-colored scar remained and would remain on his muzzle, where the dog-stealer's stick had bitten into the bone. If it had come nine months earlier, such an experience would have been bad indeed, for setbacks in puppyhood are hard to make up. But at fifteen months Finn had as perfect a physical foundation to go upon as any living creature could have.

And now came a long and rather severe winter, in which no evil thing befell Finn, and the process of "furnishing" went on in him with never a hitch of any sort and in circumstances that could not possibly have been more favorable. All day long he breathed the heartiest air in England; every day he had ample exercise and ample food, and when young summer of the next year brought him to his second birthday, Finn scaled one hundred and forty-nine pounds, and his shoulder bones just skimmed the underside of the measuring standard at thirty-six inches.

When his head was inclined upward, the tip of his nose
was more than a foot higher than his shoulder. With all four
feet on the floor, he could rest his nose on a window ledge
that was exactly four feet high. His eyes and shaggy brows
and beard, like the tip of his tail, were dark as night; there
were some extra dark hairs at his hocks, fetlocks, and shoulder blades; and all the rest of Finn was of a hard, steely gray
brindle color; the typical wolf color of northern climes, very
steely and with odd suggestions about it of ghostly fleetness,
of great speed and enduring strength. His forelegs were
straight as gun barrels, his knees flat as the palm of your
hands; his feet hard, close, round, and rather catlike, save
that his claws were more like chisels, black and hard and
strongly curved. His hind legs, on the other hand, were finely
curved, with swelling rolls of muscle in the upper thighs. The
first or upper thighs were very long and strong, curving
sharply out to hocks that were well let down and without a
hint of turn inward or outward. His loins were well arched,
his chest was deep, like an Arab stallion's, his neck long,
arched, and very strong, like the massy muscles of his fore-
arms. It was difficult to say that he had grown much since his
fifteenth month, and yet he looked a very much bigger dog,
and, above all, he looked and was very much stronger. There
was no longer anything immature or unformed about Finn.
During his next year he might possibly add half a score of
pounds to his already great weight; but on his second birthday he was set and furnished, a superb specimen of pure
breeding and perfect rearing in Irish wolfhounds.

For almost six months now Finn's only companion of his
own kind had been Tara. He had not seen Kathleen's departure from the cottage beside the Downs, and for some
days he was greatly puzzled by her absence. He even stood by
the orchard gate and growled fiercely, with the hair on his
shoulders standing almost erect, because the thought was in

his mind that Matey might have had something to do with this disappearance.

Finn need not have worried for Kathleen's sake. She had gone to a good home. Her owner paid one hundred guineas for her and would not sell her for ten times the figure. But there was no way of telling Finn these things, for though he could understand most things the Master said to him and was able to tell the Master most things he wanted to tell, yet the matter of buying and selling and its causes were naturally beyond him. He had no way of telling that the Master was in sore straits financially, though he did know that his friend was not over and above happy. Things were not prospering with the Master, and feeling that he could not part with Finn or Tara, he had been absolutely obliged to sell Kathleen.

That was by no means the end of the Master's troubles, the root of which lay in the fact that he loved the country and hated the town but was unable to earn money enough in the country to meet the various obligations with which he saddled himself and was saddled by circumstances. And so it fell out that soon after Finn's second birthday, the Master began to spend a good deal of time away from the house by the Downs. Tara liked to pass the greater part of her time in the Master's outside den with her muzzle on his slippers, but Finn was not like that. Tara was a matron getting on in years. Finn, on the other hand, was the very personification of lusty youth and tireless virility. The Mistress of the Kennels would take him out behind her bicycle while Tara lay dreaming at home, and it may be that the Mistress fancied her gentle ten- and twelve-mile runs tired Finn. She never saw him when he would set off on his hunting expeditions, in the course of which he covered every foot of the Downs for a dozen miles around. He was safe enough, too, for he would have had nothing but angry growls for any man of Matey's ilk, charmed he never so wisely with spiced meats and the

like. The weasels and the stoats, and a score of other wild
things that roamed that countryside, could have told the
Mistress of the Kennels just why Finn did not always clear
his dinner dish these days and thereby saved her an addition
to her many worries of that period. She did not like to de-
press the Master with tales of half-eaten meals, and she had
no knowledge of the half-eaten hares and rabbits and other
wild creatures that Finn left behind him on his hunting
trails.

From one point of view, Finn suffered at this stage from
the absence of the Master's eye and hand, and so did the rabbits; but, from another point of view, Finn gained. He became harder, more wily, and far more expert in hunting than
he would have been under a more disciplined regime.

There came a certain late summer's day when something
happened that Finn never quite forgot. The Master had been
away for three weeks on end, and Tara had missed him
sadly. In the evening the great bitch would often whimper
quietly as she lay outstretched, her long gray muzzle resting
on the slippers the Mistress never thought of taking from
her. Now, in the evening of the day that brought strong hints
of coming autumn with it, Finn lay beside Tara in the outside den, thinking lazily of an upland meadow, with a copse
at its far end, which he meant to hunt presently. Suddenly
there came a sound of a man's footfall on the gravel beyond
the gateway in front of the house. Tara's nostrils quivered as
her head rose. With one mighty bound she was outside the
den. The gates stood open. The Master, at the garden's far
end, called—

"Tara! Tara, girl! Here, girl!"

Finn was by Tara's flank, and he saw her leap forward,
hurtling through the air like an arrow from a box. Six great
bounds she gave, while fleet Finn galloped a good twenty
paces behind her, and then Tara stopped suddenly with a

strange, moaning cry, staggered for a moment, as the Master
ran toward her, and then fell sideways, against his knee, with
glazing eyes turned up for a last glimpse of the face she loved.
The Master was kneeling on the gravel, and Tara's shoulders
were in his arms; but at the end of two long-drawn sighs,
Tara was dead.

Finn was sniffing at his mother's back. He did not know
just what had happened, but he was profoundly conscious
that the happening was tragic and that his beautiful mother
was the victim. The shock to the Master was very great, for he
was already unhappy and he had loved this mother of heroes
very dearly But the shock to Finn, though far less complex,
was scarcely less great. He had killed many scores of times,
but it seemed that he had never seen death till now. He
recognized it clearly enough. He knew that Tara was never
going to move again; the instant his sensitive nostrils touched
her still, warm body he knew that. But there had been no
killing That was what baffled Finn and struck a kind of
terror into his heart to lend poignancy to his sorrow. One
more look he gave his mother's sightless face, this time where
it rested on the crook of the Master's arm, and then he sat
down on his haunches and, with muzzle raised high, poured
out his grief in the long-drawn Irish wolfhound howl; the
most melancholy cry in nature.

The Master had looked careworn and weary before he
called Tara to him. It was a very gray, sad face he showed
when he rose gently and bade Finn go into the coach house
and be silent. He had known that Tara's heart was weak, but
this thing that had happened he had never anticipated, and
the nature and circumstances of Tara's death were such as to
move a man deeply. In a sense, her love of the Master had
killed this beautiful hound. Her great love had burst her
heart asunder, and so she died, the very noble daughter of an
ancient, noble line.

9: A SEA CHANGE

To Finn it seemed that life was never the same after the evening of Tara's death. He did not know, of course, that changes had been set afoot during many months before his mother's end came. And in a way he was right; life never was quite the same for him. Active changes, toward which the Master's circumstances had been leading for some time past, began immediately after that strange home-coming that finally separated Finn from his own kin.

For instance, the Master seemed generally to be away from the house beside the Downs; and the Mistress of the Kennels seemed always to be busy and never to be in playful mood. Days passed without even one of those gentle runs behind a bicycle to which Finn had grown accustomed, days during which no one ever spoke to Finn except at mealtimes and the home seemed strangely silent and deserted. Finn was always locked up at night, or he would have chosen that time for hunting expeditions. As it was, however, the long days were his own, and he too devoted less and less time out of these days to the home life. He would slip through the orchard and over its gate to the open Downs; and there, roaming that countryside for hours at a stretch, he would hunt, only occasionally killing to eat and the greater part of his time hunting for the sheer pleasure of it. For so great a hound, he became wonderfully adept and cunning in the pursuit of the small creatures of the open; stalking them as silently, cautiously, and surely as a cat, and acquiring, day by day, more and more of that most distinguishing characteristic of the wild creatures: indomitable patience. Great fleetness and great strength were his by birth; tireless patience and cunning he learned in these lonely days on the Sussex Downs; and he learned

them so well that his silent, shadowy great form became a
very real terror to all the wild things of that district.

There was one wild creature, however, in this district, who
grew to know Finn well and to fear him not at all, and this
was a large male fox, born and bred in a copse not half a mile
from Finn's home. To this strong and cunning fox, Finn appeared in the light of a provider of good things, and for long
he waxed fat and lazy upon Finn's numerous kills, without
the wolfhound ever having suspected his existence. Then,
late one autumn afternoon, Finn saw Reynard descend from
a little wooded hillock and seize upon the half of a rabbit
that the wolfhound had left lying there in the valley, beside
a little brook, where he had killed it. Like a flash, Finn
wheeled and gave chase; but the fox disdained even to drop
his prize, and by reason rather of his superior woodcraft and
his knowledge of every leaf and twig in that countryside,
rather than his fleetness, Reynard was the winner of the long
race that followed.

This interested Finn more than anything that had happened for a long while. His trailing faculties, though they
had been greatly developed of late, were nothing like so
keen as those of a foxhound or a pointer or a setter, his race
having always done its hunting by sight and sheer fleetness.
But against that, the big fox had grown very lazy of late. He
had done practically no hunting at all, preferring to trail
Finn on his hunting expeditions and fare sumptuously upon
Finn's leavings. As it happened, this particular fox had never
been hunted, and during a big slice of his life he had been
wont to regard himself as the unquestioned monarch of that
countryside as far as its wildlife went.

And now, for days, Finn's great interest in life was the pursuit of the big fox. For the rest, he killed only rabbits and the
like when they came in his way; even so, he supplied ample
food for the cunning fox. At first, Finn spent his time largely

in looking for his new quarry and then giving forthright chase. But gradually he learned that the fox was his master in this work, if only by reason of its comparative smallness, which enabled it to twist and double through places that were impenetrable to the great hound who followed. So Finn fell back upon his recently acquired cunning. He killed a rabbit and left three-quarters of its carcass in an exposed, open place, while he himself crawled into a clump of brush and lay waiting, with eager, watchful eyes peering through the leaves Presently, Reynard approached from some undergrowth one hundred yards away on the other side of the kill. But he did not approach very nearly. His sharp, sensitive nose wrinkled and pointed skyward for a moment, and then, as the breeze gave him Finn's scent, he turned around promptly and trotted back to covert.

Finn gave an immense amount of reflection to this, and two days later his cunning evolved a very much cleverer scheme. He killed another rabbit and placed it in a convenient runway of the big fox's Then he trotted off on the lee side of the kill and quietly made toward his entrance to the orchard at home. But instead of entering the orchard, he circled again and, keeping religiously to leeward of his track, flew at great speed for the far end of the runway in which he had left his kill. When Reynard discovered the rabbit, he merely glanced at it and then quietly took up Finn's trail, to make sure of the wolfhound's whereabouts. This trail he followed to a point that was as near as he cared to venture to the orchard fence. Then, satisfied that Finn had gone home, he trotted back to where the kill lay, being naturally to windward all the while of Finn's second trail.

Arrived in the runway, Reynard picked up the dead rabbit and slung it carelessly across his shoulder. Then he trotted leisurely down the runway toward his own earth, where he meant to feast in security and comfort. At the end of the runway came a wide, open stretch of wasteland, on the far side of which lay the track to Reynard's cave. Well hidden by the bushes at the end of the runway on its lee side crouched Finn, every nerve tensely alert. He waited till Reynard was well clear of the runway and fairly started across the open, and then he sprang out from the place of his concealment, his leap carrying him to within a yard of Reynard's flank. The insolence of good and easy living and long mastery over the creatures that dwelt about him led the fox into perhaps two seconds of indecision in relinquishing his booty; and that cost the fox dear by reducing his starting speed. At the end of his fourth stride, he dropped the rabbit; but at the end of his fifth stride the wolfhound was abreast of him, with neck bent sideways and jaws stretched wide. Less than a second later, Finn's great jaws closed upon the back of the fox's shoulders; and that was where Finn made his first mistake. He was, for all his recent experience, quite new to the killing of such a quarry as the fox, who himself was big and strong enough for the killing of such prey as Finn had learned to hunt. The shoulders of a hare or a rabbit were easily smashed between Finn's jaws; but the shoulders of the big fox, with their mat of dense fur, were far otherwise. Finn's teeth sank deep, but they broke no bones.

Nevertheless, his weight and the force of the impact between the two brought Reynard to earth, where he rolled smartly on his back, slashing at Finn's forearm with his sharp white fangs and snarling ferociously. In the same instant almost, the fox was on his feet, but before he could leap away, Finn's jaws descended on the back of his neck, gripping him like a vice and shaking him almost as a terrier shakes a rat. With a desperate squirm the fox wriggled earthward from this terrible grip, and as Finn drew breath, stabbing at the fox with one forepaw as he would have stabbed at a still living rabbit to hold it, Reynard's fangs cut deeply into the

loose skin of his chest. As he slashed, the fox, after the manner
of his kind, leaped clear. But he had no time to run before
Finn was upon him, with a roar of awakened fury. The fox
dodged and slashed again, drawing blood from the fleshy part
of Finn's forearm. Reynard fought like a wolf or a light-
weight boxer; and after this last slash, he wheeled like lightning and flew for cover. But the wolfhound's fighting blood
was boiling in him now, and Finn swept down upon the fox,
exactly as a greyhound sweeps upon a hare. When his great
jaws closed upon the fox's neck this time, it was to kill.
Reynard squirmed valiantly; but Finn flung him on his back
and took new hold upon his throat. The fox's two hind feet,
drawn well up, scored down Finn's belly like the feet of a
lynx; but it was Reynard's last movement, for as he made it,
Finn's long fangs met in his jugular, and his warm blood
streamed upon the ground.

That was Finn's first big kill, and it marked an epoch in
his development, leaving active in him a newly wakened instinct of fierceness that had been foreign to his family for
several generations. If the big fox could have kept clear of
Finn for just two more days, he would have saved his life.
As it was, the superficial wounds the fox had inflicted upon
him were never noticed by the Master or the Mistress of the
Kennels because of other happenings in which Finn also was
concerned. His wounds were not deep, his coat was dense,
and Finn doctored himself effectively with his own tongue.

Early on the morning after his successful hunting of the
fox, Finn found several strange men about the house and
grounds. The Master had arrived home late on the previous
evening, unconscious not only of Finn's fox-hunting but also
of his foraging habits generally. All through this day Finn
pottered about the house and garden and the outside den,
observing with curiosity the behavior of the strange men

who wore green aprons. It seemed to Finn that these men were bent upon turning the whole place upside down.

The next day was one of even less comfort and more bewilderment. In addition to the men with green aprons and strongly noisy boots, there was quite a large assemblage of other people, who strode about through the rooms of the little house and in its garden, stable, and outside den as though the place belonged to them. Later on, however, these noisy menfolk drew together in one of the front rooms of the house, while one among them stood upon a kitchen chair and occasionally smote the top of a salt-box with a small white hammer. Finn prowled about in a most unhappy mood, and once the Mistress of the Kennels led him into an empty bedroom and knelt down on the floor and cried over him, while he endeavored to lick her face, whimpering the while to show his sympathy.

Then the Master and the Mistress and Finn went away together to the station, saying nothing and looking very unhappy. Finn carried his tail so low that it dragged, and its black tip picked up mud from the wet road. That night and for two subsequent nights, Finn lived unhappily in a poky London lodging with his friends; and on the third day, he walked with the Master to a railway station, while the Mistress of the Kennels drove in a cab with a mountain of baggage. Finn was not allowed in the carriage with his friends but had to travel in a van full of boxes and bags, with a rough but amiable man whose coat had shiny buttons.

Some time before this, Finn had come to the conclusion that they were all going to a dog show.

After walking some fifty or sixty yards from the train, among a great crowd of people and baggage, Finn, with the Master, entered what he supposed was the show building. The chief reason, by the way, for his conviction that he was

bound for a show lay in the fact that a long, bright steel
chain was attached to his best green collar, with its brass name
plate bearing Finn's name and the Master's. The odd thing
about this show building, however, was that there appeared
to be only two other dogs in it besides Finn; one a collie and
one an Irish terrier. Finn found these two dogs—both, of
course, unimportant small fry from his lofty standpoint—
each chained to the front part of a barrel half filled with
straw; and that seemed to the wolfhound an extremely odd
kind of show bench. But the bed to which Finn himself was
chained was a good deal more like the kind he had seen before
at shows, in that it was a flat bench, well strawed, a good foot
above the floor level; but it had solid wooden sides and roof.
And before he left, the Master fixed up some wirework before
the bench so as to shut Finn in, while on the inside of that
network a notice was hung, for the benefit of passers-by, most
of whom read the notice aloud until Finn was thoroughly
tired of hearing it. It ran like this: "Warning! Do not touch!"

After arranging this matter of the network, the Master disappeared, with a hurried wave of his hand in Finn's direction
and a "Wait there, old man!"—a rather unnecessary request
Finn may have thought, seeing that he was securely chained.

Upon the whole, Finn decided that this was the most curious show he had visited. He heard no barking beyond an
occasional yap from the Irish terrier, and among the innumerable people who passed the front of his bench, the
majority seemed to be carrying bags or bundles, and none
seemed to have come there to see dogs. After a time Finn tired
of the whole thing and, curling up on his bench, went to
sleep. He slept and waked and slept and waked again for what
seemed a very long time; and then the Master came to see
him with the Mistress of the Kennels. He was taken down
from his bench and allowed to stroll to and fro for a few
minutes, though not for any distance. Supper was given Finn

on the floor near his bench, and fresh water was placed in his dish in the front corner of the bed. Then he was chained up again, and the Master told him to be a good Finn boy and go to sleep till the next morning.

Days passed, all manner of odd things happened, and Finn saw many strange sights before he actually realized that he was not at a dog show at all but a passenger aboard a great ocean liner. And even then, when a good part of the ship had become quite familiar to him, the wolfhound did not know, of course, that they were all bound to the other side of the world, that their passages were booked for Australia. That long sea voyage was a strange, instructive experience for Finn. The preceding few months had made for rapid development upon his wilder side; they had taught him much as a hound and a hunter. This voyage developed his personality, his character, the central something that was Finn and that differentiated him from other Irish wolfhounds.

The first three or four days of the passage did, as an experience, resemble a dog show in that Finn spent almost the whole time on his bench and was only taken down for a few minutes at a time. Later on, however, when things and people had settled down into their places on board the big liner, the Master obtained permission to give Finn a good deal more freedom, on the understanding that he held himself responsible for the wolfhound's good behavior. This meant that, by day and night, Finn was given his liberty for hours together; but during the whole of that time he was never out of the sight of one or other of his two friends, and, the Mistress not being a good sailor, it meant that Finn was nearly always with the Master. This, again, meant a marked change in Finn's ways of life and a change that affected his character materially. Here was no orchard through which he could wander off to the open country, there to roam and hunt alone, out of touch with humans. Now, whether moving about or at rest, Finn was continuously within hearing and sight of the Master, and practically always within touch of him.

One result of all this was that Finn grew to understand far more of the Master's speech than he had ever understood before; he came to depend greatly upon the Master's company. With this came the development of an enduring and conscious love of the Master. With regard to other people, he was a great deal more reserved than he had been in the old days before he met Matey and before he took to hunting. He permitted their attentions courteously, and in the case of children, he would lend himself to their desires readily enough. But he never invited attention from anyone excepting the Master; and whereas he would settle down comfortably to doze on the sun-bathed deck with his muzzle resting on the Master's feet, he never volunteered to touch other people, though he accepted their caresses good-humoredly enough.

Hitherto, putting aside the exuberant demonstrativeness of early puppyhood, this had been Finn's attitude toward all humans, including even the Master. He had liked the Master and the Mistress; he had trusted them, and he had been deeply thankful to find them again after his escapade with Matey; but it could hardly have been said that he had loved them. Now he would lie for hours on his bench, waiting, watching, and listening for the sound of the footfall that he easily distinguished from among the many he heard. When they sat on the deck together at night, the Master and Finn, under the gorgeous sky that so often favors Pacific travelers by sea, the wolfhound's intercourse with the man stopped only just short of articulation and went far beyond the normal companionship of man and dog.

For instance, the Master would sometimes growl out low remarks to Finn about the Old Country, about Tara, and the

house beside the Sussex Downs; and Finn understood practically every word he said. Then the Master might wind up
by stroking his head in a heavy, lingering way that Finn
loved, saying:

"Ah, well, Finn boy; there's other good places in the
world, too. The Australian bush is a mighty big hunting
ground, I can tell you. We'll have some good times there,
Finn boy. And maybe we'll get a good home together out
there before long, old man; might even strike it rich, somehow, and go back to the Downs again."

And at such times, Finn's inability to speak after the
human fashion was no particular bar between them. Understanding was so clearly voiced in his dark, glistening eyes, in
the eager thrust of his wet, cool muzzle, and sometimes, for
emphasis, in the compelling weight of his great arm as he laid
it, with a pulling pressure, over the Master's shoulder.

And then the Master would say something about the Mistress of the Kennels, and Finn would beat the deck with his
thirty-inch tail, which was as thick and strong at its roots as
a man's arm. Or perhaps, if the weather were calm as well as
fine, the Mistress herself would come along and join them,
seated in a low deck chair; and then, though Finn's eyes
would take on a momentarily anxious look if her hand
touched the Master, he would be very happy, stretched out
between them, with his whole big heart shining out upon
the Master in the gaze that held his head always turned the
one way.

If it had not been for this remarkable development of
Finn's character, brought about by his confinement on board
ship with the Master, he would never have played the part
he did in what was really the most important event of his life
up till this time; and one, too, that taught the Master a good
deal regarding his own relationship to the great wolfhound
he had bred. It all happened on a Sunday morning when, the

weather being very hot, the captain held service on the upper
deck, under awnings, of course. Half a dozen children were
allowed, during the latter part of the service, to withdraw
and play quietly by themselves, twenty yards away from the
last row of chairs occupied by the congregation. At one end of
this last row the Master sat, with Finn beside him on the
deck. Among the children, one, a curly-headed rascal of a boy
named Tim, aged eight, was everybody's favorite and the
leader of the rest in most kinds of mischief. Exactly how he
managed it was never rightly understood, but when the piercing sound of a childish scream smote upon the Master's ears
through the droning periods of the captain's sermon, Tim
was in mid-air, halfway between the ship's rail and the sea,
and the other children were staring, horror-stricken, at the
place he had occupied a moment before, with his chubby
arms about the stem of a boat's davit and his brown legs
astride the rail.

The Master was a man given to acting swiftly upon impulse. Finn had leaped to his feet at the sound of the scream.
The Master followed on the instant and reached the ship's
side within a second or two of Finn's arrival there. Finn's
muzzle was thrust out between the white rails, and he saw
the tiny figure of Tim in the smoothly eddying water a little
abaft of the ship's beam. The Master saw it, too, and turning,
with one urgent hand on Finn's neck, he shouted:

"Over and fetch him, Finn! Over, boy!"

There was no mistaking his meaning. Finn had instant
understanding of that. But Finn was no water dog. The sea
was very far below. He let out two short nasal whimpers. The
Master swung one arm excitedly.

"Over, boy! Fetch Tim! Over!"

Then the growing love of the past few weeks spoke strongly
in Finn, overriding instinct in him, and with a whining sort
of bark of protest against the order his new love forced him

to obey, he leaped over the white rail and down, down, down through five-and-thirty feet of space into the smooth blue sea, where it swirled and rippled past the high steel walls of the ship.

This exhausted the Master's first impulse. Instantly then there flashed through his mind knowledge of the fact that Finn was no water dog, that he had never been trained to fetch from the water or to handle human beings gently with his teeth. The Master had never even seen Finn swim. That was a great love, a wonderful trust that had shone out from Finn's eyes, when, instinct protesting in his whining bark, he had leaped the rail in obedience to orders given on the impulse and without thought.

In the next moment the Master acted on his second impulse, regardless of the shouts he heard behind him. His shoes and coat were shed from him in a moment, and he, too, leaped the rail, reaching the warm blue water feet first and striking out at once toward Finn and the child. As a swimmer his powers were not at all above the average.

For all his inexperience of the water, Finn was a quicker swimmer than the Master, and he reached little Tim within a very few seconds and seized the youngster firmly between his great jaws, while turning in the water toward the ship he had left. Finn was careful enough to prevent his teeth from injuring the child. But he was no trained lifesaver, and it did not occur to him to notice which side up the child was held. Also, a few seconds later, he caught sight of the Master in the water, and that made him loose his hold of Tim, in his haste to reach one whose claim upon him he regarded as infinitely greater. This was only momentary, however. Some instinct told him he must not leave undone the task he had been set, and with a swift movement he plucked the child to him again and exerted all his great strength to reach the Master. This time little Tim's face was uppermost; but his small arms hung limply and helplessly at right angles from his body.

It was only a matter of seconds now till Finn and the Master met in the water. The Master seized Tim, and Finn seized the Master by one arm.

"Down, boy! Get down, Finn!" shouted the Master; and Finn obediently loosed his hold and swam anxiously round and round his friend in short circles, while the Master trod water and held Tim above him, head down and body bent in the middle.

It was less than three minutes later that the second officer of the liner shouted, "Way enough!" and a big white lifeboat slid past the Master's shoulder. The second officer leaned far out and snatched Tim from the Master's hands, passing him straight to the waiting arms of the ship's surgeon.

"Help the dog in!" shouted the Master, as two sailorly hands reached out toward himself. But Finn was watchfully circling behind him. It was rather an undertaking getting the great wolfhound into the lifeboat; but it was presently accomplished, the Master thrusting behind and two men in the boat tugging in front. Tim was lying on his face on the doctor's knees and gasping his way back to life under a vigorous kneading treatment. Whatever it may have been for the man and the wolfhound, it had undoubtedly been a close call for the child. There were great rejoicings on the big Australian liner during the rest of that sunshiny Sunday, and Finn came in for a good deal of flattering attention. But he paid small heed to this. What did make his heart swell within him was the little talk he had with the Master before they boarded the ship from the lifeboat. The Master had one dripping arm about Finn's wet shoulder and held it there with a warm pressure, while he muttered certain matters in Finn's right ear that sent hot blood pumping into the wolfhound's heart. The Master knew that Finn had done a big thing for love of him that day, and he would never forget it. Finn

would have leaped overboard fifty times to earn again that
pressure about his shoulders and that low murmur of loving
commendation in his ear. The half-hysterical caresses of
Tim's mother and the admiring attention of the whole ship's
company were trifles indeed after this.

The voyage to Australia took Finn into a new world in
more senses than one. Nature and the Master had endowed
him richly before. This voyage endowed him with the gift of
true love, which he had not known before; and whereas he
had come aboard that ship a very magnificent wolfhound, he
would leave it the richer by something that could almost be
called a soul, a personality developed by these long weeks
of close intercourse with a man and the final mental triumph
that had ended in his successfully rebelling against the dominion of instinct, by reason of the completeness of his devotion to the Master.

10: THE PARTING OF THE WAYS

IF Finn had been transported on a magic carpet and in an
instant of time from England to that part of Australia in
which he did eventually land, the first few months he spent
in the land of the Southern Cross would have been a desperately unhappy time. As it was, he landed under the influence
of six weeks of steady character development, his whole being
dominated by the warm personal devotion to the Master that
had taken the place with Finn of mere friendly affection.
And that made all the difference in the world in the matter
of the great wolfhound's first experience of the new land.

But it is a fact that it was not a very happy period for Finn.
The intimate understanding he had acquired regarding the

Master's moods and states of mind and spirits gave him more
than a dog's fair share of the burdens of that curious period.
It was a bad time for the Master, and for that reason, quite
apart from anything else, it was not a good time for Finn.
Some of the evil happenings of that period Finn understood
completely, and with regard to others again, all that he could
understand was their unhappy effect upon his friends and
himself. The first of them saluted Finn's friends before they
left the ship in the shape of news of the death, one week before this date, of the one man upon whom the Master had
been relying for help in establishing himself in Australia. So
that, instead of meeting with a warm welcome, Finn and his
friends had to find quarters for themselves and to spend days
in the country without a friendly word from anyone.

The man who had died suddenly was a bachelor and a
squatter on a large scale. His spacious country home was now
in the hands of the representatives of the Crown, pending its
disposal for the benefit of relatives in remote parts of the
world who had never seen the man who made it. This meant
that, instead of going up country on their arrival in Australia, the Master and the Mistress and Finn were obliged to
find economical quarters for themselves in the city.

Then came many weeks of anxiety and increasing depres-
sion, during which every sort of misfortune seemed to pursue
Finn's friends, and they were obliged at length to move into
a cheaper, smaller lodging, into which Finn was only admitted by those in authority upon sufferance; in which he
had hardly room to turn and twist his great bulk. The
Master's walks abroad at this time took him principally into
offices and places of that sort, where Finn could not accompany him, and if it had not been for the Mistress's good care,
the wolfhound's life would have been dreary indeed and
without any outdoor exercise. All these matters, however,
Finn could have endured cheerfully enough because of the

content that filled his mind when the Master was by and the anticipations that possessed him while he waited for the Master's return. But the thing that sapped Finn's spirits and vitality was his consciousness of the growing weight of unhappiness and anxiety and distress that possessed the Master. Finn knew by the manner in which his friend sat down when he entered the poor little lodging at night that things had gone evilly during the day. The touch of his friend's hand on his head, languid and inert, told the wolfhound much; and the nightly messages that reached his understanding were increasingly depressing.

But the climax of several long-drawn months of unhappiness came to them in the form of serious illness for the Mistress of the Kennels, which, for weeks, prevented the Master from seeking any further to better his fortunes. At the end of a month, in which the Master and Finn plumbed unsuspected deeps of misery, the Mistress, white and wan and desperately shaky, left her bedroom for the tiny sitting room that Finn could almost span when he stretched his mighty frame. (He measured seven feet six and a quarter inches now, from nose tip to tail tip; and when he stood absolutely erect, he could just reach the top of a door six feet six inches high with his forepaws.) By her way of it, she was to be quite herself again within a few days, but a fortnight found her practically no stronger; and the doctor spoke plainly, almost angrily, of the necessity of change of air and scene. When the Master hinted at his inability to provide this, the doctor shrugged his well-clad shoulders.

"I can only tell you that if the patient is to recover, she must leave this place. A month up in the mountains would put her right, with a liberal diet and comfortable quarters. The expense need not be great. I should say that, with care, twenty pounds might cover the whole thing."

It was then that, with a certain gruff abruptness, the

Master informed the doctor, outside the door of the sitting room, that his resources were reduced to less than half the amount mentioned and that there were bills owing. The doctor looked grave for a moment, and then shrugged his shoulders again. As he was leaving, he said:

"Why, you have a dog there that must eat as much as a man. I imagine you could sell him for twenty pounds. Indeed, there is a patient of my own who I am sure would pay that for so fine a hound."

"I dare say," said the Master sadly, "seeing that I refused one hundred guineas for him before he was fully grown. That is the finest Irish wolfhound living, a full champion, and the most valuable dog of his breed in the world. But we could not part with Finn. He—no, we could not sell Finn."

Again the young doctor shrugged his shoulders.

"Ah, well, that's your business, of course; but I have told you the patient will not recover in this place. If the dog is such a fine one as all that, perhaps you could get more for him—enough to set the patient on her feet and establish yourself in some way. In fact, I think my friend would give more if I were to ask him; he is one of the richest men in the city and a great lover of animals."

The rest of that day proved the most miserable time that the Master and Finn had spent in Australia. But a pretense at cheerfulness had to be maintained until the Mistress had retired for the night; and then, for many hours, the Master sat before an empty fireplace, with Finn's great head resting on his knees and one of his hands mechanically rubbing and stroking the wolfhound's ears, while he thought and thought and found only greater sadness in his thinking. Finn felt plainly that a crisis had arrived, and he tried to show his agreement and understanding when at long last the Master rose from his comfortless wooden chair, saying sadly:

"I don't see what else a man can do, my Finn boy; but—but it's hard."

Early next morning, the Master took a leash in his hand and set out with Finn from the poor house that sheltered them in the dingy quarter of the town where they lived. They walked for two miles through sunlit spacious streets, and then they came to the house of the doctor. The Master waited in the hall, and the doctor came to see him there, a napkin in his hands.

"Doctor," said the Master, "I want the address of that rich patient of yours who is fond of animals."

"Ah! Yes, I thought you would," answered the doctor. "Just step in here a moment, and I will give you a note for Mr. Sandbrook."

It was nearly an hour later that the Master and Finn reached the entrance to a beautiful garden, in the center of which stood a big, picturesque house, with windows overlooking the sparkling waters of a great harbor.

They were kept waiting for some time and were seated on the veranda when Mr. Sandbrook, the portly broker, merchant, and shipping agent, came to them. Finn was lying stretched at his great full length on the cedarwood planks of the veranda, forelegs far out before him, head carried high, his big dark eyes fixed lovingly on the Master's face. Mr. Sandbrook was a good-natured, kindly soul, very prosperous and very vain and little accustomed to deny himself anything that his quickly roaming little gray eyes desired. As these eyes fell upon Finn, they told him that this was the most magnificent dog he had ever seen; the handsomest dog in Australia, as indeed Finn was easily and without a doubt.

The merchant shook hands with the Master and read the note from the doctor.

And then the Master showed him Finn's printed pedigree,

with one or two newspaper descriptions of the wolfhound, a
list of his championship honors, other papers showing the
Master's own connection with the Irish Wolfhound Club, and
so forth. Mr. Sandbrook had already made up his mind that
this dog must belong to him; he almost resented, in a good-
humored way, the fact that Finn had not belonged to him
before. But he was a businessman, and he said:

"Of course, in this country no dogs have the sort of market
value that you speak of this hound having in England. That
would be regarded as absurd here."

"No price you could name, sir, would tempt me into parting with Finn; only dire necessity makes that possible. But,
in this country or any other, Finn's value, not to me, but to
the dog buyer, would be one hundred guineas; and he would
be very cheap at that. He would bring double that in England. But I will sell Finn to you, sir, for fifty guineas, because
I am assured that he would have a good home with you—
on one condition; and that is that you will let me have him
again for, say, eighty guineas, if I can offer you that sum
within a couple of years."

The merchant measured the Master with his little gray
eyes. He wanted to own that magnificent hound. So far as he
knew, no one else in the country owned such a magnificent
hound as that. He pictured Finn lying on a rug in the fine
hall of his fine house, which he was told was equal to that of
one of the stately homes of England. But then to have someone come and take his fine hound away from him—no, his
dignity forbade the thought of such a thing. He turned half
around on his heels.

"No," he said decisively. "I'm sorry, but I couldn't think
of it. I'll make it seventy-five guineas for an outright sale, and
that's my last word."

While the Master pondered over this, he had a vision of
the Mistress of the Kennels, sitting, white and shaky, in the

dismal little room on the far side of the city, waiting for the change that was to give her health again. He did hesitate for another minute; but he knew all the time that there was no alternative for him.

Five minutes later the merchant was making out a check in his study, and the Master was engaged in writing down a long list of details regarding Finn's diet and the sort of methods and system that should be followed to secure health and happiness for an Irish wolfhound. The Master used great care over the preparation of these instructions. At least, he thought, Finn would be sure of a luxuriously good home.

"You don't think he'll run away, do you?" asked the merchant.

"No; I don't think he'll run away," said the Master. "I'll tell him he mustn't do that." The merchant stared. "But for a week or two, you should be careful with him and not leave him quite at large."

They parted in the big hall, the Master and Finn, among the dim portraits. Finn had been eying the Master with desperate anxiety for some time past. At frequent intervals he had nervously wagged his tail and even made a pretense of gaiety, with jaws parted and red tongue lolling. Now he sat down on his haunches on a big rug because the Master told him to sit down. For a moment the Master dropped on one knee beside him, one arm about his shoulders. Finn gave an anxious little whine.

"Good-by, my old Finn, son! Good-by, you—you Irish hound! Now mark me, Finn, you stay here; you stay here—stay here, Finn!"

Such episodes are always suspect when seen in print. I have no wish to exaggerate by a hairsbreadth about Finn. His whole nature bade the wolfhound follow his friend. The Master said, "Stay there!" And there was no mistaking his meaning. Finn crouched down. His body did not touch the floor; his weight rested on his outstretched legs, though his position appeared to be that of lying. There he crouched; but as though the thing were too much for him to see as well as feel, he buried his muzzle well over the eyes between his forelegs, just as he might have done if a strong light had dazzled him. It was obedience such as a great soldier could appreciate. Finn stayed there, hiding his face; but as the house door closed behind the Master, a cry broke from Finn, a muffled cry by reason of the position of his head; a cry that was part bark, part whine, and part groan; a cry that smote upon the Master's ears as he stepped out upon the gravel drive in the sunlight, with the biting, stinging pain not of the parting, but of an accusation. There was a twinge of shame as well as grief in the Master's heart that day, though he knew well that what he had done was unavoidable. Still, there was the sense of shame, of treachery. Finn had been wonderfully human and close to him since they left England together.

Before noon of that day the Master was on his way to the mountains with the Mistress of the Kennels.

11: AN ADVENTURE BY NIGHT

FOR some thirty-six hours after his parting with the Master, Finn mourned silently in the big house, which overlooked the harbor and was filled with brand-new luxuries. If Finn had been a year younger, the Sandbrook family would have learned from him the exact nature of the Irish wolfhound howl, and they would not have liked it at all. But though Finn would be capable of the howl as long as he lived, he

had no mind to indulge in it now. His grief was too deep for
that and too understanding; so understanding, indeed, that
he was perfectly well aware that no howls of his would bring
the Master back to him. It was true he had not understood
the nature of the transaction that made him the property of
the Australian merchant; but he had clearly understood that
some grievous necessity had forced the Master to hand him
over to Mr. Sandbrook, and that his, Finn's, duty to the
Master involved remaining there in the house by the harbor.

But as he saw it, his duty did not make it incumbent upon
him to enter into communication with a whole pack of people who had nothing to do with the Master. In some dim
way he comprehended that he owed deference and obedience
to Mr. Sandbrook, that the Master had undertaken so much
on his behalf; but he had no wish to become familiar with
the Sandbrook household; and the consequence was that the
daughters and the servants and the lady of the house, while
they admitted the magnificence of the new acquisition's appearance, agreed in pronouncing him a rather sulky animal.
They showered caresses and foolish remarks upon him, and
he lay with his gray-black muzzle resting on outstretched
forelegs, staring through them all at the door by which the
Master had disappeared. Once when the younger daughter
of the house went so far as to sit down beside Finn and bend
her head close down to his, he submitted courteously, though
his nose wrinkled with annoyance, until the young lady
raised her head; and then, very gently, he rose, walked away
from her to the mat beside the door, and lay down there,
with his nose close to the spot on which the Master's feet
had last rested in that house.

Finn was taken out in the garden two or three times on a
leash; but he had no thought of escape. The Master had left
him and bade him stay there; and his heart was empty and
desolate within him. Now and again his dark eyes filled with

moisture, and the sadness of his face was so wonderfully striking as to impress the Misses Sandbrook.

Through the night Finn did not sleep, though he dozed occasionally for a few minutes at a time. The whole of the next day he passed in the same employment, except that, in the afternoon, he had to go through the wearisome ceremony of being introduced to a number of strange ladies, not one among whom seemed from the smell of her clothes to have anything to do with the Master.

That night Mr. Sandbrook announced that he thought Finn had quite settled in his new home and that he would now take the wolfhound for a stroll in the grounds without the leash. He did so, and when they had walked twice around a lawn and down an avenue, they came to the green gate by which Finn had first entered that place. Finn had been walking dejectedly, his head carried low and close to Mr. Sandbrook's legs, his mind still too full of mournful thoughts of his lost Master to permit his inquiring closely into the smells and other details of his immediate surroundings, which would have interested him in ordinary circumstances.

Now, as his eyes fell upon the green gate, an overpowering desire to see the Master swept through his mind. He had no intention of running away from his new owner. His one thought was just to run down to the old lodging and see the Master again. His hindquarters bent under him, and the next instant saw him neatly clearing the top of the five-foot gate with never a thought of the consternation he left behind him in poor Mr. Sandbrook's mind.

Before the portly merchant had the gate fairly open, Finn had trotted thirty or forty yards down the moonlit road in the direction from which he had approached the house with the Master on the morning of the previous day. He paused once and looked back at Mr. Sandbrook in response to agitated cries and whistles; but not being able to explain his precise object in going out, he decided that it would be better to get on with the matter in hand without delay. So he went forward again, and this time at an easy canter, which took him out of earshot of Mr. Sandbrook in less than one minute.

When Finn arrived in the streets of the city, he was more than a little confused and once or twice took a wrong turning. But he always retraced his steps and found the right turning before going far, and in due course he arrived at the house in which he had lodged with his friends. Rising on his hind feet, he pawed the front door vigorously. A few moments later the door was opened by the landlady. To her utter astonishment, Finn brushed hurriedly into the little passage and up the stairs to the door of the room the Master had used, where he paused, with one foot pressed against the closed door.

"Here, Sam!" cried the startled landlady. "You talk about your blessed menagerie; come an' look 'ere. My word, this'll surprise yer!"

The landlady's son, who had paid her a flying visit that day, appeared in the passage in his shirt sleeves, holding a small lamp. The landlady closed the front door, and together the two walked upstairs to where Finn sat, whining softly and pawing at the closed door of what had been the Master's sitting room.

"My bloomin' oath, what a dog!" exclaimed Sam, as his mother reached forward and opened the sitting-room door, leaving Finn free to plunge forward into the dark interior, which he did on the instant. In the next instant he was out again and pawing at the opposite door, leading to the bedroom. This, too, was opened for him, and in another moment he had satisfied himself that neither room had been occupied by the Master or the Mistress for a considerable time. This was a grievous blow to Finn, and as he returned to the little landing between the two rooms, he sniffed despairingly at the landlady's skirt and even nuzzled her rough hand, with a vague feeling that she might be able to produce his friends. Not that he had any serious purpose in this, however, for it was strongly borne in upon Finn now that he had lost his friends for good and all.

Sam had been eying Finn all this while with growing interest, and now he said:

"Is he savage?"

"Wouldn't hurt a sheep," replied the mother. "Wouldn't yer like to know where I got such a beauty?"

"No kidding. He's not yours," said Sam.

"Well, I reckon he could be. 'Is Master lodged 'ere these two months an' more, but 'e went off to the mountains yesterday with his sick Missis. Why, come to think of it, er course —that's what it is. 'Is Master's sold him; that's what 'e's done; and that's why 'e was able to pay me an' the doctor an' go off to the mountains yesterday. An' now the bloomin' dog's run away an' come back to look for 'im."

Sam spat reflectively on the little doormat. "Well, the dog's no use to you, Mother," he said. "You can't do nothin' with him."

"I don' know about that, Sam. I might keep 'im an' watch out fer the reward. A dawg like that's worth money."

"Too bloomin' big an' clumsy to be worth much," said Sam disparagingly. "Clumsy" was no more applicable to Finn than it would be to a panther, and Sam was well aware of it. "Tell you what," he said. "I've got to be makin' for the station in half an hour, anyway. I'll take the dog out o' yer way an' give you half a quid for him, if yer like. I shall lose on it, fer it's not likely the boss could make any use of 'im, anyway."

But the landlady knew her son tolerably well, and he could not deceive her very much. When he left the house half an hour later, he was leading Finn at the end of a rusty chain, and the poorer by twenty-five shillings than he had been an hour before. So Finn changed hands for the second time in forty-eight hours, once for seventy-five guineas and once for twenty-five shillings; and upon this second occasion the transaction was a matter of complete indifference to him. He thought vaguely of returning to Mr. Sandbrook's house later on. In the meantime, this young man seemed to want him to take a walk in another direction, and all ways were alike to Finn in his bitter disappointment over not finding the Master. He did not know that he was treading exactly the path the Master and the Mistress had trod on the previous day when leaving their lodging for the mountains. He only felt that he had now completely lost his friends and that he was rather well disposed toward long-legged Sam for the reason that Sam came from the house in which the Master had lodged.

12: THE SOUTHERN CROSS CIRCUS

THE night that followed Finn's departure from his old lodging with Sam was the most peculiar that he had ever spent in his life and, not even excepting the night in Matey's back yard in Sussex, the most unrestful.

In the first place, the greater part of the night was spent on a moving railway train; and secondly, Finn's particular resting place was a sort of wooden cage, sheathed in iron, and having another similar cage upon either side of it. In the compartment upon Finn's right were two native bears. These philosophical animals slept solidly all the time and made no noise beyond a husky sort of snoring. But they had a pronounced odor that penetrated Finn's compartment through a grating near its roof; and this odor was peculiarly disturbing to the wolfhound. In the cage on Finn's left was a full-grown, elderly, and sour-tempered Bengal tiger, who had sore places under his elbows and other troubles, which made him excessively irritable and a bad sleeper. The tiger also had a pronounced odor; and it was much more disturbing to Finn than that of the bears. In fact, it kept the wiry hair over Finn's shoulders in a state of continual agitation and his silky ears in a restlessly upright position, with only their soft tips drooping. Sometimes, when the train jolted, the tiger would roll heavily against the iron-sheathed partition between his abode and Finn's, and then Finn would spring to his feet, against the far side of the compartment, every hair on his body erect, his lips drawn right back from the pearl-white fangs they usually sheltered, his sensitive nostrils deeply serrated.

The smells and sounds about him penetrated farther into the pulsing entity that was Finn than even his experience with Matey or his hunting and killing of the fox on the Sussex Downs They stirred latent instincts that came to him from farther back in the long line of his ancestry; from just how far back one could not say, but it may well be that they came from a dim period, beyond all the generations of wolf-hunting and, earlier, of man-fighting in Ireland, when fore-bears of Finn's had been pitted against lions and tigers and bears, as well as Saxons, in Roman arenas. It was curious, the manner in which the play of these instincts affected Finn's very shape, giving to his massive depth of chest a suggestion of the hyena, to his head a marked suggestion of the wolf, and to his drooping hindquarters more than a hint of the lion. The facts that the hair along his spine stood erect like wire and that his exposed fangs and updrawn lips changed his whole facial aspect had a good deal to do with the alterations wrought in his shape by the curious position in which he found himself this night. A wiser man than Sam would have refrained from putting Finn in this predicament and more especially while he was still a stranger to the great hound.

Sam rather regretted his carelessness when he came to release Finn next morning. Since the small hours, the part of the train in which Sam had traveled had been lying in a siding, close to a little mountain station. And now the different wagons, including that containing Finn and the tiger and the bears, with a lot of paraphernalia, were being swung out upon the ground, preparatory to being drawn by road to the neighboring town. At this stage Sam had intended to take Finn out to be inspected by his employer and, if fortune willed it, sold to that gentleman for what Sam considered a handsome figure, say, fifteen or twenty pounds.

Sam was one of the underlings employed by Rutherford's famous Southern Cross traveling circus; and his idea was that Finn would be found a suitable and welcome addition to the menagerie of performing animals attached to that popular institution. But when Sam came to look at Finn by daylight and to note the extreme fierceness of the wolfhound's mien—brought about entirely by his own stupidity in locking the hound up beside a tiger and two bears—his heart failed him in the matter of releasing his prize, and he decided to wait until the camp had been formed and things had settled down a little. That cowardly decision of Sam's affected the whole of Finn's future life.

The process of transferring his cage to the road and traveling along that road, which was in reality no better than a very rough mountain track and exceedingly bumpy, worked old Killer, as the tiger was ominously called, into a frenzy of wrath. Now the tiger's frenzy meant something very like frenzy for Finn. When the tiger snarled and thrashed the inner side of his cage with his great tail, Finn's snarl became a fierce, growling bark; his forelegs stiffened, like the erect hair along his backbone, his white fangs were all exposed, and his aspect became truly terrifying. Saliva began to collect at the corners of his long mouth; his great wrath and unreasoning, instinctive fierceness and resentment made him look twice his actual size; and altogether it may be admitted that when Sam came to investigate, after the camp had been formed, Finn truly was, to all appearances, a fearsome and terrifying creature.

Sam marveled at his own courage in having led this monster through the streets and told himself that nothing would induce him to be such a fool as to take Finn out of the cage. His mother had given him both Finn's name and the name of the breed, but Sam had never before heard of an Irish wolfhound, and looking now at Finn's gleaming fangs and foamy lips, he recalled only part of the name, "Irish Wolf." It was thus that Finn was presented to the great John L. Rutherford himself, the proprietor of the circus.

"He's the Giant Irish Wolf, boss," said Sam, "and the only one in the world, as I'm told. I bought him cheap, an' I got him into that cage singlehanded, I did; an' now I'll sell him to you cheap, boss, if you'll buy him. If you don't want him, he goes to Smart's manager, who offered me twenty-five quid for him as he stood last night."

"Smart's" was the opposition circus; but the rest of Sam's remarks were imagination for the most part. As a matter of fact, the great John L. Rutherford experienced quite a thrill of satisfaction when his eyes lighted upon the raging wolfhound. He had lost his one lion from disease some weeks previously and felt that the menagerie lacked attractiveness in the way of fierce-looking and bloodthirsty creatures. Like Sam, he had never even heard of an Irish wolfhound or seen a dog of any breed who approached Finn in the matter of height and length and lissome strength.

From the point of view of one who regarded him as a wild beast and was without knowledge of the tragic chance that had made so gallant and docile a creature appear in the guise of a wild beast, Finn did actually present both an awe-inspiring and a magnificent spectacle at this moment. His cage was seven feet high, yet at one moment Finn's forepaws came within a few inches of touching its roof, as he plunged erect and snarling against the partition that separated him from the growling and spitting tiger. The next moment saw him crouched in the far corner of the cage, as though for a spring, his forelegs extended, rigid as the iron bars that enclosed him, his black eyes blazing fire and fury, his huge, naked jaws parted to admit of a snarl of terrifying ferocity, his whole great bulk twitching and trembling from the mixture of rage, bewilderment, fear, and wild killing passion with which his neighbors and his amazing situation filled him.

"Well, Sam, he sure is a dandy wolf," said the astonished Mr. John L. Rutherford.

Sam began to feel that he really was a very fine fellow and one who had accomplished great things.

"Yes, I got him into the cage singlehanded, boss; but I reckon it'll take the Professor all he knows to handle the brute." "The Professor" was the world-renowned Professor Claude Damarel, lion-tamer and performer with wild beasts, known sometimes in private life as Clem Smith.

"Giant Irish Wolf, you say," mused John L. Rutherford. "Well, he's certainly a giant right enough; big as any two wolves I ever see. My! he must stand a yard at the shoulder." Which he did, and at that moment his hackles were giving him another three inches, and his rage was giving him the effect of another foot all around.

"Well, Sam, it was smart of ye to get the beast, an' you shall have fifteen for him, though ten's his price; an' if the Professor makes a star of him, why you'll get a rise, my boy.

Say, touch him up with that stick there an' see how he takes
it."

Sam thrust a stave in between the bars of Finn's cage,
where they adjoined those of the tiger's place, and prodded
the wolfhound's side as he stood erect. The thing seemed to
come from the tiger's cage, and Finn was upon it like a whirlwind, his fangs sinking far into the tough wood till it cracked
again.

"Well, say," said the boss with warm admiration. "If he
ain't two ends an' the middle of a jim-dandy rustler from
'way back, you can search me! Say, Sam, cut along an' find
the Professor. Tell him I'd like to see him right here."

The great barred cage, with its three divisions, was now
enclosed, with various other cages and properties of the
circus, within a high canvas wall in the center of the camp.
The circus was to open that night, and much remained to be
done in the way of preparing a ring in the big main tent,
and so forth. A number of piebald horses stood in different
parts of the enclosure, nosing idly at the dusty ground and
paying not the slightest heed either to the scent of the different wild creatures or to the roaring snarls and growls that
issued continuously from Killer's cage. Familiarity had bred
indifference in them to things that would have sent a horse
from outside half crazy with fear.

The Professor arrived with Sam after a few minutes. He
wore knee boots, a vivid red shirt, and a much soiled old
leather coat that reached almost to his boots. From his right
wrist there dangled a long quilt, or cutting whip, of rhinoceros hide. He was reckoned an able tamer of wild beasts.
By stirring up the tiger, as the Professor approached, the
boss provoked a striking exhibition of savage strength and
ferocity in Finn.

"Say, Professor," he said, with a smile, "what d'ye think
of the latest? How does the Giant Irish Wolf strike you?"

The Professor inspected the furiously raging Finn with considerable interest.

"You'll not manage much taming with this fellow, Professor, will ye?" asked the boss, craftily aiming at putting the lion-tamer on his mettle.

"I'd like to know what's goin' to stop me, boss," said the Professor doughtily. "I guess you've forgotten the fact that Professor Claude Damarel was the man who tamed the Tasmanian Wolf, Satan; and the Tasmanian Wolf is about the fiercest brute in the world to tackle, next to the Tasmanian Devil; an' I had one o' them pretty near beat in Auckland till he went an' died on me. Tame this Giant Irishman—you bet your sweet life I will; an' have him cavortin' through a hoop inside of a month—or maybe a week."

"Right-ho, Professor!" said the boss good humoredly. "But I'd like to be on hand when you tackle the Giant Wolf, Professor. You might want help."

"Help! Me want help! You wait here two minutes, boss, an' I'll show you."

The boss grinned over the success of his tactics in rousing the Professor's pride and strolled around among the horses for five minutes or so till the tamer returned with Sam, carrying a brazier full of live coals, and an iron rod with a rough leather handle at one end of it. The other end of the iron rod was buried among the live coals.

Grasping the leather handle of his now red-hot rod, the Professor deftly opened the gate of Finn's cage far enough to admit of his own swift entrance, the gate being instantly slammed to behind him by Sam and bolted. Finn was lying crouched in the far corner of the cage, and if the light there had been good, the tamer would surely have seen by the expression on the wolfhound's intelligent face that he was no wild beast. On the other hand, froth still clung to Finn's jaws, the hair on his shoulders was still more or less erect, and a

few minutes before this time he had been raging like a whirlwind.

For a moment or two the Professor glared steadily at Finn.
He undoubtedly had pluck, seeing that he believed the wolfhound to be as ferocious and deadly a beast as any tiger.
Then, slowly, Finn rose from his crouching position, prepared to come forward and to treat his visitor as a friend,
even as a possible rescuer from that place of horrid durance.
The Professor's plan was all mapped out in his mind, and he
did not waver in its execution. Had he been given to waver-
ing he would long ago have been killed by some wild creature. In the instant of Finn's move toward him, the Professor
took a quick step forward and, with a growling shout of
"Down, Wolf!" smote Finn fairly across the head with the
red-hot end of his iron bar so that pungent smoke arose. One
portion of the red-hot surface of the iron caught Finn's
muzzle, causing him pain of a sort he had never known before. At the moment of the blow, a terrific snarling roar came
from the tiger's cage. Half blinded, wholly maddened, dimly
connecting this strange new agony that bit into him with the
tiger's roar, Finn sprang at the Professor with a snarl that
was itself almost a roar. The red-hot bar met him in mid-air,
biting deep into the soft skin of his lips, furrowing his beautiful neck, and stinging the tip of one silken ear. The pain
was terrible; the smell of his own burnt flesh and hair was
maddening; the deadly implacability of the attack, coming
from a man, too, was baffling beyond description. Finn
howled and sank abruptly upon his haunches, giving the Professor time for a flying glance of pride in the direction of the
admiring John L. Rutherford.

And now, had he been really a wild beast, Finn would
probably have remained cowering as far as possible from
that terrible bar of fire. Even as it was, he might have done
this if the Professor had not made the mistake of raising the

bar again with a suddenly threatening motion. Finn had greater reasoning power and greater strength of will than a wild beast. He was robbed of all restraint by his surroundings and by the Professor's absolute and crushing reversal of all his preconceived notions of the relations between man and hound. The snarl of the tiger in his ears, the smell of his own burnt flesh in his nostrils, and the pitilessness of the Professor's wholly unexpected attack filled him with a tumultuous fury of warring instincts that generations of inherited docility were powerless to overcome. But through it all, he was more capable of thought than a really wild beast, and as the hot iron was lifted the third time, he leaped in under it like lightning and with a roar of defiance brought its wielder to the ground and planted both forefeet upon his chest, while the iron bar fell clattering from the man's hand between the bars of the cage.

Be it remembered that Finn stood a foot higher at the shoulder than the average wolf and weighed fully twice as much, being long and strong in proportion to his height and weight. The Professor was momentarily expecting to feel Finn's great jaws about his throat, and his two arms were crossed below his chin for protection of that most vulnerable spot. The tiger was now furiously clawing at the partition a few inches from Finn's nose and emitting a series of the most blood-curdling snarls and roars.

"Draw him off with a stick!" shouted the Professor, who, even in his present sorry plight, was concerned most with the injury to his pride. Sam jabbed viciously at Finn's face with a long stake through the bars, and as Finn withdrew slightly, the Professor wriggled cleverly to his feet, in a crouching posture, and reached the gate of the cage. Finn growled threateningly but made no move forward, being thankful to see the retreat of his enemy. In another instant the Professor was outside the cage and the gate securely bolted. He was bruised but bore no mark of scratch or bite and so far was able to boast, having no knowledge of the fact that Finn had not thought of biting him but merely of overpowering him as a means of evading his hot iron. This the wolfhound had done easily. He could have killed the man with almost equal ease had that been his intention.

"Well, he sure is a rustler from 'way back, Professor, every single time," remarked the boss.

"You'll see him hop through a hoop when I say so inside of a week," replied the tamer sourly, as he brushed the dust from his coat. "As it is, you'll notice that he didn't dare to bite or scratch. Don't you fear but what I'll tame the beauty all right, Giant Wolf or no Giant Wolf. I've handled worse'n him."

And a couple of days before this, the younger Miss Sand-brook had been resting her carefully dressed curls against Finn's head.

13: THE MAKING OF A WILD BEAST

THE transformation begun in Finn by the night he had spent in a rocking train, caged between a tiger and two bears, was enormously accentuated and confirmed by his encounter with the Professor. If zoologists had deliberately set themselves the task of converting an Irish wolfhound into a wild beast, they could hardly have taken any more effective measures than those that had been adopted by pure chance with Finn. The mere fact of being caged behind iron bars for the first time in his life, and that between a roaring, snarling tiger and two grunting little bears, strongly odoriferous of the wild, affected Finn in somewhat the same manner that a highly excitable and nervous man of quite untrained intellect might be affected by being flung into a cell surrounded by raving maniacs.

Shortly after the episode of the red-hot iron, Finn's cage was again visited by Sam and the Professor, the former being laden with a big, blood-stained basket. From this basket the Professor took a large chunk of raw flesh and pushed it through the bars into Finn's cage. A bone was also thrust through the bars, and a fixed iron pan near the gate was filled from outside with water. The Professor eyed Finn curiously while he performed these operations and was surprised that the Giant Wolf, as they called him, did not spring forward upon the food.

Killer was already ravening furiously at the bars of his cage, his yellow eyes ablaze as he watched the meat his soul desired being thrust into Finn's cage. The tiger's roars kept Finn's hackles up and his fangs bared in a fierce snarl; so that the Professor was struck afresh with the savageness of the latest addition to the menagerie under his care. Killer's meat barely reached the floor of his cage before he had snatched and carried it to the rear, where he tore it savagely while maintaining an incessant growling snarl. But he dropped the meat as though it burned and crouched fearfully in the opposite corner of his den, when—by way of display for Sam's benefit—the Professor picked up his iron bar and threatened the tiger with it. Now Finn, on the other hand, when he saw the cruel bar raised, sprang forward with a growling roar of defiance, forefeet outstretched, bristling back curved for the leap, and white fangs flashing.

"We'll have to keep these two always caged together," said the Professor, with a careless glance at Finn and the tiger. "Old Killer works him up in great style. I guess he'll fetch the public all the time while he can hear old Killer at his antics. He certainly is the finest-lookin' beast I ever saw in the wolf line, and he's as strong and heavy as a horse. What I don't like about the beggar is you can't reckon on him. He don't fly at ye right away; he doesn't even jump for his grub, you see. He seems to lie back an' consider. He's goin' to be a rough, hard case to tame, Sam, that Giant Wolf of yours; but he's come to a hard-case tamer, too, and don't you forget it."

It was now thirty hours since Finn had tasted food and three days since he had eaten a proper meal. If his experiences of the past twenty-four hours had been in every other respect distressing, they had at least robbed him of grief about the Master. His outraged physical senses and the tremendous strain placed upon his nervous system effectually shut grief from his mind. Finn was accustomed to have meals served to him in spotless enameled dishes, and it had always been food of which a man might have partaken: well-cooked meats, bread, vegetables, and gravy, nicely cut and mixed. But hunger triumphed after a while, and with a quick, rather furtive movement, but with lips drawn back and every sign of readiness to defend his action, Finn lifted the big chunk of meat from its place by the bars and carried it into a corner at the back of the cage, where he tore it into fragments and ate it, of necessity, very much as a wolf eats, the blood of the raw meat trickling meanwhile about his jaws. To drink, Finn had to place his head close to those bars that most nearly adjoined the front of the tiger's cage. But drink was necessary to him now, and so, with his nose all furrowed, his fangs bared, and a formidable low snarl issuing from his throat, he slowly approached the water pan and lapped his fill, pausing to snarl aloud at the tiger between each three or four laps of his tongue. But Killer had fed full and crunched his bone to splinters and eaten that; so now he was preparing himself to sleep.

The hours of the day dragged slowly by, and Finn began

to suffer in new ways. He had never been confined for any
length of time before, and strict cleanliness was an instinct
with him.

At length, as the hot afternoon drew to its close, a number
of men came to the cages, and horses were hitched on to the
heavy wagon that supported them, at a level of less than three
feet from the ground. Killer woke with a start and, with his
tail, angrily flogged the partition that divided him from Finn,
while delivering himself of a snarling yawn. Finn leaped to
his feet, answering the tiger's snarl viciously, looking as savage as any of the wild kindred. The wagon moved with a
jerk; Killer rolled against his side of the partition and
growled ferociously; Finn sprang at the partition as though
he thought his great weight would carry him through it, and
his jaws snapped at the air as he sprang. The men roared with
laughter at him, and this accentuated his feeling that they
were all mad wild beasts together. Presently, Finn's cage,
with others, was ranged along the side of a canvas-covered
passageway by which the public were to approach the main
tent, where that night's performance was to be given. This
double row of cages was arranged here with a view to im-
pressing the public; a kind of foretaste of the glories they
were to behold within. The Southern Cross Circus had patent
turnstiles fixed at both ends of the main tent, those at one
end admitting only of ingress, those at the other end admitting only of egress.

It was shortly after this that Finn became conscious of a
curious grinding small sound at the back of his cage. Presently a sharp, bright point of steel entered the cage from behind, just above the level of Finn's head, as he sat on his
haunches. The steel wormed its way into the cage to a length
of fully six inches, and then it reached the side of Killer's
cage, pointing diagonally, and bored slowly through that.

The auger was well greased and made only a very slight
sound, so slight indeed that Killer was not aware of it. He
was not so highly strung as Finn at this time.

This auger hole was an idea of Sam's, for which he hoped
to derive credit from the boss. He had noted carefully the
remark of the Professor about keeping the Giant Wolf close
to the tiger, in order to lend additional fierceness to his demeanor. And so he had devised a means of improving upon
this. He took a thin iron rod and covered the end of it with
soft, porous sacking, which he moistened with the blood of
raw meat. Then, by thrusting this between the bars of Finn's
cage and jabbing violently at the wolfhound with it for several minutes, he endeavoured to impregnate the sacking on
the rod with a smell of Finn. Then he invited John L. Rutherford to take up a stand in front of the cages, as though he
were a member of the general public, and to whistle by way
of signaling that he was ready. Directly Sam heard the whistle,
he now being behind the cages, he thrust his sacking-covered
rod through the auger hole he had made from Finn's cage
into the tiger's and there rattled it to and fro to attract the
Killer's attention. Killer not only heard and saw the intrud-
ing object but smelled it, and sprang at it violently, with a
rasping savage snarl, which challenged the Giant Wolf to
come forward or be forever accursed for a coward. The rod
was withdrawn on the instant, and Finn's whole great bulk
crashed against the partition, as he answered Killer with a
roar of defiance. The great wolfhound stood erect on his
hind feet, snapping at the air with foaming jaws and tearing
impotently at the iron-sheathed partition with his powerful
claws. The boss applauded vigorously and gave Sam a shilling
for beer.

It must have been nearly two hours later, when the public
was being admitted in a regular stream to the big tent and
Sam had succeeded in working the tiger and the wolfhound

into a perfect frenzy of impotent rage, of snarling, foaming, roaring fury, that a faint odor crossed Finn's nostrils and a faint sound fell upon his ears through all the din and tumult of the conflict with his unseen enemy. In that moment, and as though he had been shot, Finn dropped from his erect position and bounded to the front bars of his cage with a sudden, appealing whine, very unlike the formidable cries with which he had been rending the pent air of his prison for the last quarter of an hour. He had heard a few words spoken in a woman's voice, and those words were:

"I cannot bear to look at them; I never do. Let us hurry straight in."

In a passion of anxiety and grief and love and remorse for not having been on the lookout, Finn poured out his very soul in a succession of long-drawn whines, plaintive and insistent as a cello's wailings, while his powerful forepaws tugged and scratched ineffectually at the solid iron bars of his cage. The woman whose voice he heard was the Mistress of the Kennels, and the man to whom she spoke, who walked beside her, looking obstinately at her and not at the cages, was the Master. Something seemed to crack in poor Finn's breast as the two humans whom he loved disappeared from his view within the great tent. He did not know that they would not pass that way again because the audience left the place by the opposite end of the tent. But he gave no thought to the future. Here, in the midst of his uttermost misery and humiliation, the Master, the light of his life, had passed within a few feet of him, and passed without a glance, without a word. For long, Finn gazed miserably out between the bars, sniffing hopelessly at the air through which his friends had passed. Then, slowly, he retired to the furthermost corner of his cage and curled down there, with his muzzle between his paws.

14: MARTYRDOM

It may be that a good deal of the wisdom and philosophy of mankind is born of grief and suffering. It is certain that a good deal of philosophy came to Finn as the aftermath of that evening upon which he retired, heartbroken, to the farthest corner of his cage after seeing the Master and the Mistress of the Kennels pass him without a word or a glance. His mind did not deal in niceties. He did not tell himself that if the Master had only guessed at his presence there, all would have been different. He was conscious only of the apparently brutal fact that the Master had walked past his cage and ignored him; left him there in his horrible confinement. And so he lay, all through that night, silent, sorrowful, and blind to his surroundings.

The natural result was that sleep came to him after a while when all was dark and silent. And this sleep he badly needed. While he slept, the burns on his muzzle and ear were healing, the searing heat of his grief was subsiding, and his body and nervous system were adapting themselves to his situation and recharging themselves after the great drain made upon them during the past couple of days.

When Killer's long, snarling yawn woke Finn in the morning, he did not fling himself against the partition that hid the tiger from him. He did not even bark or snarl a defiant reply. He only bared his white fangs in silence and breathed somewhat harshly through his nostrils, while the hair over his shoulders rose a little in token of instinctive resentment. This comparatively mild demonstration cost Finn a great deal less in the way of expenditure of vitality than his previous day's reception of the tiger's snarls and left him just so

much the better fitted to cope with other ordeals that lay
before him.

If Finn had been a wild beast, his experience in the Southern Cross Circus would have been a far less trying one for
him than it was. He would have learned early that the Professor was a practically all-powerful tyrant who had to be
obeyed because he had the power and the will to-inflict great
suffering upon those of the wild kindred who refused him
obedience. That he was a tyrant and an enemy the wild
creature would have accepted from the outset as a natural
and an inevitable fact. In Finn's case the matter was far
otherwise. His instinct and inclination bade him regard a
man as a probable friend. Naturally, if the Professor had
been aware of this, he would never have approached Finn
with a hot iron, and their relations would have been quite
different from the beginning. As it was, or as Finn saw it,
anyhow, the Professor had proved himself a creature absolutely beyond the pale; a mad wild beast disguised as a man;
a devil who met friendly advances with repeated blows of a
magic weapon, a stick made of fire, against which no living
thing might stand. However he might disguise his intentions,
his purpose clearly was Finn's destruction. That was how
Finn saw it, and he acted accordingly and consistently, not
from malice but upon the dictates of common sense and self-
preservation as he understood them.

It is hardly necessary to add that Finn suffered greatly during the next few weeks of his life, for had not the Professor
sworn to make the Giant Wolf his obedient creature and a
docile performer in the circus? That he never did. His boast
was never made good, though with a real wolf it might have
been; and again it almost certainly would have been had he
ever guessed that Finn was not a wolf at all but one of the
most aristocratic hounds and friends of man ever bred. But

his failure cost Finn dear, in pain, humiliation, fear, and suffering of diverse kinds.

The boss jeered at the Professor when the failure to tame Finn had extended over a week; and that added greatly to the severity of Finn's ordeal. The Professor was on his mettle; and now, while he made no further spoken boasts, he swore to himself that he would break the Giant Wolf's spirit or kill him. He never guessed that his whole failure rested upon one initial mistake. To the wild beast the red-hot iron bar was merely the terrible insignia of the Professor's indubitable might and mastery; a very compelling invitation to docility and respectful obedience. To Finn it was not that at all but merely terrible and unmistakable evidence of basest treachery and malevolent madness. And it was largely with the red-hot iron that the Professor sought to tame Finn, believing, as he did, that this was necessary to his own, the Professor's, preservation.

Upon one occasion—one brilliantly sunny morning of Finn's martyrdom—it did dimly occur to the Professor that it might be the hot iron that somehow stood between him and the mastery of Finn. Accordingly, he twisted some wire around the end of his quilt, or cutting whip, and entered the cage without the iron, while Sam stood outside with the brazier, ready to pass in the iron if that should prove necessary. Finn absolutely mistrusted the man, of course—he had suffered what he believed to be the man's insane lust of cruelty for a fortnight now—but yet he saw that the iron was not in the cage, and so he made no hostile demonstration; and that was a notable concession on his part, for of late the Professor's tactics, so far from taming him, had taught the naturally gracious and kindly wolfhound to fly at the man with snapping jaws the instant he came within reach. Now the man moved slowly, very slowly, nearer and nearer to Finn's corner, using ingratiating words. When it seemed that he meant to come near enough for touch, Finn decided that he would slip across the cage to its opposite far corner in order to avoid the hated contact. He did not snarl; he did not even uncover his fangs, for the fiery instrument of torture was not there. He rose from his crouching position, and of necessity that brought him a few inches nearer to the Professor before he could move toward the far side of the cage.

"Would yer? Down, ye brute!" snarled the man, in his best awe-inspiring tone. And in that instant the wire-bound rhinoceros hide whistled down across Finn's face, cutting him almost as painfully as the hot iron was wont to sear him. He snarled ferociously. Down came the lash again, and this time a loose end of wire stabbed the corner of one of his eyes. The next instant saw the Professor flung back at length against the bars of the cage; and in his face he felt Finn's breath and heard and saw the flashing, clashing gleam of Finn's white fangs. Sam thrust the white-hot bar in, stabbing Finn's neck with its hissing end. The Professor seized the bar and beat Finn off with it; not for protection now but in sheer, savage anger. Then he withdrew from the cage and, seizing a long pole, beat Finn crushingly with that through the bars till his arms ached. Meantime, Finn fought the pole like a mad thing; and the Professor, unable to think of any other way of inflicting punishment upon the untameable Giant Wolf, took his food from the basket and gave it to Killer before Finn's eyes, leaving the wolfhound to go empty for the day.

That was the result of the Professor's one attempt, according to his lights, at humoring the Giant Wolf by approaching him without the iron. That also was a specimen of the kind of daily interviews he had with Finn.

By this time the wolfhound actually was a very fierce and savage creature. But he was not at all like the magnificently

raging whirlwind of wrath that had aroused the boss's admiring wonder on the day he first saw Finn. Killer might
growl and snarl himself hoarse now for all the notice Finn
took of the great beast. Scarred from nose to flank with
burns, bruised and battered and aching in every limb, Finn
remained always curled in the darkest farthest corner of his
cage now, roused only by the daily fight, the daily torture,
of his interviews with the Professor. At other times, as the
boss said bitterly, he might have been dead or a lap dog for
all the spectacle he offered to the curious who visited his
cage. All they saw was a coiled iron-gray mass and two burning black eyes with a glint of red in them and a blood-colored
triangle in their upper corners.

Now and again, in the midst of the night, Finn would rise
and go down to the bars of his cage and stand there, motion-
less, for an hour at a stretch, his scarred muzzle protruding
between two bars, his aching nostrils, hot and dry, drinking
in the night air, his eyes robbed of their resentful fire and
pitiably softened by the great tears that stood in them. At the
end of such an hour he would sometimes begin to walk softly
to and fro inside the bars, the four paces that his cage allowed
him. Thus he would pad back and forth silently for another
hour, with tail curled toward his belly and nose on a level
with his knees, almost brushing the bars as he passed them.
He made no sound at all, even when the moon's silvery light
flooded his cage or when Killer snarled in his sleep. But always, before returning to his corner, he would systematically
test every bar at its base with teeth and paws and then sigh,
like a very weary man, as he slouched despairingly back to
his corner.

But for all the glowering misery that possessed him by day
and the despair to which he would give rein by night, it was
always with dauntless ferocity that the tortured wolfhound
faced his enemy, the Professor. Short of starving him to death

or killing him outright with the iron bar, the Professor could see no way of making the Giant Wolf cringe to him; he could devise no method of breaking that fierce spirit, though he exhausted every kind of severity and every sort of cruelty that his wide experience in the handling of fierce animals could furnish. For anyone who could have comprehended the true nature of that situation, its tragedy would have lain in the reflection that, had he but known it, Finn could without difficulty have earned not alone ease and good treatment but high honors in the Southern Cross Circus. But Finn had no means of guessing that the Professor merely desired to master him and to teach him to stand erect or leap through a hoop at the word of command. No sign of any such desire that Finn could possibly read had been furnished. On the contrary, the one thing made evident to the wolfhound's understanding was that here was a bloodthirsty man in a leather coat who desired to burn him to death when not engaged in beating him with a pole or thrusting at him viciously through the bars of his cage with a stick or slashing at him with a whip that cut through hair and skin.

There came a day when, other matters occupying his attention, the Professor did not trouble to pay one of his futile visits to Finn's cage. Sam fed him as usual when Killer was fed. (One of the features of Finn's captivity, which while in his confinement it helped to injure his physical condition, also helped to make him the more fierce, was the fact that his diet consisted exclusively of raw meat.) Finn waited through the long day for the Professor, steeling himself for the daily struggle and the daily suffering. His body free of new pains, he rested that night more thoroughly than he had rested for a long time; and there were faint stirrings of hope in his mind. Next morning the boss happened to walk past the cages with the Professor, and when they came to Finn's place, the Professor said:

"I reckon I'll give that brute best, unless you'd like him killed. I'll tackle that job for you with pleasure, but your Giant Wolf's no good for the show."

"He sure is twice as sulky as any beast I ever saw. An' that blame book-writin' chap from the city the other night said he reckoned the Giant was a dog an' not a wolf at all!"

"You should have asked the gent to go in his cage an' try 'im with a bit of sugar. He wouldn't have written any more books!"

If the Professor had continued his daily attempts to cow Finn, as a preliminary to training, he would have been likely to succeed at about this time, for the wolfhound was losing strength daily, and though the fire of wrath and fierceness burned strongly when he saw the leather-coated man, it had little to feed on now and must soon have died down under the hot bar and the wired whip. But the Professor could not be expected to know this. He had had as many as sixty futile struggles with Finn and, as he thought, had only stopped short of killing the Giant outright. But idleness or some other cause did lead him to make one other attempt, on a hot afternoon, just before the hour of tea and of dressing for the evening show. The Professor did not know how near to the breaking point Finn's despair had reached. There was little sign of it in the roaring fierceness with which he faced the iron and whip. Finn fought with the courage of a brave man who has reached the last ditch and with the ferocity that came to him out of the ancient days in which his warrior ancestors were never known either to give or to receive quarter.

The Professor felt that this was a last attempt, and he did not greatly care whether the great hound lived or died. The Giant Wolf had defeated him as a trainer; but the Giant Wolf should never forget the price paid for the defeat. It was a cruel onslaught. The iron bit deep. The Professor himself was aching and sore when he flung passionately out from

Finn's cage and slammed the iron gate to; and as for Finn, I have no words in which to explain how his body ached and was sore. If the iron had been stone cold, Finn would still have been a terribly badly beaten hound when he staggered to his corner after this last visit from the mad beastman in the leather coat. He lay in his corner quivering and shuddering and did not even find the heart to lick his wounds till long hours afterwards, when silence ruled in the field where the circus was encamped that night.

The field was on the outskirts of a considerable township; the twenty-second that Finn had visited with Southern Cross Circus. The authorities had refused to allow the boss to come closer in, and so one side of his camping place was walled by virgin bush; a dense tract of blue gum and ironbark stretching almost as far as the eye could reach, to the foothills of a gaunt mountain range. For a mile or so from the circus camp the trees had all been ring-barked a couple of seasons or more before this time, with the result that they were now the very haggard skeletons of mighty trees, naked for the most part, their white bones open to all the winds of heaven, but here and there sporting a ghastly kind of drapery, remnants of their grave clothes as it might be, in the shape of long hanging streamers of dead bark, which moaned and rustled eerily in the night breezes.

Finn could just see the ghostly extremities of these spectral trees over the top of the main tent as he lay crouched in his corner after devoting an hour to the licking of his sores. Presently, an almost full moon rose among the trees' fleshless limbs and painted their nakedness in more than ever ghostly guise. It was then that Finn rose, painfully and slowly, to his feet and moved, like an old, old man, across the floor of his cage to the bars, the bars that were of an inky blackness in that silvery light. For almost an hour this great hound, this tortured prince of a kingly race, stood sadly there, staring

out at the moonlight between the bars of his prison; and for
almost an hour, big clear drops kept forming in his black
eyes and trickling along his scarred muzzle till they pattered
down upon the floor of the cage.

Near as Finn was to the limit of his endurance, his brave
spirit lived within him yet, and he did not forgo the nightly
habit he had formed long since of trying the bars that made
him a prisoner. The process was not made easier by Finn's
latest wounds Both his forelegs and his muzzle had suffered
severely under the iron that day; and it was with these that
he now tested his bars, slowly, conscientiously, and with painful thoroughness. It was the bottom of the bars that Finn
always tried, where they entered the floor of the cage. He took
each between his teeth and pushed and pulled, sometimes
pushing or pulling with his paws as well. And the result, on
this night of bright moonlight and great pain, was as it had
always been. The iron did not change.

Having reached the end of his task, Finn sat erect on his
haunches for it may have been a quarter of an hour, gazing
out at the risen moon, which sailed serenely now high above
the praying hands of the skeleton trees. Certainly, Finn's
spirit was near to the breaking point. He rose, meaning to
seek his corner again as after so many other futile testings of
his bars; but something moved him first to look out as far
as he could, over the tent top, to the great world beyond. Sore
though his body was, he rose erect upon his hind feet, placed
his forefeet against the upper half of the gate, and only nar-
rowly escaped falling forward through the gate to the ground
beneath. In his passion the Professor had slammed the barred
gate to as usual and, in flinging himself angrily off from the
place, had omitted to slip the two thick bolts that normally
held it secure. The gate fitted closely and was rusty, besides;
so that Finn's jaws, tugging at its extreme foot, and upon this
particular occasion less strongly no doubt than usual, had not

shifted it. But his weight pressing against the upper half was quite another matter; and now the gate stood wide open before him.

For an instant, Finn's heart swelled within him so sharply and so greatly that a little whine burst from him, and it seemed he was unable to move. In the next instant he dropped quietly to the earth and was lost in the inky shadow of the main tent.

15: FREEDOM

VERY wonderful and wolflike, catlike, too, in some respects, was Finn's progress through the circus encampment on that bright moonlight night. The field was full of silvery moonlight; but never a glint of all that liquid silver touched Finn's outline for a moment. Finn was sore and aching from many wounds and stiff from long confinement. He knew that everyone connected with the circus was sleeping; but on this occasion he took no risks.

A fiery picture of the issues at stake was floating in Finn's mind as he crept in and out among the tents and wagons of the enclosure, and he was conscious neither of wounds nor weakness nor stiffness, but only of his great resolve, based upon the wonderful chance that had come to him. Once he came to a place where ten feet of brilliant moonlight lay between the black shadow he occupied and the next. He paused for a moment or two, looking about him upon every side with all the cunning of the truly wild kindred; and then, with a very good imitation of the lightness and elasticity of other, happier days, he sprang clear from the one shadow to the other, landing as delicately and silently as a cat, though the impact jarred all his stiffened joints and touched, as with living fire, every one of his almost innumerable wounds.

Then he came to the outer canvas wall of the big enclosure. It was too high to jump, a good twelve feet. An attempt to jump and scramble over it might have led to noise. Finn approached it in the deep shadow cast by a caravan wagon and, thrusting his muzzle underneath the canvas, midway between two stakes, easily forced it up and crawled under it into the open. When he was halfway out, the boss's fox terrier gave one sleepy half-bark, too languid and indifferent a sound to be taken as a warning; and for the rest, complete silence paid tribute to the extreme deftness of Finn's passage through the sleeping camp. In the next moment, almost as silently as a passing cloud shadow, the great wolfhound streaked across the thirty yards of moonlit paddock that divided the camp from the ring-barked bush and melted away among that crowded assembly of tree ghosts. The barbed-wire fence of the paddock was no more than four feet high, and this Finn took in his stride, without appreciable pause.

The ring-barking of trees admits sunlight and air to the earth, and this means rich "feed" and a sturdy undergrowth. Finn was amazed by the wealth and variety of wildlife he saw as he loped swiftly through the few miles of bush lying between the circus camp and the foothills of the mountains beyond. His immediate purpose, of putting a considerable distance between himself and the place of his captivity, was too urgent to admit of delays, no matter what the temptation; and accordingly, Finn made no pauses. But it added greatly to the joy of his escape to find himself surrounded by so great an abundance of creatures that instinct made him regard as game for him. Upon every hand there were rustlings and whisperings, tiny footfalls and scufflings among dead leaves and twigs; and here and there, as the great gray, shadowy wolfhound swept along between the white tree trunks, he had glimpses of rabbits, bandicoots, kangaroo rats, and many of the lesser marsupials, all busy about their different night affairs, all half paralyzed by amazement at his passage through their midst. Once he heard a venomous spitting overhead and, as he hurried on, caught a flying glimpse of a native cat, who had pinned an adventurous young possum on the lower limb of a giant blackbutt.

The ring-barked country was soon left behind, and then Finn found himself among dense living bush, climbing a steep ascent. Here his speed was necessarily a great deal slower. There was a good deal of undergrowth upon the mountainside, besides much heavy timber; and hidden among this lush undergrowth were occasional boulders and innumerable fallen tree trunks.

Dawn was not far off when Finn emerged, with heaving flank and lolling tongue, into the green but stony glade that formed the ridge and crest of the Tinnaburra range. The last one hundred yards of his progress had been a good deal of a scramble through thick scrub and over lichen-covered boulders on a very steep rise. And now that he had reached the cool glade of topmost Tinnaburra, he found that his arrival had caused considerable perturbation among a small mob of brumbies, or wild horses, consisting of some seven or eight mares and foals, led by a flea-bitten old gray stallion, who snorted angrily as he saw Finn and minced forward toward the wolfhound, his long chisel teeth bared, his four-foot tail billowing out behind him like a flag, and his black hoofs rising and falling from the dewy earth like spring hammers.

Finn devoted the little breath he could spare to the rather whining note of explanation that means: "Don't fear me! I pursue my own affairs only, and they are harmless for you!" But the old stallion was taking no chances. Also, Finn brought a baffling mixture of scents with him, including those of men

and of wild creatures such as the stallion had never seen and
did not wish to see. So he continued his threateningly minc-
ing progress toward Finn and whinnied out a declaration to
the effect that this could be no resting place for dingoes, however huge and diversified in their smells. Finn was not in the
least like a dingo; but, on the other hand, he was not like a
kangaroo hound. He was very nearly twice the size of a dingo
and a good seven inches taller than the biggest kangaroo
hound the stallion had seen.

Finn was in no mood for disputes of any sort, and so,
though exceedingly weary now, he made a wide detour to
satisfy the nervousness of the flea-bitten gray stallion and began a diagonal descent upon the south side of Tinnaburra.
Just as the sun cleared the horizon over his right shoulder,
Finn dropped wearily down from a clump of wattle upon
a broad, flat ledge of many-colored rock, which caught the
sun's first glinting rays upon its queer enamel of red and
brown and yellow lichen. From this point Finn looked down
a densely wooded mountainside and out across a tolerably
well-timbered plain to hills, which stood nearly forty miles
away. It would have made an eyrie for a king eagle. Finn
had already slaked his thirst hurriedly a mile back, in a chat-
tering, rock-bedded mountain streamlet. And now he was
weary beyond all further endurance. He had been sick and
sore and stiff and sadly out of condition when he started; and
he had been traveling now for six hours. A feeling of security
had stolen over him since he reached the topmost ridge of
Tinnaburra. The very fragrance of the air told him, as he
drew it in through his nostrils, that he was far from the works
of men. Food he could not think of while every bone and
muscle in his great body ached from weariness. By the edge
of the rock was a sandy hollow, over which a feathery shrub
drooped three or four of its graceful branches at a height of
three feet from the ground. Finn eyed this inviting spot

steadily for two or three minutes, while his aching sides continued to heave and his long tongue to sway from one side of his jaws. Then he stepped cautiously into the sheltered nook, turned completely around in it three or four times, and finally sank to rest there in a compact coil and with a little grunt of contentment and relief.

Finn opened his eyes and half opened them many times during the day, once, to his utter amazement, when a huge wedge-tailed eagle swept gloriously past with a lamb in its talons no more than ten feet from his nose; but the day was practically done and nightfall approaching when the wolfhound finally rose from his sandy bed and stretched his seven-foot length from nose to tail. The long stretch drew a sharp whine from him toward its end when the stiffness and soreness of his limbs and of some of his more recent burns and bruises found him out. But now that he was broad awake and in the hushed gray twilight looked out across forty miles of wild open land, with never a sign of tent or house or other work of man, his heart swelled within him with satisfaction and content, and he drew deep breaths of grateful pleasure and relief before setting out upon the descent of Tinnaburra and, if it might be, the capture of a supper.

Before Finn had traveled half a mile along the hillside, he made his first painful acquaintance with snakes. In descending at a sharp angle from the side of a fallen tree, his forefeet just scraped the end of the tail of a nine-foot carpet snake, whose coloring was vivid and fresh. Before Finn knew what had happened, one coil of the sinuous reptile's body was about his left hind leg, and as the startled wolfhound wheeled in his tracks, the big snake's head rose at him with a forbidding, long-drawn "Ps-s-s-s-t!" of defiance. The rapidly tightening pressure about his muscular lower thigh produced something like panic in Finn's breast; but, luckily enough, his panic resulted in speeding him toward precisely the right course of action. He feinted in the direction of his hind leg, and then, as the snake plunged for his neck, his jaws flashed back and caught the reptile just behind the head. A single bite was sufficient, for it smashed the snake's vertebrae and almost divided it. A moment later Finn's teeth were at the coil about his hind leg, and in another instant he was free. But he was too greatly shocked to make a meal upon the remains of his enemy, which is what he should have done, and after taking a good look at its long, brilliantly colored body, he was glad to make off down the hill, traveling now with a good deal more caution than he had shown before. It was a merciful thing for Finn that his first contact with the snake folk should have brought him in touch only with the powerful and courageous carpet snake and not with one of the many deadly, venomous members of his tribe.

This experience rather shook Finn by its utter strangeness to him. He recalled the spitting venom of the native cat, of whose kill he had caught a fleeting glimpse on the previous night. That again was rather strange and outside his experience. Just then a laughing jackass started a hoarse chuckle above Finn's head, and a big white cockatoo, startled by the jackass, flew out screaming from the branches of a gray gum with the agonized note in its cry that these birds seem to favor at all seasons and quite irrespective of the nature of their occupations at the moment. The loose skin on Finn's shoulders moved uneasily as he trotted along, using the most extreme care.

But with all his care, he was in strange surroundings, and his bush lore was all to learn; and because of his strangeness, his most careful gait seemed a noisy and clumsy one to the little wild folk of that mountainside, and Finn saw none of them. By chance he saw one of the larger kind, however, and the sight of it added to his sense of strangeness, for it was unlike any other beast he had ever seen. This was a large

female rock wallaby, a big gray doe with her young one. The
youngster was at the awkward age, free of the teat yet unable
to travel alone. It was nibbling and playing some distance
from its big mother when she had her first warning of Finn's
approach in the crackling of dead twigs under his powerful
feet. The youngster showed awkwardness in getting to its
snug retreat in the mother's pouch, and so, by these delays,
Finn was given his glimpse of a big marsupial in the act of
taking a fifteen-foot leap through the scrub. Finn almost sat
down on his haunches from astonishment. But, unlike the
snake, the wallaby inspired him with no sort of fear, possibly
by reason of its evident fear of him.

It seems absurd to suggest that the great wolfhound may
have been suffering from loneliness, seeing that he had never
been so thankful for anything else in his whole life as he was
for his escape from the circus, with its small army of menfolk
and animals. But it is a fact that as Finn plodded along
through the wild bush to the south of Tinnaburra, he began
to be haunted by a sense of isolation and friendlessness. It was
now thirty hours since he had tasted food, and it seemed that
game shunned his trail, for he saw none of the many small
animals he had passed on the previous night. Finn inherited
fighting instincts and savage ferocity under persecution from
a long and noble line of hunting and fighting ancestors. But
he inherited few instincts that bore practically upon the matter of picking up his own living, of walking alone, of depend-
ing exclusively upon himself, and of leading the solitary life
of the really wild Carnivora. As it was, the big snake, the
huge eagle, the screaming cockatoo, the nerve-shaking caco-
phony of the jackass, and the half-flying progress of the big
wallaby, all combined with the huge wildness of the country
and its vegetation to oppress Finn with the sense of being a
lone outcast, an outlier in a foreign land that was full of
sinister possibilities. Also, he was getting very hungry.

While these impressions were sinking into the wolfhound's mind, the country through which he was traveling was becoming more open, more like a long-neglected park, in which many of the trees were dead and all had a gaunt and scraggy look, with their thin, pointed gray-green leaves, their curiously tortured-looking limbs, and their long, rustling streamers of decaying bark. But, however Finn might feel in the matter of loneliness, it was with a pang of something like horror that he came presently upon a barbed-wire fence, exactly like the one he had leaped over the previous night directly after leaving the circus. Could it be possible that the circus had been moved during the day to this place and the barbed-wire fence brought with it? Finn prowled cautiously up and down that fence for a couple of hundred yards in each direction, peering beyond it and sniffing and listening with the extreme of suspiciousness before he finally leaped the wire and continued his way in a southeasterly direction.

Five minutes later he saw a rabbit, and though he lost it, because it was sitting within a foot of its burrow and disappeared with lightning-like rapidity at sight of Finn, yet he was cheered by this homely sight and pursued his way with renewed hope in the matter of supper. A moment later, he stopped dead in his tracks as though shot and then crawled softly aside to take cover behind a thicket of scrub.

In topping an abrupt little ridge, he had come suddenly into full view of a bark gunyah or shanty, in the triangular opening of which, beside a bright fire, sat a man and a big black hound. A billycan swung over the fire on a tripod of stakes, and the man was engaged with his supper. Finn did not know, of course, that the man was a boundary rider and his dog a not very well-bred kangaroo hound. The wind was northwest or the kangaroo hound would surely have scented Finn's approach and given tongue.

For a long time Finn lay under the cover of his thicket,

peering through the darkness at the boundary rider and his
dog. The thing that most impressed Finn in the picture he
saw was the figure of the black hound, stretched at ease beside the fire, steadily eying its master. Every once in a while
the man would break a chunk from his damper or cut a
morsel from his meat and toss it to the kangaroo hound, who
opened and closed its jaws like a steel trap and gulped the
gift with portentous solemnity and absolutely without visible
sign of any emotion whatever. The hound showed only
watchfulness. Finn heard its jaws snap and could almost hear
the gulp that disposed of each morsel. The sight and the
sound gave an edge to the wolfhound's already keen appetite,
and almost unconsciously, he drew nearer and yet nearer to
the gunyah, crouching low to the ground as he moved, his
hindquarters gathered under him ready for springing, like
a huge cat.

There was no suggestion of circuses or cages or cruelty
about the picture Finn saw; but his recent experiences had
been far too severe to admit of anything like the old simple
trustfulness in his attitude. That could never be again. Even
hunger would never make this wolfhound trustful again. But
for all that, there was something in the picture of the campfire and the pair who sat beside it that drew Finn strongly.
So far as his own life in the world went, this was the first
campfire Finn had ever seen. One could not say exactly how
or why it should have been so, but it is a fact that, while
crouching, Finn gazed upon and crept closer to that campfire, his mind was full of affectionate thoughts and memories
of the Master and of the old days of their happy companionship. Up till this evening he had not thought of the Master
for many days.

It was doubtless the campfire picture that filled the lone
wolfhound's mind with thoughts of the Master; but it was

nonetheless an odd coincidence that, at the very hour of
Finn's approach to a campfire in the bush, a dozen miles and
more to the southeast of Tinnaburra, the Master should have
been approaching the big house by the harbor outside the
capital city, three hundred miles away, with a mind full of
Finn.

The Mistress of the Kennels had more than justified the
doctor's prophecies. Less than a month of life in the mountains had given her back her old energy and strength. The
third week there had given her also the acquaintance, soon
to ripen into friendship, of a certain squatter's wife, who was
spending a few weeks in the hills with her husband and three
children. Before the acquaintance was a week old, the Mistress of the Kennels had been pressingly invited to make her
home with the squatter and his wife at their station, for a
time at all events, in order that she might supervise the education of the three youngsters and also give the squatter's
wife the benefit of some of her experience in the rearing of
dogs. The Master could have found a minor opening on the
same station but decided that he could not afford to take up
a life that offered no particular prospect of advancement, and
he was confirmed in his decision by an offer that was made
to him at this time to join, in a working capacity, a small
prospecting party setting out for a tract of back-block country said to be extremely rich in gold, copper, and silver. And
so, for a time, the Master and the Mistress had parted company.

Less than three weeks after the outset of this particular
expedition, the party had pegged out a considerable number
of rich claims. Some of these claims had been of a kind that
admitted of a good deal of highly profitable alluvial working; but the majority called for the use of machinery and the
outlay of capital. Accordingly, the party gathered to themselves such surface gold as was obtainable—the Master's share

came to two hundred and sixty pounds—and then, laden with samples of ore, returned townward with a view to selling their claims to mining capitalists before starting out upon a second and more protracted journey. The fascination of the prospector's calling had gripped the Master strongly, and he gladly agreed to remain a member of the party. But, in the meantime, having reached the city, he had determined to pay a visit to Mr. Sandbrook's house; first, that he might have the satisfaction of seeing Finn again, and, secondly, in order that he might try the effect of a substantial money offer in the matter of regaining possession of his wolfhound. And so now the Master strode up the hill overlooking the city and the harbor.

Mr. and Mrs. Sandbrook were both away from home, but one of the daughters of the house explained to the Master how, after "sulking desperately for two whole days," the wolfhound had basely deserted his luxurious new home and never been heard of since. She showed the Master an advertisement offering a reward of five-and-twenty pounds for Finn's recovery and was at some pains to make clear the indubitable fact that her father had paid very dearly indeed for the doubtful privilege of possessing for two days a wolfhound who had "treated everybody as if they were dirt under his feet." The Master expressed sympathy in sentences that were meant to be loyal excuses for Finn; and then he turned and walked back to the city, heavy at heart for the loss of the great wolfhound whom he had loved and feeling vaguely that the money he had made was not such a very precious thing after all. He placed the greater part of it at the disposal of the Mistress of the Kennels and went back to his fellow prospectors.

16: THE DOMESTIC LURE

As Finn drew closer to the campfire, the savory smell of the stewed mutton the man by the gunyah was eating came sailing down the breeze into his nostrils. But the wolfhound's desire for food was nothing like so keen a thing as his dread of renewed captivity, and his approach to the campfire was an illustration of the extreme of animal caution. His powerful limbs were all the time gathered well under him, prepared for instant flight.

Suddenly and simultaneously two things happened. A log on the fire broke in half, allowing a long tongue of flame to leap up and light the ground for fifty yards around, and the kangaroo hound turned its greyhound-like muzzle sharply to one side and saw Finn. In the next instant three things happened together: the man's eyes followed those of his dog and saw Finn, the dog leaped to its feet and barked loudly; and Finn jumped sideways and backwards, a distance of three yards. Then the man said, "By ghost!" and the kangaroo hound bounded forward toward Finn.

Now it was not in Finn's nature to run from a dog, and so, as the boundary rider did not move, he held his ground. But his recent experiences had all made for hostility and the fighting attitude toward other animals; and so Finn held his hindquarters bunched well under him ready for springing, his forelegs stretched well before him, his jaws slightly parted, and the lips lifted considerably from his fangs.

But apparently the black kangaroo hound was not very greatly impressed. It is practically certain that this dog knew at a glance that Finn was not really of the wild kindred; also, she was a brave creature, a fearless hunter, and a hound who stood twenty-eight inches at the shoulder; eight inches lower than the giant wolfhound it is true, but even so, taller, bigger, and heavier than a typical greyhound of her sex. She showed not the slightest fear of the wolfhound but flew right up to him, barking loudly, with every sign of readiness for fight. Finn growled warningly, and as the stranger snapped at him, he leaped aside. It was then, as his jaws parted in anger, that consciousness of the black hound's sex came to him, in the subtle way that his kind acquire such facts, and his jaws promptly closed upon space. When the kangaroo hound snapped a second time, Finn turned his shoulder to her meekly and gave a little friendly whinny of a whine. This was repeated two or three times, Finn evading the black hound's snapping jaws (one could see that her bites no longer meant serious business; they were more ceremonial than punishing), but showing not the slightest intention to make reprisals. Finn was obeying the law of his kind where the weaker sex is concerned.

After a minute, the kangaroo hound began to sniff curiously at Finn instead of snapping at him, and at this the wolfhound drew himself up proudly and remained perfectly still and very erect, his long tail curving grandly behind him, legs well apart, and his magnificent head carried high, save when, as opportunity offered, he took a passing sniff at any portion of the kangaroo hound's anatomy that happened to come near his muzzle.

All this while—these elaborate formalities had occupied no more than three minutes altogether—the boundary rider, who was a knowledgeable person with animals, had been standing quite still beside his fire, watching Finn and his own dog with intent curiosity. He had never seen a dog at all like Finn, but he felt certain Finn was a dog and not a creature of the wild, if only by reason of his own black hound's attitude. He pictured himself hunting kangaroo with Finn and Jess (the black hound), and the prospect pleased him mightily. So

now he picked up a piece of mutton from the dish beside the
fire and took a couple of steps in Finn's direction, holding
the meat out before him and saying in a friendly way:

"Come on in, then, good dog! Here, boy! Here then!"

Finn eyed the man hesitatingly for a moment. The meat
was tempting. But Finn's memories and fear were strong,
and he moved slowly backwards as the man advanced. For a
little distance they progressed in this wise: the man slowly
advancing and calling, Finn slowly retiring backwards, and
the kangaroo hound playing and sniffing about him.

The man was the first to tire of this, as was natural, and
when he came to a standstill, he tossed the meat from him to
Finn, with a "Here then, boy; eat it there, if you like." But
Jess had no notion of carrying hospitality as far as all this.
She sprang upon the bit of meat and growled savagely as her
nose grazed Finn's. She had forestalled the wolfhound and
was likely to continue to do so, since the law of their kind
prevented him from exerting his superior strength against
her.

Then the man walked slowly back to the shanty, calling
both dogs over his shoulder as he went. Jess obediently ran
to him and then danced back, encouragingly, to Finn. Finn
advanced with her till the man reached the fire and resumed
his seat on the ground. Then Finn stopped dead, his hindquarters well drawn up and ready for a spring; and no
blandishment that Jess could exercise proved sufficient to
draw him closer to the fire. Seeing this, the man called Jess
sharply, after a while, and ordered her to lie down beside
him, which she did. Then he cut off a good-sized chunk of
meat and tossed it to Finn, saying, "Here, good dog; come in
and feed then!" He carefully threw the meat to a point about
three yards nearer the fire than where Finn stood but still a
good six or seven paces from it. Finn watched the meat fall

and sniffed its fragrance from the dry grass. The man, after all, was sitting down, and humans always occupied quite a long time in rising to their feet. Very slowly, very warily, and with eyes fixed steadily on the man, Finn covered the three yards between himself and the meat and, as he seized it in his jaws, moved backwards again at least one yard.

The warm mutton was exceedingly gratifying to Finn, and he showed little hesitation about advancing the necessary four or five feet to secure a second and larger piece thrown down for him by the man. But again he withdrew about a yard before swallowing it. Then the man held another piece of meat out to him at arm's length and invited him to come and take it for himself. Finn advanced one yard and then definitely stopped at, say, eight paces from the man's hand and waited. Still the man held the meat and would not throw it. Finn waited, head held a little on one side, black eyes fixed intently on the man's face Then, slowly, he lowered his great length to the ground, without for an instant removing his gaze from the boundary rider's face, and lay with forelegs outstretched, watching and waiting and resting at the same time. Evidently the man regarded this as some sort of a step forward, for he yielded now and flung the piece of meat so that it fell beside Finn's paws. The great wolfhound half rose in gulping down the meat but resumed his lying position a moment later, still watching and waiting. The man smiled.

"Well, sonny," he said with a chuckle, "you play a mighty safe game, don't you? You're not takin' any chances on the cards. I believe you reckon I've got the joker up my sleeve, hey? But you're wrong, 'cos me sleeves is rolled up. Now, how d'ye like plain damper? Just see how Wallaby Bill's tombstones strike ye!"

As he spoke, the man called Wallaby Bill flung Finn a solid chunk of very indigestible damper, which the wolfhound gratefully disposed of with two bites and three gulps before plainly asking for more. This was Finn's first taste of food other than raw meat for some months, and he enjoyed it.

"Well, say, Wolf, I suppose your belly has a bottom to it, somewhere, what? Here; don't mind me; take the lot!"

With this, having first broken up a good large section of damper in it, he pushed the dish along the dry grass as far as he could in Finn's direction, with all that was left of the meat cooked that evening, a fairly ample meal for a hound, apart from what had come before. The boundary rider lay on the ground to push the dish as far toward Finn as he could and then recovered his sitting position and pretended to become absorbed in the filling of a pipe, while continuing to watch Finn out of the corners of his eyes. The dish was now perhaps three yards from where Bill sat and a yard and a half from Finn. The man appeared to be wrapped up in his own concerns, and Finn's hunger was far from being satisfied. Very cautiously, then, he advanced till he could reach the lip of the dish with his teeth; then, still moving with the most watchful care, he gripped the tin dish and softly drew it back about a couple of feet. Then he began to eat from it, his eyes still fixed upon the half-recumbent figure of the man, who was now contentedly smoking and pulling Jess's ears.

Finn polished the tin dish clean and bright and then retired into the shadows.

"There's gratitude for you!" growled Bill. But he did not move, being the knowledgeable person with animals that he was. Finn had only gone as far as the water hole he had seen, some thirty or forty yards from the shanty. There the wolfhound drank his fill and drew back, licking his jaws with zest.

Slowly, and with only a little less caution than before, Finn now approached the camp a second time and heard Bill say to the kangaroo hound: "All right, Jess; go to him, then!" In another moment, Jess came prancing out toward him, and Finn spread out his forelegs and lowered his great frame to the earth, while his hindquarters remained erect and ready for a pivoting movement. Jess now imitated Finn's attitude, and when his nose had almost touched hers, she bounded from him sideways and backwards, sometimes wheeling completely around and barking with pretended ferocity, till she stooped again and repeated the process.

Wallaby Bill was pleasantly interested in watching this amiable performance, but it would have impressed him vastly more if he could have pictured to himself the sort of spectacle Finn had presented a couple of days before, when, with foaming jaws, gleaming fangs, raised hackles, and straining limbs, the great wolfhound had pitted himself, with roaring fury, against the leather-coated man who wielded the hot iron. To lend verisimilitude to the game, Finn had to growl low down in his throat at intervals, while Jess snarled and barked; but when Finn laid one paw on the kangaroo hound's curved back, as he frequently did at different phases of the game, his touch, for all his huge bulk and weight, was one that would not have incommoded a newborn pup.

Wallaby Bill's pipe had burned itself out before the hounds tired of their play and stretched themselves upon the ground, Jess lying a good yard and a half nearer to the fire than Finn ventured. But Finn moved only very slightly now when Bill rose slowly to his feet and stretched his arms, while taking careful observations of the newcomer. In the bright firelight, he was just able to make out the bigger among Finn's scars, where the Professor's iron had burned through the wolfhound's wiry coat. Finn half rose, with ears cocked and muscles ready for the spring, when Bill yawned and said:

"Well, Wolf, you are the biggest thing in your line ever I did see. But it seems to me you've been havin' a pretty rough

house with somebody." He took one slow step forward; and
Finn immediately took three backwards, in one quick jump.
"All right, sonny; keep your hair on now, do. I only want to
get the dish an' wash up after your royal highness. Can't I
move then? You're too suspicious, Wolf, my son." And then,
in a lower tone, "My oath, but someone's handled you pretty
meanly before today, I reckon."

Bill's notion of washing up was distinctly primitive. He
took a long drink of tea from the billy and then used what
was left to rinse out the dish that Finn had polished. Then
he wiped it carefully on his towel and hung it up inside the
gunyah. Finn had returned to his old place by this time but
hesitated to lie down while Bill moved about.

"Now, just you take a rest, Wolf," said the boundary rider
satirically. "I'm goin' to turn in now, an' I don't attack thun-
derin' great gray wolf dogs while I'm undressin'. An' jest you
remember, my boy, that where I sleeps I breakfasts—sure
thing—an' where I breakfasts, there's apt to be oddments goin'
for great big gray wolf dogs as well as black kangaroo bitches;
so don't you forget it, Wolf. So long, son!"

And with that the man retired to his bunk, which consisted of two flour sacks stretched on saplings, supported a
few inches above the ground by forked sticks, a very comfortable bed indeed. As for Finn, the feeling inspired in him by
Bill's talk, to say nothing of Bill's supper and Bill's fire and
the black hound, was something really not far removed from
affection; but it was nothing at all like complete trust. Finn
did not lie down again until his ears had satisfied him that
the man was lying down within the bark shanty. Yet it was
not many months since Finn had faced the whole world of
menfolk with the most complete and unquestionable confidence and trust. So much the Professor had accomplished
in his attempt at "taming" the "Giant Wolf." But, well fed
and cheered by companionship, Finn rested more happily

that night than he had rested since his parting with the Master. It was very delightful to slide gradually off into sleep with the sound of Jess's regular breathing in his ears and the warm glow of the smoldering log fire in his half-closed eyes.

17: THE SUNDAY HUNT

FINN'S new friends were distinctly an odd couple. Wallaby Bill had been a small farmer, a "cockatoo," at one time, with land of his own, but when he received a check for stock or for a crop, it was his wont to leave the farm for days together while he "blew in his check" in the township. After that, he would have to buy flour on credit, eat kangaroo flesh and rabbit, and his stock would have to live upon what they could pick up for themselves in the bush. So naturally, an end had come to Bill's farming.

His present life could only be described as nomadic; and it seemed to be the only life he cared for. He was an excellent boundary rider, shrewd, capable, and farseeing. As such, he would work for weeks, and even, occasionally, for months at a stretch, utterly alone, save for his dog, and apparently quite content. Then, without apparent reason and certainly without any kind of warning, he would make tracks for the nearest township and be seen no more outside its "hotel" till every penny he could lay hands upon was transferred to the publican's till.

This man had reared Jess by hand with the aid of a cracked teapot; and the kangaroo hound bitch knew him better than anyone else did. For her, he was the only human being who counted seriously; and it was said that she had come near to killing a certain publican who had attempted to "go through"

Bill's pockets when he was drunk. She accompanied Bill everywhere and, whatever his occupation or condition, was never far from his side.

Bill had probably never been guilty of willful meanness or cruelty in his life, though, upon occasion, he could display a certain rough brutality. His normal attitude of mind was one of careless, kindly good-humor. From Finn's point of view, he was an extremely good sort of fellow, of a type new and strange to the wolfhound; one of whom nothing could be predicted with any certainty. Six months before, Bill's obvious good nature would have been ample passport to Finn's confidence and friendship. But all that had been changed, and everything and everybody strange was now suspect to Finn.

The wolfhound was the first to wake in the very early morning of the day following his arrival at the boundary rider's gunyah. His movement waked Jess, and together they stretched and walked around the camp. Then Finn trotted off toward the denser bush that lay some hundreds of yards eastward of the camp. Jess ran with him for perhaps a score of yards, and then, determined not to lose sight of her man's abode, she turned and trotted back to camp. This surprised Finn but did not affect his plans. He noted a warm little ridge some distance ahead, which looked as though it contained rabbit earths. This spot he approached by means of a flanking movement, which enabled him to reach it from the rear, moving with the care and delicacy of a great cat. As he peered over the edge of the little ridge, he saw three rabbits performing their morning toilet, perhaps a score of paces beyond the bank. He eyed them with interest for about a minute, and then, having decided that the middle one carried the most flesh, he pursed himself together and leaped. As he landed, ten or a dozen paces from the rabbits, they separated, two flying diagonally for the bank and the middle one leap-

ing off ahead, meaning to describe a considerable curve before reaching its earth. But Finn was something of an expert
in the pursuit of rabbits and, besides being very fleet, had
learned to wheel swiftly and to cut off corners. Two seconds
later that rabbit was dead and, holding it firmly between his
great jaws, Finn had started off at a leisurely trot for the camp.

As Finn arrived beside the gunyah, Bill appeared at its
entrance, yawning and stretching his muscular arms.

"Hullo there, Wolf," he said lazily. "Early bird catches the
worm, hey? Good on ye, my son."

Finn had stopped dead at sight of the man, and now Jess
bounded toward him, full of interest. Finn dropped the rabbit before her, quite prepared to share his breakfast with the
kangaroo hound. That had been his intention, in fact, in
bringing his kill back to camp. But to his surprise Jess
snatched up the rabbit and wheeled away from him.

"Come in here, Jess! Come in!" growled the man sharply.
"Come in here an' drop it."

Whereupon, Jess trotted docilely up to the humpy and laid
her stolen prize at Bill's feet. Bill whipped out his sheath
knife and, with one or two deft cuts and tugs, skinned the
rabbit. The pelt he placed on a log beside the gunyah, and
the carcass he cut in half across the backbone. Then he tossed
the head half to Jess and the other, and slightly larger portion, to Finn.

So the hounds fed while Bill washed and prepared his own
breakfast. Jess ate beside the bark hut, but Finn withdrew to
a more respectful distance and lay down with his portion of
the rabbit some twenty yards from the camp.

After breakfast, the man took a bridle in his hand and set
out to find his horse, who carried a bell but was never
hobbled. Jess walked sedately one yard behind her man's
heels; Finn strolled after them at a distance of fifteen or
twenty yards. Occasionally Jess would turn and trot back to

the wolfhound for a friendly sniff; but while receiving her advances amiably, Finn never responded to her invitations to join her in close attendance upon the man. Once Bill was mounted, Jess seemed satisfied to leave twenty or thirty yards, or even more, between herself and her man; and this being so, the two hounds ran together and shared all their little discoveries and interests. Bill rode a good many miles that day, always beside a wire fence; and occasionally he would stop, dismount, and busy himself in some small repair where a fencepost had sagged down or the wire become twisted or slack.

At such times, while Bill was busy, Finn and Jess would cover quite a good deal of ground, always within a half-mile radius of the man; and in these small excursions Finn began to learn a good deal in the way of bushcraft from the wily Jess. Once she snapped at his shoulder suddenly and thrust him aside from a log he was just about to clamber upon. As Finn drew back wonderingly, a short black snake rose between him and the log, hissed angrily at the hounds once, and then darted away around the log's butt end. He had now seen a death adder, the snake whose bite kills inside of fifteen minutes; and, so much more apt are the dog kind in some matters than ourselves, that Finn would never again require reminding or instructing about this particular form of danger.

On the other hand, when a sudden pungent scent and a rustle among the twigs set Finn leaping forward after the strangest-looking beast his eyes had ever seen, Jess joined with him in a good-humored, rather indifferent manner, and between them they just missed a big iguana. This particular 'guana had a tail rather more than twice its own length, and the last foot of this paid forfeit in Finn's jaws for the animal's lack of agility. Though when one says lack of agility, it is fair to add that only a very swiftly moving creature could have escaped the two hounds at all; and once it reached a tree trunk, this reptile showed wonderful cleverness in climbing, running up fifty feet of ironbark trunk as quickly as it could cover the level ground, and keeping always on the far side of the tree from the dogs, its long, ugly wedge-shaped head constantly turning from side to side in keen, listening observation.

After four days of this sort of life, during practically every hour of which Finn was learning bushcraft from Jess, the wolfhound began to feel almost as thoroughly at home in the bush as he had felt on his own hunting ground in Sussex. But rather curiously, perhaps, he advanced hardly at all in the intimacy of his relations with Bill. The wolfhound was conscious that the boundary rider was friendly; but, on the other hand, he had points in common with the circus people, whose doings had burned right into Finn's very soul. It was extremely pleasant to lie near the campfire with Jess of a night and to run with Jess in the bush by day; but nothing would induce Finn to approach the gunyah more nearly, or to allow Bill's hand to come within a yard of him.

As for Bill, he seemed content. Finn brought rabbits to the camp every day, with occasional bandicoots, and in the evening, sometimes, a kangaroo rat. Bill never thought of making any use of the overplentiful supply of rabbits for the replenishment of his own larder. He regarded rabbits as English people regard rats and would never have eaten them while any other kind of meat was available. And as Finn found later, the same pronounced distaste for rabbits' flesh holds good, not alone among the menfolk of the country, but with practically all its wild folk, also; even the highly carnivorous and fierce native cat paid no heed to them as game.

The fifth day of Finn's acquaintance with Bill and Jess was a Sunday, and the boundary rider was a strict observer of the Sabbath. His observation of it might not have particularly commended itself to orthodox Sabbatarians, but such as it was, Bill never departed from it. Directly after breakfast he washed the shirt and vest he had been wearing during the previous week and hung them out to dry. Then he brought in his horse and trifled with it for a while, examining its feet and rubbing its ears and giving it a few handfuls of bread. Then he took a very early lunch and went off hunting. He had no gun, but he had a formidable sheath knife, his horse, and Jess. And now, in a way, he had Finn as well. He had been wondering all the week about Finn's quality as a hunter and looking forward to the opportunity of testing the wolf-hound. As for Jess, she knew perfectly well when a Sunday had arrived.

On the previous day, Bill had paid particular attention to some tracks he had seen on the far side of a gully some three or four miles from the gunyah; and Jess had shown herself amazingly anxious to make further investigations at the time, until brought sternly to heel by Bill with the suggestion that, "You've got mixed up in your almanac, old lady. This is Saturday."

Now, with a tomahawk stuck in the saddle cleat he had made to hold it and a stock whip dangling from one hand, the bushman ambled off on his roan-colored mare in the direction of this same gully. Jess, full of suppressed excitement, circled about the horse's head for some few minutes till bidden to "Sober up, there, Jess!" when she fell back and trotted beside Finn, a dozen yards from the horse. Arrived at the gully, Bill reined in to a very slow walk and peered about him carefully upon the ground. It was Jess who found what her man was questing: the quite fresh tracks of a kangaroo; and Finn was keenly interested in the discovery. He noted carefully every scratch in the tracks as Jess nosed them and noted also, as the result of long strong breaths drawn through his nostrils, the exact scent that hung about them. This scent alone proved the tracks quite fresh.

In starting away from the gully, Bill rode at a walk and with extreme care, Jess going in front and Finn, not as yet so clever in tracking, following up the rear and taking very careful observations, not alone of the trail, but also of fallen timber and likely places for snakes. They progressed in this way, in a curving line, for between two and three miles when Jess came to a momentary halt and gave one loud bark. Next instant they were all traveling at the gallop for a thick clump of scrub, which stood alone in a comparatively clear patch. On the edge of this scrub Finn had a momentary glimpse of their quarry, a big red old-man kangaroo, sitting on his haunches and delicately eating leaves.

The kangaroo covered over twenty feet of ground in his first leap. By the time the hunters had reached the scrub, the quarry was between two and three hundred yards distant, traveling at a great rate in fairly open country. Bill had urged his horse to the top of its gallop, and Finn was close behind them. He could have passed them but was not as yet sufficiently familiar with the man to do so. He felt safer with Bill in full view; and, in any case, the roan mare was a very fast traveler and kept as close to Jess's flying feet as was safe The old man seemed confident of his power to outrun his pursuers, for he made no attempt at dodging, taking a straight-ahead course over ground that left him clearly visible almost all the time That his confidence in his superior speed was misplaced became quite evident at the end of the first mile, for by that time there was not much more than one hundred yards between Jess and himself, in spite of the enormous bounds he took, which made his progress resemble flying. He could take a fallen log in his jump easily enough, but whenever the course rose at all sharply, the old man lost ground, his jumps appearing to fall very short then.

At the end of the third mile Jess, who was galloping in greyhound style, was within twenty feet of the kangaroo; Bill

and the roan mare were twelve or fifteen feet behind her, and
Finn, running a little wide of the trail, was abreast of the
mare's flanks with a fierce, killing light in his eyes. In that
order they entered a steep gully, which, if the old man had
been on thoroughly familiar ground, he would have avoided.
Be this as it may, the red old man plunged straight down and
then, fearing to attempt the comparatively slow process of
mounting the other side, turned at a tangent and bounded
along the bottom of the gully. With a gasping bark, as of
triumph, Jess wheeled after him, and the roan mare, unable
to turn quite so swiftly, left Finn to shoot ahead for the first
time, perhaps fifteen paces behind Jess.

But, unfortunately for the kangaroo, this was a blind gully,
and Jess knew it. Two minutes later the old man found himself facing a quite precipitous rocky ascent at the gully's end,
and so, there being no alternative that he could see, he turned
at bay to face his pursuers. Jess was tremendously excited by
the three-mile chase, and it may be that the sound of Finn's
powerful strides behind her gave the black hound more than
ordinary recklessness. At all events, with practically no per-
ceptible slackening of speed, she flew straight for the old
man's throat and received the cruel stroke of his hind leg
fairly upon her chest, being flung backward fully five yards,
with blood spouting from her.

Finn had a full view of poor Jess's terrible reception, and
with him, as with all his kind, action follows thought with
electrical swiftness. He saw in that instant exactly the old
man's method of defense: the cowlike kick, with a leg strong
enough to propel its weighty owner five-and-twenty feet in a
bound and armed at its extremity with claws like chisels. He
swerved sharply from his course and then leaped with all his
strength for the old man's throat from the slightly higher
level of the gully's bank.

Now, the old man weighed two hundred and forty pounds

and measured nine feet from the tip of his snout to the tip of his long tail. But, as against that, he was sitting still, while Finn came with the tremendous momentum of a powerful spring from higher ground than that occupied by the kangaroo. And Finn weighed one hundred and forty odd pounds—not of fat and loose skin, but of muscle and bone, without a pound of superfluous flesh. The impact of Finn's landing on the old man was terrific; but the kangaroo was not bowled over, though he did sway for a moment on his haunches. But it was a terribly punishing hold upon his neck that Finn's jaws had taken, and Finn's great claws were planted firmly in the old man's side and back. The kangaroo made a desperate effort to free one hind leg sufficiently from Finn's clinging weight to be able to take a raking thrust at the wolfhound by shaking him sideways; and if he had succeeded in this, the result for Finn would have been very severe. Meantime, however, the whole strength of Finn's muscular neck and jaws was concentrated upon dragging the kangaroo's head back, upon breaking his neck, in fact. An old-man kangaroo, such as this one, is generally able to give a pretty good account of himself in the face of four or five hounds; but the hounds he meets are of Jess's type and weight and not of Finn's sort.

However, whether or not Finn would have succeeded in his task of breaking this old man's neck was never known, for with a suddenness that surprised the wolfhound into suffering momentary contact with Bill's arm, the boundary rider slipped into the fight, having first picked up the old man's tail so that he could not kick. He then leaned across Finn from behind and slit the marsupial's throat with his sheath knife. Finn growled fiercely as he felt the weight of the man's arm pressed across his shoulders and sprang clear at the same moment that the kangaroo toppled over dead, Bill's practiced hand having severed its jugular vein.

The black hound could do no more hunting for some time to come. Finn was already sympathetically licking Jess when Bill turned away from the dead kangaroo; but as the man came forward, Finn retreated, his lips lifted slightly and his hackles rising. He was not quite sure of Bill's intentions and had been greatly disturbed by the pressure of the boundary rider's arm across his shoulders. He did not realize that Bill, and not he himself, had killed the old man. However, Bill was not paying any heed to Finn just now.

With a single blow the kangaroo had practically laid open the whole of one side of Jess's body. The gash his terrible foot had made extended from the front of the breast down to the inside of the flank; and it was far from being simply a skin wound. Down the chest it had reached the bone; in the belly it had carved a furrow that suggested the wound of an ax. Bill sighed as he told himself that poor Jess's chances were problematical.

A surgeon would have been vastly interested by Bill's operations now. First, he walked along the gully to where he had seen a little water and, bringing this back in his felt hat, proceeded carefully to cleanse parts of the torn flesh as well as he could. Then he unbuckled a big belt that he wore and, opening a pouch on it, drew out two or three needles and some strong white thread. Having threaded one of the needles, he began now, in as matter-of-course a manner as though he were mending a shirt, to stitch up the whole great wound so as to draw its sides together. During the whole lengthy operation the black hound only moved her head twice, in a faint, undecided manner, and almost as though from an intelligent desire to watch Bill's progress; certainly with no hint of any wish to interfere with it.

Then Bill filled a pipe and smoked it for a time, while watching the filmy eyes of his hound. Presently he rose and brought more water in his hat. This he held under Jess's muzzle in such a position as to enable her to loll her tongue in it and lap a little. The gratitude that shone in her eyes was very touching and unmistakable. Bill waited for another quarter of an hour, and then he stooped over the black hound and raised her bodily in his arms with great care, much as a nurse carries a baby. In this position, stopping occasionally for short rests, Bill carried Jess the whole way back to the camp, a distance of about three and a half miles. (The course taken by the kangaroo had been a curve that ended rather nearer to the gunyah than it began.) Finn followed, twenty paces behind the man, with head and tail carried low.

Arrived at the camp, Bill made a bed of leaves for Jess beside the gunyah and placed her down upon it very gently, with an old blanket of his own folded around her body in such a way that she could not reach the wound with her mouth. Then he mounted the horse, which he had driven before him, and galloped back to the blind gully armed with a small coil of line.

When Bill returned with the old man lashed on his horse's back, he found Finn affectionately licking the black hound's muzzle. Jess had not moved an inch.

18: THREE DINGOES WENT A-WALKING

WALLABY BILL showed himself a kind and shrewd nurse where Jess, his one intimate friend, was concerned. For her part, Jess was too weak and ill to be likely to interfere with the wound; even the slight lifting of her head to lap a little broth seemed to tax her strength to the utmost. All night Finn lay within a couple of yards of the kangaroo hound; and in the morning, soon after dawn, he brought her a fresh-killed rabbit and laid it at her feet. Finn meant well, but Jess did not even lick the kill, and as soon as Bill appeared, he looked in a friendly way at Finn and then removed the rabbit. But he afterwards skinned and boiled it for Finn's own delectation, and at the time he said:

"You're a mighty good sort, Wolf, and you can say I said so."

After making the black hound as comfortable as he could, Bill rode off for his day's work. He had rigged a good shelter over Jess with the help of a couple of sheets of stringy bark and a few stakes. He gave her a breakfast of broth and left a dish of water within an inch of her nose, where she could reach it without moving her body. Lastly, as a precaution against the possibility of movement on Jess's part, he stitched the old blanket behind her in such way as to prevent its leaving her wound exposed. He looked over his shoulder several times after riding away, thinking that Finn would be likely to follow him. But the wolfhound remained standing some twenty paces from Jess's shelter, and when the man was almost out of sight, stepped forward and lay down within a yard or two of the kangaroo hound.

It was an odd and very interesting and pleasant life that Finn led now, his time divided pretty evenly between bearing the wounded kangaroo hound company and foraging on his own account in the bush within a radius of two or three miles of the gunyah. He did not know then that the country he traversed, all within four miles of the camp, was but the fringe of a vastly more interesting tract of bush; and, in the meantime, the range he did learn to know thoroughly proved sufficiently absorbing and various.

Five miles from Bill's gunyah, in a direct southerly line, stood the big, rambling station homestead where Bill's bachelor employer had lived for many years. He did not live there now because six months before this time he had died, and his station had reverted to distant relatives in other countries.

Jacob Wilton Hall, the man who had made Warrimoo station, had all his life long been something of an eccentric. He had been an indiscriminate admirer of animals and an interested student of the manners and customs of all the creatures of the wild. When the rabbit pest first began to be severely felt in the neighborhood of his home station, he had tried a variety of methods of coping with it, and in the execution of some of these methods he had met with a good deal of opposition and ridicule from his neighbors. He had, for instance, imported fifty ferrets and weasels of both sexes and turned them loose in pairs, in rabbit earths situated in different outlying portions of his land. These fierce little creatures were a scourge to the countryside by reason of their attacks upon poultry; but it was freely stated that they adopted the curious attitude of nearly all the native-born animals in ignoring the rabbits they had been expected to prey upon.

Jacob Hall had then imported two pairs of wild cats and turned these loose in the back blocks of his land, besides encouraging a number of cats of the domesticated variety to take to the bush life and become wild, as they had been doing all over Australia for many years. With great difficulty and considerable expenditure of money, the eccentric squatter had succeeded in securing a pair of Tasmanian wolves and a pair of Tasmanian devils, and having successfully evaded the customs and quarantine authorities, he turned these exceptionally fierce and bloodthirsty creatures loose in the wildest part of his land. It was supposed that the persistent efforts of hunters and boundary riders had resulted in these wild creatures being driven well into the back country; and it is certain that, despite an occasional strange story from bushmen regarding the animals whose tracks they had come upon in the back blocks, nothing was ever actually seen of Jacob Hall's more fantastic importations. It was said, however, that there

were already notable modifications in certain of the wild
kindred of that countryside. There was talk of wild cats of
hitherto unheard-of size and fierceness and of dingoes having
suggestions about them of the untamably fierce marsupial
wolf of Tasmania.

Naturally, Finn and Jess knew nothing of these things.
They lived for themselves, these two; but Jess was deeply
interested in the return of her man to the camp each night,
and Finn was equally keen and interested in his daily for-
agings and explorations in the bush. They neither of them
knew that they themselves were objects of the greatest interest to a very large circle of the wild folk. But they were.

Within twenty-four hours of the fight with the old-man
kangaroo in the blind gully, the news had gone abroad among
all the wild folk in the strip of bush that surrounded the
camp that a redoubtable hunter had been laid low and was
lying near to death and quite helpless beside the gunyah.
Jess, having always been well fed by her man, had never been
a great hunter of small game; but she had accounted for a
goodly number of wallabies and had played her part in the
pulling down of a respectable number of kangaroos. And
though she had seldom troubled to run down the smaller fry,
she was as greatly feared by them as though she lived only
for their destruction; and innumerable small marsupials,
from the tiny, delicate little kangaroo mouse up to the fleet
and muscular wallaby hare, with bandicoots, kangaroo rats
(bushy-tailed and desperately furtive), possums, native cats,
and even a couple of amiable and sleepy-headed native bears,
and a surly, solitary wombat—all took an opportunity of peering out from the nearest point of dense covert for the sake of
having a glimpse of the helpless kangaroo hound.

News reached the rocky hills behind Warrimoo of Jess's
condition, and during the second night of her helplessness
three dingoes left their hunting range to come and look into

this matter for themselves. A dying hound might prove well worth investigating, they thought. The movements of these dingoes, once they reached within a couple of miles of Bill's gunyah, would have interested any student of the wild. The caution with which they advanced was extraordinary. Not a dry leaf or a dead twig on the trail but they scanned it shrewdly with an eye for possible traps or pitfalls. They moved as noiselessly as shadows and poured in and out among the scrub like liquid vegetation of some sort. When the three dingoes from the hills reached the edge of the clear patch in which the gunyah stood, they saw the almost black, smoldering remains of a campfire and, stretched within a couple of yards of the ashes, Finn. His shaggy coat was not that of a kangaroo hound, and his place beside the man-made fire seemed to forbid the possibility of his being a monster dingo. Vaguely, the dingoes told themselves that Finn must be some kind of giant among wolves who was connected in some mysterious way with menfolk.

In the meantime, it was quite evident to the dingoes' sensitive nostrils that man inhabited the gunyah at that moment, and that, therefore, quite apart from the presence of the huge strange beast near the fire, it would never do to investigate the shelter at the gunyah's side just then. The dingoes ate where they made their kills that night, within a couple of miles of the camp, thereby spreading terror wide and deep throughout the range.

When dawn came, the three dingoes were crouched in a favorable watching place opposite the gunyah and saw Finn rise, stretch his great length, and stroll off leisurely in the direction of the bush on the shanty's far side. They looked meaningly one at the other, with lips drawn back, as they noted Finn's massive bulk, great height, long jaws, and springy tread. They decided that the wolfhound might, after all, be of the wild kindred, since he evidently had no mind to face the owner of the gunyah by daylight. Then, with hackles raised and bodies shrinking backward among the leaves, they saw Bill come out, yawn, stretch his arms, and go to look at Jess under her shelter. Now as it happened, Finn stumbled upon a fresh wallaby trail that morning, a trail not many minutes old; and he followed it with growing excitement for a number of miles. Finn's hunting of the wallaby took him a good deal farther from the humpy than he had been before, since his first arrival there; and so it fell out that Bill left upon his day's round without having seen the wolfhound that morning.

"I guess he's after an extra special breakfast of his own," muttered Bill before he left. "But I'll leave him this half a rabbit in case." The patient dingoes watched the whole performance closely, licking their chops while Bill ate his breakfast and again when he placed the cooked half-rabbit on the log. The whole proceeding was also watched by several crows. It was largely as a protection against these, rather than against the elements, that Bill had given Jess her substantial bark shelter, under which the crows would be afraid to pass. Otherwise, as Bill well knew, Jess would have been likely to lose her eyes before she had lain there very long.

After Bill's departure, the crows were the first to descend upon the camp; and they soon had the meat left for Finn torn to shreds and swallowed. Then they swaggered impudently about the fire, picking up crumbs. The presence of these wicked black marauders gave courage to the waiting dingoes, and they determined to proceed at once with the business in hand: the examination of the dying kangaroo hound of which they had heard. As for the huge spectral wolf, it was evident that he had no real connection with the camp.

The three dingoes advanced, still exhibiting caution in every step but marching abreast because neither would give any advantage to the others in a case of this sort. When they got to within five-and-twenty paces of the shelter, poor Jess winded them, and it was borne in upon her that the hour of her last fight had arrived. She knew herself unable to run a yard, probably unable to stand; and the dingo scent, as she understood it, had no hint of mercy in it. With an effort that racked her whole frame with burning pain, the helpless bitch turned upon her chest and raised her head so that she might see her doom approaching. She gave a little gulp when her eyes fell upon the stalwart forms of no fewer than three full-grown dingoes, stocky of build, massive in legs and shoulders, plentifully coated, and fanged for the killing of meat. Their eyes had the killing light in them too, and a snarl curled her lips. Even three such well-grown dingoes as these would never have dared to attack her if she had been in normal condition.

Very slowly the three dingoes approached a little nearer in fan-shaped formation, and with a brave effort, Jess succeeded in bringing forth a bark, which ended in something between growl and howl by reason of the cutting pain it caused her. The three dingoes leaped backward, each three paces, like clockwork machinery. Jess glared out at them from under her thatch of bark, her fangs uncovered, her nose wrinkled, and her short, close hair on end. The dingoes watched her thoughtfully, pondering upon her probable reserves of strength. Then, too, there was her shelter; that was endowed with some of the mysterious atmosphere that surrounds man. But the biggest of the dingoes had once stolen half a sheep from a shepherd's humpy, and no disaster had overtaken him. He advanced three feet before his companions, and that spurred them to movement. And now, as the dingoes drew nearer, inch by inch, the black kangaroo hound braced herself to die biting and to sell her flesh as dearly as might be.

As the snout of the foremost dingo, the largest of the three, showed under the eave of Jess's shelter, she managed to hunch her wounded body a little farther back against the side of the gunyah, meaning thereby to draw the dingo a little farther in and give herself a better chance of catching some part of him between her jaws. With a desperate effort she drew back her forelegs a little, raising herself almost into a sitting position against the side of the gunyah. The faint groans that the pain of moving forced from her were of real service to her in a way, for they made the foremost dingo think she was in her death agony and gave a sort of recklessness to his plunge forward under the thatch. He meant to end the business at once and slake his blood thirst at the hound's throat.

In the instant of the big dingo's plunge for Jess's throat, several things happened. First, Jess's powerful jaws came together about the thick part of the dingo's right foreleg and took firm hold there, while the snarling and now terrified dingo snapped at the back of her neck, the rough edge of the bark thatch on the middle of his back producing in him a horrible sense of being trapped. Another thing was that the two lesser dingoes between them produced a yelp of pure terror and, wheeling like lightning, streaked across the clear patch of the scrub, bellies to earth and tails flying in a straight line from their spines. And the third thing that happened in that instant was the arrival at the end of the gunyah of Finn. There was something elemental about it and something, too, suggestive of magic. The wolfhound had caught his first glimpse of the two lesser dingoes as he reached the far side of the clear patch, and for an instant he had stood still. He was dragging a young wallaby over one shoulder. Then it came over him that these were enemies attacking his crippled friend Jess. He made no sound but, dropping his burden, flew across the clearing with deadly swiftness. As he reached the end of the gunyah, a kind of roar burst from his swelling chest and, in that instant, the two dingoes flung themselves forward in flight, Finn after them. Five huge strides he took

in their rear; and then the power of thought or telepathy
or something of the sort stopped him dead in the middle of
his stride, and he almost turned a somersault in wheeling
around to Jess's assistance.

As Finn plunged forward again toward Jess, the big dingo
succeeded, by means of a desperate wrench, in freeing his leg
from the kangaroo hound's jaws and with a swift turning
movement leaped clear of the shelter. Then the big dingo of
the back ranges found himself facing Finn and realized that
he must fight for his life.

The dingo has been called a skunk and a cur and a coward
and by most other names that are bad and contemptuous. But
the dingo at bay is as brave as a weasel; and no lion in all
Africa is braver than a weasel at bay. Finn had brought himself to a standstill with an effort, a towering figure of blazing
wrath. He had made one good kill that morning; his blood
was hot; the picture of these dogs of the wild kindred attacking his helpless friend had roused to fighting fury every last
drop of blood in his whole great body. Rage almost blinded
him. He flung himself upon the big dingo as though he were
a projectile of some sort. And then he learned that the creatures born in the wild are swifter than the swiftest of other
creatures. He had learned it before, as a matter of fact; he had
seen a striking illustration of it only a few days before when
the kangaroo stretched Jess helpless on the ground at a single
stroke. Finn only grazed the dingo's haunch, while the dingo
slashed a three-inch wound in his right shoulder as he passed.
Even while Finn was in the act of turning, the wild dog's
fangs clashed against his flank, ripping his skin as though it
were stretched silk.

It may be imagined that Finn's wrath was not lessened, but
his blind rage was, and he pulled himself together with a
jerk, a cold determination to kill cooling his brain like water.
This time he allowed the dingo to rush him, which the beast

did with admirable dexterity, aiming low for the legs. Finn
plunged for the back of the dingo's neck and missed by the
breadth of two hairs. Then he pivoted on his hind legs and
feinted low for the dingo's legs. The dingo flashed by him,
aiming a cutting snap at his lower thigh—for the wild dog was
a master of fighting and worked deliberately to cripple his
big opponent and not to kill him outright—and that gave
Finn the chance for which he had played in his feint. Next
moment his great fangs were buried in the thickly furred
coat of the dingo's neck, and his whole weight was bearing
the wild dog to earth.

His legs lost to him, by reason of Finn's crushing weight,
the frenzy of despair filled the dingo, and he fought like ten
dogs, snarling, snapping, writhing, and scratching, all at the
same time. Despite Finn's vicelike hold, the dingo did considerable execution with his razor-edged fangs in the lower
part of the wolfhound's forelegs. But his race was run. Finn
gradually shifted his hold till the front teeth gripped the soft
part of the dingo's throat, and then he bit with all the mighty
strength of his great jaws, closer, closer, and closer, till the red
blood poured out on the ground and the struggles of the wild
dog grew fainter and fainter. Finally, Finn gave a great shake
of his head, lifting the dingo clear of the ground and flinging him back upon it, limp and still.

For two whole minutes Finn glared down at the body of
the dingo, while licking the blood from his own lips and working the torn skin of his body backward and forward as
though it tickled him. Then he turned to look to Jess, and an
extraordinary thing happened, the sort of thing that does not
happen save in the life of a dingo; the thing, in short, that
couldn't happen, but that just does sometimes. That dingo's
glazing eyes opened wide and looked at Finn's back. Then
the slain dingo (Finn had almost torn out its throat) dragged
itself to its feet and staggered off like a drunken man toward

the bush. A feeble snarl escaped from Jess, whose head faced this way. Finn, who had been licking her, wheeled like a cat and in that amazing moment saw the dingo he supposed he had killed staggering toward the scrub thirty paces distant. Five seconds later the still living dingo was on its back and its throat was being scattered over the surrounding ground.

When Wallaby Bill came to look at that corpse some hours later he said:

"Well, by ghost! If I didn't tell that wolf this very morning that he was a mighty good sort. My oath, but that blessed dingo has been killed good an' plenty, and a steam hammer couldn't kill him no more!"

There was a wallaby lying beside the fire, Finn having been too busy licking his own wounds and comforting Jess to think of feeding, though common prudence had reminded him to bring in his kill from the edge of the clear patch. Bill gave a deal of time and attention to Jess that night, but Finn was fed royally on roughly cooked wallaby steaks and damper. But even upon this special occasion the wolfhound, still mindful of his awful circus experience, refused to come within touch of the man.

19: A BREAKUP IN ARCADIA

Jess's struggles on the day of the dingo fight naturally retarded the healing of her wound, but before the week was out, Bill was able to remove his rude stitches, and the great gash showed every sign of healing cleanly. Yet, in spite of the kangaroo hound's wonderful hardihood and her advantages in the matter of pure, healing air, almost another week had passed before she was able to move about around the camp, and a full ten days more were gone before she cared to resume her old activities.

During all this time Finn played the part of a very loyal and watchful protector. The wild folk of the bush situated within a mile of the camp became as much accustomed to his presence as though he were in truth one of themselves, so thoroughly and constantly did he patrol their range during his guardianship of the wounded hound In this period he learned to know every twig in that strip of country and practically every creature that lived or hunted there. The snake folk, brown, tiger, carpet, diamond, black, and death adder— he came to know them all from a very respectful distance; and he studied their habits and methods of progression and of hunting with the deepest interest.

For instance, on one occasion, toward evening, Finn saw a carpet snake pin a big kangaroo rat close to a fallen log. With a swiftness that Finn's sharp eyes were unable to follow exactly, the snake twisted two coils of his shining body around the marsupial and crushed the little beast to death. Then slowly, and as though the process gave him great satisfaction, the snake worked his coils downward, from the head to the tail of the kangaroo rat, crunching its body flat and breaking all its joints. Then, very slowly, the snake took its victim's head between its jaws and, advancing first one jaw and then the other, an eighth of an inch at a time, very gradually swallowed the whole animal, the operation occupying altogether a full ten minutes. When the snake had quite finished, Finn leaped upon it from his hiding place, killing the creature with one snap of his jaws immediately behind the head. Bill was just dismounting beside the gunyah when Finn arrived, trailing twelve feet of gorged snake beside him.

But this was only one small incident among the daily, almost hourly, adventures and lessons that came to the wolfhound during this period of Jess's convalescence. He actually caught a half-grown koala, or native bear, one hot afternoon when Jess was beginning to stroll about the clear patch; and finding that the queer little creature offered no fight but only swayed its tubby body to and fro, moaning and wailing and generally behaving like a distressed child, Finn made no attempt to kill it but simply took firm hold of the loose, furry skin about its thick neck and dragged it, complaining piteously, through the bush to the gunyah, where he deposited it gingerly upon the ground for Jess's inspection. Bill found the two hounds playing with the koala on his return to camp that night. It was a one-sided kind of game, for the bear only sat up on his haunches between the hounds, rocking to and fro and sobbing and moaning with grotesque, appealing pathos, while Finn and Jess gamboled about him, occasionally toppling him over with a thrust of their muzzles and growling angrily at him till he sat up again, when they appeared quite satisfied. Bill sat on his horse and shook with laughter as he watched the game. But long laughter moved his good-nature, and after a while he called Jess off and drove the bear away into the scrub. He did not call Finn because that was unnecessary. Finn withdrew immediately upon Bill's approach.

It was perhaps a week after the bear-baiting episode, when for several days Jess had been following her man by day in the same manner as before her hurt, that both hounds began to notice that Bill was undergoing a change of some sort. He never talked to them now. He took not the smallest notice of Finn and but rarely looked at Jess. When she approached him of an evening, he would gruffly bid her lie down, and once he thrust her from him with his foot when she had nosed close up to him beside the fire. Jess had vague recollections of similar changes in her man having occurred before this time, and she had vague, uncomfortable stirrings that told her that further change of some sort was imminent. This made the

kangaroo hound restless and uneasy, and before long her uneasiness communicated itself to Finn. All this made the wolfhound more shy than ever where Bill was concerned and more
like a creature of the real wild in all his movements and general demeanor. He slept a little farther from the gunyah now
and relied almost entirely upon his own hunting for food.
Still, he had no wish to leave the camp and regarded Jess as
his fast friend.

One evening the now definitely surly and irritable Bill devoted half an hour to counting and recounting some money
in the light of the campfire. He had visited the station homestead that day and drawn his pay from the manager.

"Ger-r-router that, damn ye!" he growled at poor Jess when
she crept toward him with watchful, affectionate eyes. So Jess
got out, to the extent of a dozen yards, with the mark of one
of Bill's heavy boots on her glossy flank. She bore not a trace
of malice and would have cheerfully fought to the death for
her man at that moment; but she was full of vague distress
and whimpering uneasiness, of dim, unhappy presentiments.

In the morning Bill hardly took the trouble to prepare
a breakfast for himself, and the clothes he wore were not
those that Finn had always seen him in before. Bill presently tied up the hanging door of the gunyah and mounted
his horse. Jess and Finn followed him, but their hearts were
sad, and Bill's glowering looks gave them no encouragement.
For almost seven miles they followed Bill, and then, after
leaping a low "dog-leg" fence, they found themselves in the
wide street of Nargoola township. Bill cantered slowly down
the empty road till he came to the First Nugget Hotel, and
there he drew rein and finally hitched his horse's bridle to a
veranda post. Then he strode across the veranda and disappeared within the hotel, and Jess remembered—many things.

Finn remained with Jess, a few yards from the horse, waiting; but whereas the experienced Jess lay down in the dust,

Finn stood erect and watchful beside her. He was already rather nearer to the house than he cared to be; and the air was heavy with the scent of man and his works. Finn was acutely uncomfortable and told Jess so as plainly as he could, with a hint as to the advantages of returning to the bush. But Jess urged patience and tucked her nose under one of her hind legs.

Presently one or two men came straggling down the street and made overtures to Finn, after standing and gazing upon him with admiring astonishment and slowly piecing together his connection with Bill and Jess through the horse.

"My oath!" exclaimed one of the men. "I guess old man Hall's pets have been busy back in the hills there. Wonder how Bill got a-holt o' *him!*"

And then, with every sign of deferential friendliness, the man endeavored to approach Finn. But though Jess lay still, showing only pointed indifference where the men were concerned, Finn leaped backward like a stag and kept a good score of paces between the menfolk and himself.

Out of consideration for the patient Jess, Finn endured the discomfort of waiting beside the First Nugget all through that day, though he never ventured to sit down even for a moment; there among the man smells and the threatening shadows of the houses, each one of which he regarded as the possible headquarters of a circus, the possible home of a "Professor." But when evening set in and Jess still showed no sign of forsaking her post, Finn could endure it no longer and told his friend several times over that he must go; that he would return to the camp in the bush and wait there. The nuzzling touches of Jess's nose said plainly, "Wait a bit, yet! What's your hurry?" But Finn was in deadly earnest now. Jess pleaded for delay and licked his nose most persuasively. But Finn's mind was made up, and he turned his shoulder coldly upon the bitch, while still waiting for some sign of yielding on her part. But Jess was bound to her post by ties far stronger than any consideration of her own comfort or well-being. Also, of course, she had not Finn's violent distaste for the neighborhood of man and his works. She had never been in a circus. She had never been suddenly awakened from complete trust in mankind to knowledge of the existence of mad man-beasts with hot iron bars.

In the end, Finn gave a cold bark of displeasure and trotted off into the gathering twilight, leaping the fence and plunging into the bush the moment he had passed the last house of the township. Half an hour later he killed a fat bandicoot, who was engaged at that moment in killing a tiny marsupial mouse. A quarter of an hour after that, Finn lay down beside the ashes of the fire before the gunyah, his kill between his forelegs. He rested there for a few minutes and then, tearing off its furry skin in strips, devoured the greater part of the bandicoot before settling down for the night; as much, that is, as he ever did settle down these days. His eyes were not often completely closed; less often at night, perhaps, than in the daytime. But he dozed now, out there in the clear patch where the gunyah stood, free of all thoughts of men and cages. And the bush air seemed sweeter than ever to him tonight after his brief stay in the man-haunted township.

20: THE OUTCAST

For nine consecutive days and nights Finn continued to regard the empty gunyah in the clear patch as his home, to eat there, and to rest there, beside the ashes of the fire or in the shadow of the shanty itself. And still Jess and her man did not come, and the wolfhound was left in sole possession. Once, when the heat of the day was past, Finn trotted down the trail to the township and peered long and earnestly through the dog-leg fence in the direction of the First Nugget. But he saw no trace of Jess or her man; and, for his part, he was glad to get back to the clear patch again and to take his ease beside the gunyah.

He had recently struck up a more than bowing acquaintance with the koala that he had once dragged through a quarter of a mile of scrub to the gunyah and was now in the habit of meeting this quaint little bear nearly every day. For his part, Koala never presumed to make the slightest advance in Finn's direction, but he had come to realize that the great wolfhound wished him no harm, and though his conversation seldom went beyond plaintive complainings and lugubrious assertions of his own complete inoffensiveness, Finn liked to sit near the little beast occasionally and watch his fubsy antics and listen to his plaint.

Another of the wild folk that Finn met for the first time in his life during these nine days and continued to meet on a friendly footing was a large native porcupine, or echidna. Finn was sniffing one afternoon at what he took to be the opening to a rabbit's burrow when, greatly to his surprise, Echidna showed up, some three or four yards away, from one of the exits of the same earth. The creature's shock of fretful quills was not inviting, and Finn discovered no inclination to risk touching it with his nose; but having jumped forward in such a way as to shut Echidna off from his home, Finn was left face to face with him for a few moments. Then, he decided that he had no wish to slay the ant-eating porcupine, and Echnidna, for his part, made up his exceedingly rudimentary little mind that Finn was a fairly harmless creature. So they sat looking at one another, and Finn marveled that the world should contain so curious a creature as his new acquaintance. Then the flying tail of a bandicoot caught

Finn's attention, and the passing that way of an unusually fat bull-dog ant drew Echidna from reflection to business, and the oddly ill-matched couple parted after their first meeting. After this, they frequently exchanged civil greeting when their paths happened to cross in the bush.

But unlike the large majority of Australia's wild folk, Finn was exclusively a carnivorous animal, and this fact rather placed him out of court in the matter of striking up acquaintances in the bush. Finn would have been delighted, really, to make friends with creatures like the bandicoot folk and to enjoy their society at intervals—when he was well fed. But the bandicoots and their kind could never forget that they were, after all, food in the wolfhound's eyes, and it was not possible to know for certain exactly when his appetite was likely to rise within him and claim attention—and bandicoots. Therefore, full or empty, hunting or lounging, Finn was a scourge and an enemy in the eyes of these small folk and, as such, something to be avoided at all cost and at all seasons.

The hunting in the neighborhood of the gunyah was still amply sufficient for Finn's needs; and as he continually expected the return of Bill and Jess, he did not forage very far from the clear patch. He generally dozed and rested beside the humpy during the afternoon, preparatory to hunting in the dusk for the kill that represented his night meal. It was on the evening of his tenth day of solitude, and rather later than his usual hour for the evening prowl, that Finn woke with a start in his place beside the gunyah to hear the sound of a horse's feet entering the clear patch from the direction of the station homestead. There was no sign of Jess that nose or eye or ear could detect, but Finn told himself as he moved away from the gunyah that this was doubtless Bill and that Jess would be likely to follow. As his custom was, Finn took up his stand about five-and-twenty paces from the humpy, prepared gravely to observe the boundary rider's evening tasks: the fire lighting and so forth. As the newcomer began to think of dismounting, he caught a dim glimpse of Finn's figure through the growing darkness. It was only a dim glimpse the man caught, and he took Finn for a dingo, made wondrous large in appearance, somehow, by the darkness. He was both astonished and exceedingly indignant that a dingo should have the brazen impudence to stand and stare at him, within thirty yards of camp, too. In his hand he carried a stock whip, with its fifteen-foot fall neatly coiled about its taper end. Swinging this by the head of its fall, he flung it with all his might at Finn, at the same time rising erect in the saddle and spurring his horse forward at the gallop to ride the supposed dingo down.

"G-r-r-r, you thieving swine! I'll teach ye!"

The voice was strange to Finn and very hoarse and harsh. The wolfhound cantered lightly off, and the rider followed him right into the scrub before wheeling his horse and turning back toward the camp. Before he moved, Finn gave one snarling growl; the heavy butt end of the stock-whip handle had caught him fairly in the ribs and almost taken his breath away.

From the shelter of the bush, Finn peered for a long while at the camp from which he had been driven. He saw the man gather twigs and light a fire, just as Bill had been wont to do. But he knew now that the man was not Bill. He heard the man growling and swearing to himself, just as a creature of the wild does sometimes over its meals. As a matter of fact, this particular man had been removed from a post that he liked and sent to this place because Bill had left the district; and he was irritable and annoyed about it. Otherwise, he probably would not have been so savage in driving Finn off. But the wolfhound had no means of knowing these things.

All his life long, up till the time of his separation from the Master, Finn had been treated with uniform kindness and

consideration, save during the one very brief interval in
Sussex. Then, for months, he had been treated with what
seemed to him utterly purposeless and reasonless cruelty and
ferocity. But it had been reserved for Wallaby Bill's suc-
cessor to implant in Finn's mind the true spirit of the wild
creature, by the simple process of driving him forth from the
neighborhood of civilization—such as it was—into the bush.
Finn had been cruelly beaten; he had been tortured in the
past. He had never until this evening been driven away from
the haunts of men.

Finn desired none of man's society, and during all the time
that he had regarded the camp in that clearing as his home,
he had never sought anything at man's hands nor approached
man more nearly than at a distance of a dozen paces or so.
But now he was savagely given to understand that even the
neighborhood of the camp was no place for him, that it was
forbidden ground. Man was actively hostile to him, would
fling something at him on sight. Man declared war on him
and drove him out into the wild. Well, and what of the wild?

The wild yielded him unlimited food and unlimited interest. The wild was clean and free, it hampered him in no way;
it had offered no sort of hostile demonstration against him.
Altogether, it was with a curiously disturbed and divided
mind, in which bitterness and resentment were uppermost,
that the wolfhound gazed now at the man sitting in the firelight by Bill's gunyah. Vague thoughts, too, of the Master
drifted through Finn's mind as he watched the stranger at his
supper; and, somehow, the circle of firelit grass attracted. For-
giveness came naturally to the wolfhound, and for the moment, he forgot the humiliation and the bitterness of being
driven out as a creature of the wild.

Slowly, not with any particular caution but with stately,
gracious step, Finn moved forward toward the firelight, in-
tending to take up his old resting place, perhaps a score of

paces from the fire. No sooner had Finn entered the outer-most ring of dim firelight than the man looked up and saw not the whole of him but the light flickering on his legs.

"Well, if that ain't the limit!" gasped the man, as he sprang to his feet. He snatched a three-foot length of burning sapling from the fire and, rushing forward, flung it so truly after the retreating wolfhound that it fell across his neck, singeing his coat and enveloping him from nose to tail in a cloud of glowing sparks. A stone followed the burning wood, and the man himself, shouting and cursing, followed the stone. But he had no need to run. The flying sparks, the smell of burned hair, the horrible suggestion of the red-hot iron bar—these were amply sufficient for Finn, without the added humili-ation of the stone and the curses and the man's loud, blunder-ing footfalls. The wolfhound broke into a gallop, shocked, amazed, alarmed, and beyond words embittered. He snarled as he ran, and he ran till the camp was a mile behind him, beyond scent and hearing.

There was no mistaking this for anything but what it was. The burning sapling made a most profound impression upon Finn and roused bitter hostility and resentment in him. From time immemorial men have frightened and chased wolves from their chosen neighborhood with burning faggots. Finn had never before experienced it, and yet, in some vague way, it seemed he had known of such a thing. His ancestors for fifteen hundred years had been the admired companions and champions of the leaders among men. Certain it is that noth-ing else in his life had been quite so full of hostile significance for Finn as this fact of his having been driven out from the camp in the clear patch with a faggot of burning wood. This was man's message to him; thus, then, he was sent to his place, and his place was the wild.

The wild folk of that particular section of the Tinnaburra country will never forget the strange happenings of that

night, which they will always remember as the night of the
madness of the Giant Wolf—only they thought of him as the
Giant Dingo. For four mortal hours the Irish wolfhound who
had been driven out from the haunts of men raged furiously
up and down a five-mile belt of Tinnaburra country, slaying
and maiming wantonly and implanting desperate fear in the
hearts of every living thing in that countryside.

Once, in the farthest of his gallops, he reached the fringe
of the wild, rocky hill country that lies behind this belt; and
there, as luck would have it, he met in full flight one of the
two dingoes that had escaped him on the day of the attack
upon wounded Jess. It was an evil chance for that dingo. A
fanged whirlwind smote him and rent him limb from limb
before he realized that the devastating thing had come, scattering his vital parts among the scrub and tearing wildly
at his mangled remains. Lesser creatures succumbed under
the blinding stabs of Finn's feet; and once he leaped like a
cat clear into the lower branches of a bastard oak tree and
pinned a possum into instant death before swinging back to
earth on the limb's far side. He killed that night from fury
and not to eat; and when he laid him down to rest at length
on the rocky edge of a gully fully four miles from the camp,
there was not a living thing in that district but felt the terror
of his presence, and cowered from sight or sound of his flying feet and rending, blood-stained fangs. It was as the night
of an earthquake or a bush fire to the wild folk of that range;
and the cause and meaning of it all was that Finn, the Irish
wolfhound, had been hunted out of the menfolk's world into
the world of the wild.

21: MATED

Iᴆ Finn had deliberately thought out a bad way of beginning his life as one of the wild folk, who have no concern at all with humans, he could have devised nothing much worse or more disadvantageous to himself than the indulgence of his wild burst of berserk-like fury after being driven out of the clear patch. And of this he was made aware when he set forth the next morning in quest of a breakfast. Every one of his hunting trails in the neighborhood of the encampment he ranged with growing thoroughness and care without finding so much as a mouse with which to satisfy his appetite. It was as though a blight had descended upon the countryside, and the only living thing Finn saw that morning, besides the crows, was a laughing jackass on the stump of a blasted stringybark tree, who jeered at him hoarsely as he passed. Disconsolate and rather sore, as the result of his frenzied exertions of the night, Finn curled himself up in the sandy bed of a little gully and slept again, without food. The many small scavengers of the bush had already made away with the remains of the different creatures he had slain during his madness.

Finn did not know it, but hundreds of small bright eyes had watched him as he ranged the trails that morning; and most of these eyes had in them the light of resentment, as well as fear. Finn had been guilty of real crime according to the standards of the wild; and had he been a lesser creature, swift punishment would have descended upon him. As it was, he was left to work out his own punishment by finding that his hunting was ruined. These wild folk, who were judging Finn now, tacitly admitted the right of all flesh-eating creatures to kill for food. But willful slaughter, particularly when

accompanied by all the evidences of reckless fury, was a crime
not readily to be forgiven. It was not merely a cruel affliction
for those needlessly slain and their relatives (some of whom
depended for life upon their exertions); but it was also an
affliction for all the rest, in that it spoiled hunting for the
carnivorous, rendered feeding extremely difficult for the non-
carnivorous, and generally upset the ordered balance of
things that made life worth living for the wild creatures of
that range. Finn had been feared and respected in that corner of the Tinnaburra, while by some of the wild folk who,
from one cause or another, were able to afford the indulgence
in such an emotion, he had been admired. He was now feared
and hated.

When Finn rose from his day sleep, it was to realization of
the uncomfortable fact that he was stark empty of food. The
next thing he realized—and this was before he had walked
many hundred yards through the falling light of late afternoon—was the solid atmosphere of hatred that surrounded
him in his own range of bush. He did not get the full sting
of it at first—that bit into him gradually during the night—
but he was aware of its existence almost at once. And he
found it singularly daunting. True, he was the undisputed
lord of that range. No creature lived there that could think
of meeting him in single combat. But the concentrated and
silent hatred of the entire populace was none the less a thing
to chill the heart even of a giant Irish wolfhound.

The silence of the ghostly bush, in that brief half-light that
preceded darkness, spoke loudly and eloquently of this hatred
and resentment. The empty runways of the little grass-eating
animals were full of it. The still trees thrust it upon Finn as
he threaded in and out among their hoary trunks. The sightless scrub glared hatred at him till the skin twitched over his
shoulders, and he took to flinging swift glances to left and
right as he walked—glances little in keeping with his char-

acter as hunter and more suggestive of the conduct of the lesser hunted creatures. When a long streamer of hanging bark rustled suddenly behind Finn, he wheeled upon it with a snarl; and the humiliation of his discovery of what had startled him partook of the nature of fear when his gaze met the coldly glittering eyes of a bush cat (whose body he could not discern in that dim light) that glared down at him from twenty feet above his head.

It was with a sense of genuine humility, and something like gratitude, that Finn met Koala a few minutes later, passing hurriedly—for him—between the trunks of the two trees in which he made his home at that time. Koala stopped at once when Finn faced him—not from any desire for conversation but from fear to move—and waved his queer little hands in an apparent ecstasy of grief and perturbation. Finn whispered through his nose a most friendly assurance that he had too much respect and affection for Koala to think of harming him, and the little bear sat up on his haunches to acknowledge this condescension tearfully, while reiterating the time-honored assertion that there was no more inoffensive or helpless creature living than himself. With a view to establishing more confidence, Finn lay down on his chest, with forelegs outstretched, and began to pump Koala regarding the chilling attitude of the creatures of that range toward himself. In his own dolorous fashion Koala succeeded in conveying to Finn what the wolfhound already knew quite well in his heart of hearts, that the attitude he complained of was simply the penalty of his running amuck on the previous night. Finn gathered that the native-born wild creatures would never forgive him or relax their attitude of silently watchful hatred, but that there were some rabbits who were feeding in the open a little farther on, in the neighborhood of the clear patch.

It was not for any pleasure in hunting but because he was

very empty that Finn proceeded in the direction indicated
by the bear. He had developed the Australian taste in the
matter of rabbits and regarded their flesh with cold disfavor.
Still, he was hungry now, and when he had stalked and killed
the fattest of the bunch of rabbits he found furtively grazing
a quarter of a mile from the clear patch, he carried it well
away into the bush and devoured it steadily.

During a good part of that night Finn strolled about the
familiar tract of bush he had ranged now for many weeks,
observing and taking note of all the many signs which,
though plain reading enough for him, would have been quite
illegible to the average man. And he decided that what he
saw was not good, that it boded ill for his future comfort
and well-being. The simple fact was that he had outraged all
the proprieties of the wild in that quarter and was being
severely ostracized in consequence. The lesser creatures were
still sharper of scent and hearing than he was, and their senses
all made more acute by their fear and indignation, they succeeded in keeping absolutely out of the wolfhound's sight.
It was shortly after midnight when a crow and a flying fox
saw Finn curl down to sleep in his sandy gully, and by making
use of the curious system of animal telepathy, they soon had
the news spread all over the range. The lesser marsupials and
other groundlings were glad to have this intelligence, and
the approach of dawn found them all busily feeding, watchful
only with regard to the ordinary enemies among their own
kind, the small carnivorous animals and the snake folk. Indeed, they fed so busily that a pair of wedgetailed eagles, who
descended among them with the first dim approach of the
new day, obtained fat breakfasts almost without looking for
them, a fact that, unreasonably enough, earned new hatred
for Finn among the circle upon which the eagles swooped.

For another three days Finn continued in his old hunting
ground, and during the whole of that time he had to content

himself with a diet consisting exclusively of rabbit meat. Indeed, during the last couple of days he found that even the despised rabbit required a good deal of careful stalking, so deeply had the fear and hatred of the wolfhound penetrated into the minds and hearts of that particular wild community. If it had not been for the rabbits' incorrigible habit of forgetting caution during the hours of twilight and daybreak, Finn might have gone hungry altogether. Apart from their hatred and resentment, the wild creatures of that range felt the giant's madness might return to him at any moment, and that for this reason alone it would be unsafe to permit any relaxation in their attitude toward him.

On the fourth evening, with a rather sad heart, Finn turned his back on the familiar trails and hunted west and south from the little gully in which he slept, heading toward the back ranges and the stony foot of Mount Desolation. For a mile or more, even in this direction, he found that his evil fame had preceded him, and no good hunting came his way. But presently a flanking movement to the eastward was rewarded by a glimpse of a fat wallaby hare, which Finn stalked with the most exquisite patience till he was able to spring upon it with a snap of his great jaws. Finn carried this fat kill back to his den and feasted royally that night for the first time since he was expelled from the purlieus of the gunyah and the easy-going old life. These few days had changed the wolfhound a good deal. He walked the trails now with far less of gracious pride and dignity and more of eager, watchful stealth than he had been wont to use. He walked more silently; he stalked more carefully and sprang more swiftly and bit more fiercely. He was no longer the amateur of the wild life but an actual part of it, and subject to all its laws and customs.

Thus it was that, in the afternoon of the day following, he leaped in a single instant from full sleep to fullest wakeful-

ness in response to the sound of a tiny twig rolling down the
side of his little gully. There, facing him from the western lip
of the gully, with a rather eager, curious, inviting sort of
look upon her intelligent face, stood a fine, upstanding, red-
brown female dingo, or warrigal The stranger stood fully
twenty-three inches high at the shoulder and was unusually
long in the body for such a height—thirteen inches less than
Finn's shoulder height it is true, but yet about the same
measurement as a big foxhound and of greater proportionate
length. Her ruddy brown tail was bushy and handsome, and
at this moment she was carrying it high and flirtatiously
curled. Also, she wagged it encouragingly when Finn's eyes
met her own, which were of a pale greenish hue Her hind
feet were planted well apart; she stood almost as a show cob
stands, her tail twitching slightly and her nostrils contracting
and expanding in eloquent inquiry. She had heard of Finn
some time since, this belle of the back ranges, but it was only
on that day, when Nature recommended her to find a mate,
that she had thought of coming in quest of the great wolfhound. Now she eyed him from her vantage point fearlessly
and with invitation in every line of her lissome form.

Finn sniffed hard and began a conciliatory whine, which
terminated in a friendly bark as he scrambled up the gully
side, his own thirty-inch tail waving high above the level
of his haunches. Warrigal fled—for ten paces, wheeling around
then, in kittenish fashion, and stooping till her muzzle
touched the ground between her forefeet But no sooner had
Finn's nose touched hers than the wild coquette was off
again, and this time a little farther into the bush. To and
fro and back and forth the shining bushy-coated dingo
played the great wolfhound, and twilight had darkened into
night when, at length, she yielded herself utterly to his masterful charms and nominally surrendered to the suit she had
actually won. As is always the case with the wild folk, the

courtship was fiery and brief, but one would not say that it was the less passionately earnest for that; and, at the time, Warrigal seemed to Finn the most gloriously handsome and eminently desirable of all her sex.

When their relations had grown temperately fond and familiar, they took to the western trail together, and presently Warrigal "pointed" a big bandicoot for Finn, and Finn, delighted to exhibit his prowess, stalked and slew the creature with a good deal of style. Then the two fed together, Finn politely yielding the hindquarters to his mate. And then they lay and licked and nosed and chatted amicably for an hour. After this, Warrigal rose and stretched her handsome figure to its full length—there was not a white hair about her nor any other trace of cross-breeding—her nose pointing west and by south a little for the back ranges, whence she came. When she trotted sedately off in that direction, Finn followed her as a matter of course, though he had never been this way before. There were no longer any ties that bound him to his old hunting ground. It was not in nature to spare a thought for lugubrious Koala or prickly Echidna when Warrigal waved her bushy tail and trotted on before. Finn had never before been appealed to by the scent of any of the wild people, but there was a subtle atmosphere about Warrigal's thick red-brown coat that drew him to her strongly.

Finn knew the life of his own range pretty well and was familiar with the life of the wild generally. Yet when he contentedly took up the trail with Warrigal, after their supper together upon the bandicoot he had slain, Finn was absolutely and entirely ignorant of the life of the world in which the handsome dingo had spent her days and attained her high position as the acknowledged belle and beauty of her range. One hour afterwards, however, he knew quite a good deal about it.

Possibly from a sense of gallantry, or it may have been because the trail was a new one to him, Finn trotted slightly
behind his mate, his muzzle about level with her flank. He
went warily, with hindquarters carried well under him ready
for springing, and that suggestion of tenseness about his
whole body made it actually, as well as apparently, lower to
the ground than when he stood erect. As for Warrigal, she
trod a home trail and one in which she was accustomed to
meet with deferential treatment from all and sundry. The
law of her race prevented a male dingo from attacking her,
and no female in that countryside would have cared to face
Warrigal in single combat.

The country grew wilder and more rugged as the pair advanced, and as they drew near the foothills surrounding
Mount Desolation, the bush thinned out and the ground became stony, with here and there big lichen-covered boulders
standing alone, like huge bowls upon a giants' green. Then
came a patch of thin, starveling-looking trees, mere bones of
trees, half of whose skin was missing. Suddenly Warrigal gave
a hard, long sniff and then a growl of warning to Finn. She
would have barked if she had known how, but her race do
not bark, though they can growl and snarl with the best.
Besides, they have a peculiar cry of their own, which is not
easy to describe other than as something midway between
a howl and a roar. Finn recognized the growl as warning
clearly enough, and all his muscles were gathered together
for action on the instant; but he had no idea what sort of
danger to expect or whether it was danger or merely the need
of hunting care that his mate had in mind. He knew all
about it some two seconds later, however.

The starveling trees, with the mean, wiry scrub that grew
between them, had served as cover for two lusty males of
Warrigal's tribe—cousins of hers they were, as a matter of
fact, though she had never known the kinship—both of whom

had waked that day to the fact that Warrigal was eminently desirable as a mate. Now, in one instant, they both flew at Finn, one from either side of the trail on which he trotted with Warrigal. Warrigal herself slid forward, a swiftly moving shadow, her brush to the earth, her hindquarters seeming to melt into nothingness, as the jaws of her cousins flashed behind her on either side of Finn's throat. Then, when there were a dozen paces between herself and her new mate, she wheeled and stopped, sitting erect on her haunches, a well-behaved and deeply interested spectator.

Finn suffered for his ignorance of what to expect, as in the wild all folk must suffer for ignorance. The penalty he paid was that he was cut to the bone upon his right and his left shoulders by the flashing teeth of his mate's stalwart young cousins. They had both aimed for the more deadly mark, the throat, but were not accustomed to foes of Finn's great height and had not gauged his stature correctly as he trotted down the trail. Their own shoulder bones were a good foot nearer the earth than Finn's, and his neck towered above the point their jaws reached when they sprang. Wolflike, they leaped aside after the first blow, making no attempt to hold on to their prey. And now, before the keenly watchful eyes of Warrigal, there began the finest fight of her experience. Regarding her mate's good looks she had more than satisfied herself; here was her opportunity to judge of his prowess, in a world where all questions are submitted to the arbitration of tooth and claw in physical combat. And keenly the handsome dingo judged; watchfully she weighed the varying chances of the fray; not a single movement in all the dazzling swiftness of that fight but received her studious and calculating attention, her expert appraisement of its precise value.

In the first moments of that fight the two dingoes were half drunk from pride. It seemed certain to them that they would easily overcome the giant stranger. Indeed, Blacktip, the bigger of the two, who had a black bush at the end of his fine tail, actually seized the opportunity of taking a lightning cut at one of the forelegs of his cousin in the confusion of a rush in upon the wolfhound, feeling that it was as well to get what start he could in dealing with the remaining claimant for Warrigal. He counted the wolfhound dead and wanted to reduce his cousin's chances in the subsequent fight that he knew would be waged to secure possession of Warrigal.

Finn took much longer than one of Blacktip's kindred would have taken to realize the exact nature of his situation and to act accordingly; but, as against that, he was a terrible foe when once he did settle down to work, and further, his mighty muscles and magnificent stature, though they could not justify either recklessness or slackness—which nothing ever can justify in the wild—did certainly enable him to take certain liberties in a fight that would have meant death for a lesser creature. But Finn had been learning a good deal lately, and now, once he had gotten into his stride, so to say, he fought a good deal more in wolf fashion than he would have done a few months earlier; and, in addition, he had his own old fashion and powers the dingoes knew not of in reserve.

At first, he snapped savagely upon one side only, leaving his unprotected side open to the swift lacerations of Blacktip's sharp fangs. But even then he was backing gradually toward a boulder beside the trail, and the moment he felt the friendly touch of the lichen-covered stone behind him his onslaught became double-edged and as terrible as forked lightning.

He was kept too busy as yet to think of death blows; both dingoes saw to that for him, their jaws being never far from one side or the other of his neck or his forelegs. But though, as yet, he gave them nothing of his great weight, he was slashing them cruelly about the necks and shoulders, and once he managed to pluck Blacktip's cousin bodily from the earth and fling him by the neck clean over a low bush. A piece of the dingo's neck remained in Finn's jaws and spoiled half the effect of his next slash at Blacktip's shoulder. But from that moment Blacktip lost for good and all his illusion in the matter of the stranger being as good as dead.

When the sorely wounded dingo, who had been flung aside as if he were a rat, returned to the fray, his eyes were like red coals, and his heart was as full of deadly venom as a death adder's fangs. His neck was tolerably red, too; it was from there that his eyes drew their bloody glare. He crawled around the far side of the boulder, close to the ground like a weasel, and, despairing of the throat hold, fastened his fangs into one of Finn's thighs, with a view to hamstringing while the wolfhound was occupied in feinting for a plunge at Blacktip's bristling neck. It was the death hold that Finn aimed at, but the sudden grip of fire in his thigh was a matter claiming instant attention. He leaped straight up into the air, with the sorely wounded cousin hanging to his thigh and Blacktip snapping at his near foreleg, and in mid-air he twisted his whole great body so that he descended to earth again in a coil, with his mighty jaws closed in the throat of Blacktip's cousin. His fangs met, he gave one terrible shake of his massive neck and head, and when the dingo fell from his jaws this time, two clear yards away, its throat was open to the night air.

Finn was bleeding now from a dozen notable wounds, but it was not in nature that Blacktip singlehanded should overcome him, and Blacktip knew it. The big dingo ceased now to think of killing and concentrated his flagging energies solely upon two points—getting away alive and putting up a fight that should not disgrace him in Warrigal's watchful eyes. He achieved his end, partly by virtue of his own pluck and dexterity and partly because his smell reminded Finn of Warrigal and so softened the killing lust in the wolfhound.

Finn could handle the one dingo with great ease, even wounded as he was, and because of that smell, he had no particular desire to kill. Indeed, he rolled Blacktip over once and could have torn the throat from him but caught him by the loose skin and coat instead and flung him aside with a ferocious, growling snarl.

And Blacktip, with life before him and desire in his heart where Warrigal was concerned, was exceedingly glad of the chance to bound off into the scrub with a long, fierce snarl, which he hoped would place him well in Warrigal's esteem, though he was perfectly aware that it could not deceive Finn.

Then, when it was quite clear that Blacktip had really gone, having taken all the fight he could stand, Warrigal stepped forward mincingly and fell to licking Finn's wounds, with strongly approving tenderness and assiduity. Her mate had fought valiantly and doughtily for Warrigal, and she was proud of him. A savage creature was Warrigal and a brave and quite relentless enemy, the marks of whose fangs more than one fighting member of her race and more than one powerful kangaroo would carry always. But she was very feminine with it all, and the remarks she murmured to her great gray lord, while her solicitous tongue smoothed down the edges of his wounds, were sweetly flattering and vastly stimulating to Finn's passion and his pride.

And then, when between the two busy tongues every wound had received its share of healing attention and antiseptic dressing, Warrigal moved slowly off down the trail, throwing a winsome look of unqualified invitation over her right shoulder to Finn, so that the wolfhound stepped grandly after her, with assumed unconsciousness of his many wounds.

Immediately below the crest of a sharply rising spur of the great mountain they came upon the entrance to Warrigal's own den, which was masked and roofed in by the spreading roots of a fallen tree. The mouth of the den was narrow and very low for one of Finn's stature, but he bent his aching body gladly and followed his mate in to find that the den itself was comparatively roomy and capable of accommodating half a dozen dingoes.

Finn sniffed curiously all around the walls of the den and, finding them permeated with the scent of Warrigal and with that scent only, he lay down there restfully, stretching himself to the full extent of his great length and sighing out his pleasure in being at ease. Warrigal sat gravely erect beside him, admiring the vast spread of his limbs. From tip of nose to tip of tail he covered practically the whole width of the den, which was a shade over seven and one-half feet. The dingo looked over her mate's wounds once more, giving an occasional lick here and there, and then, with a little grunt of gratified pride and content, she curled herself around, after circling three or four times, and went to sleep under the lee of Finn's mighty hindquarters, her muzzle tucked under the spreading hair of her tail and one eye, half opened, resting upon her lord.

Two hours later, Warrigal rose softly and went out to inspect the night. She found the world bathed in a shining glory of silken moonlight, bright as day but infinitely more alluring and mysteriously beautiful. After gazing out at this wonderful panorama for a few minutes and drawing in information through her nostrils of the doings of the wild, Warrigal sat down on her haunches and raised her not very melodious voice in the curious dingo cry, which is a sort of growling howl. Next instant Finn was beside her, with lolling tongue and sensitively questioning nostrils.

Then the two began to play together like young cats, there on the sandy ledge of moon-kissed stone that stretched for yards on either side of the den's mouth. Perhaps it was then,

rather than in the afternoon hours that came earlier, that
Finn courted Warrigal. The stinging of his wounds, caused
by the rapid, sinuous movements with which he danced about
his mate, seemed only to add zest to his love-making. They
were, after all, no more than love tokens, these fang marks
and scratches, and Finn rejoiced in them as such. He had
fought for Warrigal and was ready and willing to fight for
her again. And his mate was most sweet to him; so deft,
so agile, and so swift, so strong and supple, and withal so
instant in response to his gallantries. The night air was sweet,
too, to headiness, and the moonlight seemed to run like quicksilver in Finn's veins. Certainly, he told himself, this new life
in the wild, this life of matehood, was a good thing.

22: THE PACK AND ITS MASTERS

When Finn and Warrigal tired of their play on the flat ledge
outside their den, the moon had set, and in the eastern sky
there was visible the first gray hint of coming dawn. In that
strange, ghostly light, which gave a certain cloak of mystery
even to such common objects as tree stumps and boulders of
rock, Finn saw two unfamiliar figures emerge from the scrub
below the spur next to that of Warrigal's den and begin
slowly to climb toward Mount Desolation itself. There was a
deep, steep-sided gully between Finn and these strange figures, but even at that distance the wolfhound was conscious
of a strong sense of hostility toward the creatures he watched.
Their scent had not reached him because the spur they
climbed was to leeward, yet his hackles rose as he gazed at the
ghostly figures, whose shapes loomed huge and threatening

against the violet-gray skyline. The wolfhound and his mate were just about to enter their den, and Finn touched Warrigal with his muzzle, "pointing" meaningly at the strangers. Warrigal looked, and though her shoulder hairs did not rise at all, her lips curled backward a little from white fangs as she indicated that these figures were perfectly well known to her.

The foremost of them was of great length and bulk, low to the ground, and a savage in every line of his massive frame. His tail, carried without any curve in it, was smooth and tapering, like a rat's tail; his chest was of immense depth, and his truncated muzzle was carried high, jaws slightly parted, long yellow tusks exposed. In general outline he was not unlike a hyena, but with more of strength and fleetness in his general make-up, more, perhaps, of the suggestion of a great wolf, with an unusually savage-looking head and an abnormally massive shoulder. From spine to flank, on either side, the strange creature was striped like a zebra, the ground color of his coat being a light yellowish gray and the stripes black.

This was old Tasman, the zebra wolf, who had been turned loose in that countryside six years before with a mate of his species, who had died during the first year of their life in the Tinnaburra. Behind Tasman, burdened with the weight of a fat wallaby, which he dragged over one shoulder, marched Lupus, his son, now almost four years old and the acknowledged master of Mount Desolation. Lupus had none of his sire's stripes, and his tail, though not so bushy as a dingo's, was well covered with hair. He was, in fact, a half-breed dingo, differing from other dingoes of the Mount Desolation pack only in that he was greater than the rest, more massive in trunk and shoulder, more terrible in tooth and claw. His feet were weapons almost as deadly as a bear's feet. His loins and thighs were those of a fleet runner, and his forepart, in every hair of it, was that of a killer. Tasman was feared on that range rather as a tradition than as a killer; Lupus was feared and obeyed as an actual, living ruler.

It was many months since Warrigal had seen the old wolf Tasman, but Lupus was abroad every night of his life. Also, his eyes, unlike those of his terrible old sire, could face the daylight. All the wild folk knew that Tasman was like an owl by day; light actually hurt him. Lupus was not fond of the light, but he could endure it well enough and kill by it if need be, as was well known. He still shared with his savage old sire the den in which he had been born, deep in the heart of Mount Desolation, and it was stated among the wild folk that he had killed his own mother toward the end of his first year of life and that he and Tasman had devoured her body during a season of drought and poor hunting. Be that as it may, her blood had given Lupus his rating in the Mount Desolation country as a dingo, and his own prowess and ferocity had given him his unquestioned rank as leader and master of the pack. He had never openly preyed upon the pack, but he had killed a round half dozen of its members who had dared to thwart him at different times. It was supposed that Tasman did not hunt now and that Lupus hunted for him, but venturesome creatures of the wild, who had dared to climb the upper slopes of Mount Desolation, claimed to have seen Tasman foraging there after insects and grubs; and as for Lupus, his hunting was sufficiently well known to all on the lower ground. And, in the meantime, though Tasman was credited with very great age, there was no creature in that countryside who would have dared to face the old wolf alone.

It was not very much of all this that Warrigal managed to convey to her mate as they stared out through the gray mist at these strange creatures, but Finn was profoundly and resentfully impressed by what he did gather from her. The shuddering way in which she wriggled her shoulders and

shook her bushy coat before turning into the den for rest after
their long play in the moonlight told Finn a good deal, and
it was information he never forgot. It did not seem fitting to
the great wolfhound that his brave, lissome mate should be
moved to precisely that shuddering kind of shoulder movement by the sight of any living thing, and now, before following her into the den, he stepped well forward to the edge of
the flat rock and barked fierce defiance in the direction of old
Tasman and his redoubtable son. Lupus dropped his burden
in sheer amazement, and father and son both faced around in
Finn's direction and glared at him across the intervening
ravine. It was a fine picture they saw through the ghostly,
misty gray half-light.

Finn was standing, royally erect, at the extreme edge of his
flat table of rock, from which the side of the gully sloped
precipitously. His tail curved grandly out behind him, carried
high, like his massive head. The sight was awe-inspiring and
a far more formidable picture than any dingo in the world
could possibly present. Tasman and Lupus glared at this picture for fully two minutes, while themselves emitting a continuous snarling growl of singular, concentrated intensity and
ferocity.

As the light in the east strengthened, old Tasman's eyes
blinked furiously, and his snarl died down to a savagely
irritable grunt as he turned again to the mountain. Lupus
bent his head, still snarling, to pick up his heavy kill, and
together the two trailed off up the mountainside to their den,
full of angry bitterness.

Barking fiercely at intervals, Finn watched the savage lords
of Mount Desolation ascending till their forms were lost
among the crevices and boulders of the hillside, and then,
with a final, far-reaching roar, he turned and entered the den
where Warrigal sat waiting for him and softly growling a
response to his war cries. This defiance of the admitted lords

of the range was not altogether without its ground of alarm
for Warrigal; its utter recklessness made the skin over her
shoulders twitch, but it was something to have a mate who
could dare so much, even in ignorance. Long after Finn had
closed his eyes in sleep, Warrigal lay watching him, with a
queer light of pride and admiring devotion in her wild yellow eyes.

The afternoon was well advanced when Finn and Warrigal
finally sallied forth from their den in quest of food. Now,
before they crossed the patch of starveling bush that skirted
the foot of their particular ridge, they were approached by
Blacktip and two friends of his, who were also preparing for
the evening hunt. Warrigal growled warningly as the three
dingoes approached, but it seemed that Blacktip had spread
abroad news of the coming of the wolfhound in such a manner
as to disarm hostility. It was with the most exaggerated re-
spectfulness that the dingoes circled, sniffing, about Finn's
legs, their bushy tails carried deferentially near the ground.
Seeing the friendliness of their intentions, Finn wagged his
tail at them, at which they all leaped from him in sudden
alarm, as though he had snapped. His great tail continued
to wag, while he gave friendly greeting through his nostrils
and made it quite clear that he entertained no hostile feeling toward his mate's kindred.

After this the dingoes took heart, and there was a general
all-round sniffing, which occupied fully ten minutes. Finally,
the five of them trotted off into the bush, and then it was
noticeable that Warrigal clung closely to Finn's near side. If
any small accident of the trail caused a change in the position
of the dingoes, Finn instantly dropped back a pace or two,
and a quick look from him was sufficient to send the straying
dingo back to his place on the wolfhound's off side. There
was no talk about it; but from the beginning it was clearly

understood, first, that Finn was absolutely master there, and, secondly, that place on his near side was strictly reserved for his mate and for his mate only; that no creature might approach her except through him.

Finn appeared to lead the hunting party, but its real leader that evening was Warrigal, who had taken note on the previous day of the exact whereabouts of a big mother kangaroo. She now desired two things: a good supper and an opportunity of displaying before the three dingoes the fighting prowess of her lord. Blacktip had had his lesson, as various open wounds on his body then testified, but it was as well that his friends should see something of Finn's might for themselves. That was how Warrigal thought of it, and she knew a good deal about mother kangaroos as well as dingoes. She knew, for instance, that they were more feared by dingoes than the "old men" of their species and that, even with the assistance of his two friends and herself, Blacktip would not have thought of attacking such prey while there were lesser creatures in plenty to be hunted.

In due course Warrigal winded the mother kangaroo and conveyed instant warning to Finn and the others by a sudden checking of her pace. Silent as wraiths between the shadowy tree trunks then, Finn and the four dingoes stalked their prey, describing a considerable circle in order to approach from good cover. To Warrigal's keen disappointment, they found as they topped a little scrub-covered ridge that the mother kangaroo was feeding with a mob of seven, under the guidance of a big red old man. Then she conceived the bold plan of "cutting out" the mother kangaroo from the mob and trusting to Finn to pull her down. This plan she conveyed to her fellow hunters by means of that telepathic method of communication that is as yet little comprehended by men. One quick look and thrust of her muzzle asked Finn to play

his independent part, and another, flung with apparent carelessness across her right shoulder, bade the three dingoes follow her in the work of cutting out.

It was a careful, silent stalk until the hunters were within
ten yards of the quarry, and then with a terrifying yowl of
triumph, a living rope of dingoes—four of them, nose to tail
—was flung between the big mother kangaroo and the rest of
the mob. The red old man gave one panic-stricken look
around his flock, and then they were off like the wind, in big
twenty-foot bounds. But the mother could not bring herself
to leap in their direction because of the yowling streak of
snapping dingoes, which had flung itself between them. She
sprang off at a tangent, and as she made her seventh or eighth
bound, terror filled her heart almost to bursting. A roaring
gray cloud swept upon her from her right quarter, and she
felt the burning thrust of Finn's fangs in her neck. She sat up
valiantly to fight for her life and the young life in her pouch,
and her left hind leg, with its chisel claws, sawed the air like
a pump handle. The dingoes knew that it would be death for
one or two of them, at all events, to face those outthrust
chisels. They surrounded the big beast in a snarling, yowling
circle and gnashed their white fangs together with a view to
establishing the paralysis of terror. But they did not advance
as yet. Finn slipped once, when he tried to take fresh hold,
and in that instant the kangaroo slashed him deeply in the
groin. But the wound was her own death warrant, for it filled
the wolfhound with fighting rage, and in another instant
there was a broken neck between his jaws and blood was
running over the red-brown fur of the kangaroo, as her body
fell sideways, with Finn upon it.

The three other dingoes approached the kill with Warrigal,
but she snarled at them, and a swift turn of Finn's head told
them to beware. In the end Warrigal settled down to make a
meal at one side of the kangaroo's hindquarters, Finn took

the other side, and the three dingoes were given their will of
the forepart. There was more than enough for all, and
though, when they left the kill to the lesser carnivora of that
quarter, Finn carried a good meal with him between his jaws,
it was not that he needed it for himself but that he wished to
place it in the den at Warrigal's disposal—a little attention
that earned for him various marks of his mate's cordial ap-
proval. She was extremely pleased to have this evidence of
Finn's forethought as a breadwinner. Instinct told her the
value and importance of this quality in a mate. And while she
carefully dressed the wound in her lord's groin that night,
Blacktip and his friends, with much chop-licking, spread
abroad the story of their glorious hunting and of Finn's might
as a killer. They vowed that a more terrible fighter and a
greater master than Lupus, or than his even more terrible
sire, whom few of them had seen, had come to Mount Desolation, and old dingoes shook their gray heads, feeling that
they lived in strange and troublous times. But as for Lupus,
he was ranging trails at that moment on an empty stomach
in savage quest of no other than this same stranger, who had
dared to defy him.

23: SINGLE COMBAT

EVEN while he hunted, the irritating thought of the creature
who had barked defiantly at him remained with Lupus and
was not softened by the fact that he missed two kills and
failed to find other game. He was in no real need of killing,
for he had fed during the afternoon on the remains of the
wallaby he had dragged up the hill early that morning. This

was probably why he missed two kills; when empty, it was
rare indeed for him to miss.

And, now, with irritation added to the anger of his recollection of the wolfhound, he happened by pure chance upon
the warm trail of Warrigal and the others who had accompanied Finn that night. This led him to the remains of the
mother kangaroo, where he disturbed some lesser creatures
who were supping at their ease. Lupus had no mind to leave
bones with good fresh meat on them, and when he turned
away again on Finn's trail, the unfamiliar scent of which
raised the stiff bristles on his back till he looked like a hyena,
there was nothing much left for the ants or the flesh-eating
rats and mice of the bush.

Finn's home trail was still fresh, and Lupus followed it
easily. He licked his chops, then, over a recollection of sundry
whiffs and glimpses that had interested him of late in Warrigal, and as his nose dropped low over her trail on the near
side of Finn's, it was borne in upon Lupus that it would be
well for him to have a mate and that Warrigal would be a
pleasing occupant of that post. The stranger must be removed, once and for all. Lupus growled low in his throat. So
he pieced the matter out in his mind while loping heavily
along Finn's trail; while among the starveling trees near the
mountain's foot, Blacktip and his friends discussed the newcomer's prowess; while in the den on the first spur Finn lay
dozing under the admiring eyes of his mate, who did not
greatly care for sleep at night.

Before Lupus touched the first loose stone of the trail leading up the hill to Warrigal's den, the creatures of the scrub
below were all aware of his passage, and Blacktip, with seven
other dingoes who did not happen to be away hunting, were
following up the same trail, in fan-shaped formation and at
a respectful distance behind the master of the range. Halfway
up the rugged side of the spur, his unbeaten insolence be-

trayed Lupus into what the wild folk considered an unsports-
manlike and stupid mistake. He paused for a moment and
bellowed forth a threatening and peremptory announcement
of his coming in the form of a hoarse, grating howl of challenge, which could have been heard a mile away. Then he
proceeded on his upward way slowly because he was fully
fed, carelessly because he had never known defeat, but de-
terminedly because he was bent upon ridding the range of
one who had flung defiance at him across the gully, and because, the more he thought of it, the more ardent became his
desire to possess Warrigal for a mate

Warrigal's friendly warning to Finn was not needed. In the
same instant that Lupus's hoarse cry fell upon his ears he
was awake and alert. He recognized the voice and read clearly
enough the meaning of the cry. He knew that this was a more
considerable enemy than any he had faced as yet, and there
was time in the moment of his waking for regret to flash
through his mind that the challenge should have come now,
while his whole body was scarred with unhealed wounds and
his left thigh was stiff from the punishing slash of the kangaroo's mailed foot. In the next moment he was outside the
mouth of the den, his deep, fierce bark rending the silence
of the night. The eight dingoes who followed in Lupus's trail
heard the bark and glanced one at another in meaning comment. Never was a leader of men or beasts more cordially
hated than Lupus Blacktip experienced a generous sensation
of sympathy and pity for Finn, and so did the two friends of
his who had fed that night upon good fresh kangaroo flesh.
But they, like all the others, were keen to see the coming
fight and—to act accordingly. The question of what was to
become of Warrigal had occurred with interest to each one
of them, for she was eminently desirable just then to all her
kind.

Fierce, savage, and justly feared, though he was, physically,

Lupus was mentally a sluggish beast and not overintelligent. In this he favored his sire, who was slow-moving, sluggish, but as fierce as any weasel and immensely powerful. When Lupus caught his first glimpse of the creature he had come to slay, he had a momentary thrill of uneasiness, but it was no more than momentary. Finn's towering form stood out clearly in the moonlight as he waited, with tail curved upward and hackles erect, on the stone ledge outside the den. Lupus was scaling an extremely steep section of the trail at the moment, and seen against the skyline, Finn seemed monstrous. But Lupus knew nothing of fear. It was only that for a moment, as he dragged his full-fed weight upward over the stones, the thought passed through his dull mind that this was surely a strange sort of dingo and extraordinarily tall. But Lupus always had killed every animal that he had met in combat, and it did not for an instant occur to him that he might fail to kill this newcomer. And then there was Warrigal—he got her scent now as she emerged, crouching, from the den. He wanted Warrigal for his mate and he would have her.

Finn was standing in the middle of the flat ledge outside the den, and he neither advanced nor retreated a single step as Lupus drew nearer. He simply bayed, at intervals, like a minute gun and scratched a little at the sandy rock beneath him with his right forefoot. Once, Warrigal, snarling savagely, ranged up alongside him, but he sent her back to the mouth of the den with a peremptory growl, which admitted of no argument. And Warrigal, like the good spouse she was, retreated to the mouth of the den. Just then Lupus landed on the rock ledge with a hectoring snarl. He plunged forward upon Finn with the clumsiness of a buffalo and, for his instruction, received a slashing bite across one shoulder and a chest thrust, which sent him rolling backward off the ledge to the trail below on his back.

A dingo in Finn's place would have leaped upon him then,

and, it may be, the fight would have ended suddenly; for even
so redoubtable a foe as Lupus is of no very great account if he
can be seized when on his back, with all four feet in the air.
Blacktip and his companions in the rear drew in their breath
sharply. They had never before seen Lupus on his back, and
if he had stayed there another second, he would have had
their fangs to reckon with. But his reception by the stranger
taught Lupus something, and the enemy that faced Finn for
the second assault was a far more deadly one than the Lupus
of a few moments earlier. Finn had scorned to pursue his
fallen foe, but it would have been better for him if he had
had less pride. The fan-shaped line of watching dingoes
closed in a little as Lupus remounted the rocky ledge with a
blood-curdling snarl and an awe-inspiring exposure of his
gleaming fangs. In another instant the two were at grips, and
Finn realized that he was engaged in a fight for life and a far
more serious combat than any he had known before. The
mere weight of impact with the wolf dingo was sufficient to
tell Finn this, and for the infinitesimal fraction of an instant
he felt a sense of fatality and doom when his opponent's tremendously powerful jaws closed over the upper part of his
right foreleg.

In the next instant Finn had torn one of Lupus's ears in
half, and the terrible grip on his leg was relaxed. The wolfhound sprang completely over the wolf dingo and took a
slashing bite at the creature's haunches as he descended. Then
they rose one at the other, like bears standing erect, and meeting jaw to jaw in mid-air, with a flashing and clashing of
fangs, which sent a thrill of excitement along the line of
watchful dingoes, who realized now that they were looking
on at the greatest spectacle of their lives. Lupus missed his
grip that time, but so did Finn, being unable to withstand
the violent sidelong wrench that snatched the enemy's neck
from his jaws. And, as they came to earth again, Lupus se-

cured firm hold upon Finn's leg in the same grip that he had
obtained before. The grip was so vicelike and punishing as
to flash panic into Finn's very soul, such as an animal knows
when trapped by a man's device in unyielding steel. It was
only by a violent twist of his neck that he could bring his
jaws into action upon Lupus at all. But panic drove, and the
long, immensely powerful neck was curved sufficiently. His
jaws took the wolf dingo at the back of the head, and one of
his lower canines actually penetrated Lupus's lower jaw, causing him the most excruciating pain, so that he emitted a
sound more like a hoarse scream than a growl and snatched
his head back swiftly from so terrible a punishment. That
was the last time in this fight that Finn's legs were in serious
danger. He had learned his lesson, and from that point onward, no matter what punishment his shoulders might receive, his hanging jaws, from which the blood dripped now,
effectually guarded his legs.

From this point, too, Lupus seemed to have centered all his
desires upon the wolfhound's throat; an underhold was what
he sought, and in the pursuit of that he seemed prepared for,
and capable of standing, any amount of punishment. The
line of watching dingoes was still and silent as a line of
statues; it seemed they hardly drew breath, so intent was their
preoccupation. Warrigal, too, stuck closely to her position,
but she was not silent; a low, continuous snarl issued from her
parted jaws, and the updrawn line of her lips showed white
and glistening in the moonlight. She had been ordered to the
rear by her mate, but the waiting dingoes on the trail below
realized that if Finn were to be laid low, there would still be
fighting to be done on that ledge of rock, and fighting of a
deadly sort, at that, from which there would be no escaping.

In one sense the wolfhound's great height was against him
now, since it placed Lupus in a more favorable position for
securing the underhold upon which he was intent. But, as

against that, it gave Finn readier access to the hold that in all his fights hitherto he had made fatal: the hold a terrier takes upon a rat. But Lupus was no rat, and Finn had already found more than once that even his mighty jaws were not powerful enough to give killing pressure through all the mass of harsh bristles and thick rolling skin and flesh that protected Lupus's spinal chord at the neck. Three times during the later stages of the fight Lupus managed to ward off attack with a lightning stroke of one forefoot, the claws of which scored deep into Finn's muzzle and neck, in one case opening a lesser vein and sending the red blood rushing over his iron-gray coat. It seemed the long claws of the wolf dingo were almost more deadly than his snapping jaws.

The flow of his own blood seemed to madden Finn, and he made a plunge for his enemy's neck. Lupus sat erect and, like a boxer or a big bear, warded off the plunge with a violent, sweeping blow of his right paw. There was a quick flash of bloody, foam-flecked fangs, and the deadly paw was crushed between Finn's jaws. The pain of the crushing drew a screeching howl from Lupus, and in that same instant a powerful upward twist of Finn's neck threw him fairly on his back, snarling despairingly. One could not measure the fraction of time that elapsed between Finn's release of the crushed foot and his seizure of the throat—the deadly underhold. The wolf dingo's bristles were thin there and the skin comparatively soft. The fight was for life, and it was the whole of the wolf-hound's great strength that he put into his grip. Lupus's entire frame, every inch of it, writhed and twisted convulsively, like the body of a huge cat in torment. Finn's fangs sank half an inch deeper. The wolf dingo's claws tore impotently at space, and his body squirmed almost into a ball. Finn's fangs sank half an inch deeper, and hot blood gushed between them. Lupus's great body hunched itself into an almost erect position from the shoulder blades; he was standing on his shoulders. Then, as in a convulsion, one of his hind legs was lowered in order that it might saw upward, scoring three deep furrows down the side of the wolfhound's neck. Finn's fangs met in the red center of his enemy's throat. There was a faint grunt, a final spasm of muscular activity, and then Finn drew back and shook his dripping muzzle in the air. The fierce lord of Mount Desolation had entered upon the long sleep; his lordship was ended.

Finn sank back upon his haunches, gasping, with a length of scarlet foam-streaked tongue dangling from one side of his jaws. The watching line of dingoes advanced two paces. War-rigal, stepping forward to her mate's side, snarled warningly. But Finn pushed her gently with his lacerated muzzle, and turning then to the watchful dingoes below, he emitted a little whinnying sound that said plainly: "You are welcome here!" Acting upon this, Blacktip moved slowly, deferentially forward and climbed the flat ledge of rock, his bushy tail re-spectfully curled between his legs. Long and thoroughly he sniffed at the dead body of the terrible Lupus, and then he looked around at his still waiting companions and whined as he walked back toward them. In twos and threes the dingoes followed Blacktip's lead and climbed the flat rock to sniff their dead tyrant and satisfy themselves that he had in-deed entered upon the long sleep. And the gesture in Finn's direction, with which they turned away from the rock, was as near to being a salutation, an obeisance, as anything that mortal dingo has ever achieved. And when the last of the band, reinforced now by half a dozen others who had been hastily summoned from their hunting nearby, had paid his visit of inspection, Finn did a curious thing, which probably no dingo would ever have done. He moved slowly forward on his aching limbs, gripped the dead body firmly by the neck, and heaved it down from the flat rock to the trail below. Then he barked aloud a message that said plainly:

"Here is your old lord and tyrant! Take him away and leave me now!"

Blacktip and half a dozen of his comrades seized upon the carcass of the tyrant and dragged it away down the trail. I cannot say what was done with the remains of Lupus, the terrible son of Tasman; but Finn and Warrigal saw them no more, and for three days after that night of the slaying of Lupus, the bush folk saw nothing of the wolfhound. They saw Warrigal hunt alone each evening, and doubtless with thoughts of Finn in their minds, they respected her trail and sought no speech of her. These young bloods, by the way, began to mutter now of the desirability of banding together to beard old Tasman in his den and rid themselves of the shadow and tradition of tyranny, as well as its actuality. But the counsel of the elders strongly favored delay. "Let us wait and see what the Great One will do when he is healed of his wounds," was what they thought and, after their own fashion, said to the ambitious youngsters.

24: DOMESTIC LIFE IN THE DEN

WHEN the wolfhound and his admiring mate between them had thoroughly licked and cleansed his numerous wounds, he stretched himself deliberately across the rear corner of the den, and there lay, sleeping soundly, until the next morning was well advanced. His body was lacerated by the wounds of three considerable fights. But even the ten hours that Finn gave to sleep—he opened his eyes two or three times during that period but did not move—brought a wonderful change in these numerous wounds. Now they were submitted to another thorough licking. Then Finn crept out into the sunlight beside the cave's mouth and slept again, fitfully, till evening came. Then he sat up and licked all his wounds over again with painstaking and scrupulous care. They were healing nicely, and the healing process made Finn stiff and sore. So he crept painfully into the den again and lay down to sleep once more, while Warrigal, with a friendly, wifely look at her lord, went out hunting.

In this way three full days and nights passed, and on the fourth night Finn killed for himself—a small kill and not far from home, but a kill, nonetheless, that required a certain agility, of which he already found himself quite capable. The wolfhound had immense reserves to draw upon—greater reserves, really, than any of the wild folk possessed; for, in his youth, he had never known scarcity of food or lack of warmth or undue exposure; and his system had been deliberately built up and fortified by the best sort of diet that the skill and science of man could devise.

From this point onward, Finn's wounds troubled him very little, and in the healing air of that countryside they soon ceased to be apparent to the eye. An ordinary dingo would have been obliged to fight many fights before obtaining ascendancy over the Mount Desolation pack; but the mastery fell naturally to Finn without calling for any effort upon his part. He had slain the redoubtable old leader and tyrant of the pack. He had soundly trounced one of the strongest among the fully-grown young dingoes, Blacktip, and killed another in singlehanded fight against two. Most of the pack had taken good measure of his prowess on the night of the slaying of Lupus, and that was enough for them, so far as mastery went. Further, the pack found Finn a generous leader, a kingly sort of friend; slow to anger and merciful even in wrath; open as the day and never, in any circumstances, tyrannical or aggressive. Then in the matter of his kills, Finn was generosity itself. As a hunter of big game, he was more formidable than any three dingoes and, withal, never rapacious. Three portions he would take from his kill; one to satisfy his own hunger, one for Warrigal to satisfy her hunger upon, and a third to be set aside and taken back to the den against the time when Warrigal should care to dispose of it. For the rest, be his kill what it might, Finn made the pack free of it.

But no sort of temptation seemed strong enough to take the wolfhound near to the haunts of men. It came to be understood that Finn would not touch sheep, and reasoning it out amongst themselves, the rest of the pack accepted this as a prohibition meant to apply to all of them; so that Finn's mastership was an exceedingly good thing for the squatters and their flocks all through the Tinnaburra. But a full-grown kangaroo, no matter how heavy and strong in the leg, never seemed too much for Finn; and so, all dingoes liking big game better than small, it came about that every night saw the Mount Desolation dingoes hunting in pack formation at the heels of the great wolfhound. Finn thoroughly enjoyed the hunting and did not care how many fed at his kill, so that his mate and he had ample.

Once, the two youngest members of the pack, puppies quite new to the trail, were attacked and driven from the remains of a big kill the leader had made by an outlier, a strange dingo from some other range. The youngsters, bleeding and yelping, carried their woes to the scrub below the mountain, and within the hour Finn learned of it. Followed by Blacktip and one or two others of the more adventurous sort, he set out upon the trail of the outlier, now full fed, ran it down at the end of four or five miles' hard galloping, pinned the unfortunate creature to the earth, and shook it into the long sleep almost before they had come to a standstill together. This was true leadership the pack felt, a thing Lupus would never have done; something to be placed to the great wolfhound's credit and not forgotten.

During this time a subtle change crept over Finn's appearance. Though he fed well and plentifully and his life was not a hard one, since he only did that which pleased him, yet Finn had acquired now the hard, spare look of the creatures of the wild. In his alertness, in the blaze of his eyes and the gleam of his fangs when hunting, in his extreme wariness and in the silence of his movements, and in his deadly swiftness in attack, Finn had become one of his mate's own kindred. He differed from them in his great bulk, his essentially commanding appearance, in his dignity, and in a certain lordly generosity, which always characterized him. He never disputed; he never indulged in threats or recrimination. He gave warning when warning was needed; he punished when punishment was needed; and he killed if killing was desirable; making no sort of fuss about either process. Also, upon occasion, though not often, he barked. Otherwise, he was thoroughly of the wild kindred and the unquestioned master of the Mount Desolation range.

Some six or seven weeks after his arrival upon that range, Finn began to notice that Warrigal was changing in some way, and he did not like the change. It seemed to him that his mate no longer cared for him so much as she had cared. She spent more time in lying about in or near the den and showed no eagerness to accompany him in his excursions, to gambol with him, or even to lie with him on the warm flat ledge outside the den. However, life was very full of independent interest for the wolfhound, and it was only in odd moments that he noticed these things. One night he was thoroughly surprised when Warrigal snarled at him in a surly manner, without any apparent cause at all, unless because he had touched her with his nose by way of inviting her to accompany him, bound for the trail in quest of that night's supper.

Finn walked out of the den, carrying his nose as high as he could in view of the stoop necessary at the entrance. A dingo in his place would have snarled back at Warrigal, and, it may be, have wrangled about it for half an hour. Finn's dignity would not permit of this, but he was hurt and decided that his spouse needed a lesson in courtesy. Since she responded so rudely to his invitation to join him in the hunt, she might go supperless; he would eat where he killed and bring home nothing.

Finn killed a half-grown kangaroo that night, and he, with Blacktip and two or three others of the pack, fed upon this before going down to the creek together to drink. In the small hours the wolfhound wended his way alone to his den on the first spur, prepared, as many a male human has been in like case, to seek his rest without taking any notice of his mate, unless he found her in a repentant mood. At the mouth of the cave he stooped low, as he was bound to do, to gain admittance, and in that moment he was brought to a halt by a long, angry, threatening snarl from within. Warrigal was very plainly telling her mate to remain outside unless he was looking for trouble. This was unprecedented, and he was a very angry and outraged wolfhound, who withdrew slowly with as much dignity as might be in walking backward with lowered head and shoulders.

He selected a comfortable sleeping place in the shadow of a bush some half a dozen paces away from the mouth of the den. And then, being well fed and rather tired, he fell into a sound sleep until just after daybreak, when he woke to the sound of an unfamiliar small cry. With head slightly on one side and ears cocked sharply, Finn listened. The small cry was repeated. It certainly was not Warrigal's voice, though it came from the inside of the den. Also, there were a number of other small sounds that were strange—weak, quaint, gurgling sounds. It was extremely puzzling and interesting, and he decided to investigate.

Finn stooped low in the entrance, and Warrigal snarled. But this time there was no note of aggression in her snarl. Indeed, to her mate, there was a hint of appeal in the salutation, which said clearly: "Be careful! Please be careful!" He advanced with extreme caution into the den and saw his spouse lying at full length on her side, her bushy tail curled around to form a background for the smallest of four sleek puppies, of a yellowish gray color, whom she was nursing assiduously. Moving with the utmost delicacy and care, Finn sniffed all around his mate, refraining from touching the puppies by way of humoring Warrigal, in whose throat a low growl sounded whenever his nose approached the little strangers. Then Finn stood and stared at the domestic group with hanging head and parted jaws, his tongue lolling, and his eyes saying plainly:

"Well! Who'd have thought of this! They are nice little creatures, in their insignificant way, though I don't quite see why their presence should make you snarl at your own lawful mate."

Seeing that her lord entertained no shadow of a hostile intention toward the family, Warrigal raised her nose in friendly fashion to the wolfhound and permitted him to lick her, which he did in the most affectionate manner. Then she gave a little whine and glanced around the walls of the den Finn barked quietly, bidding his mate rest assured that all would be well, and ten minutes later he was descending upon a rabbit earth that he knew of, a moving shadow of death among young rabbits assembled to welcome the dewy warmth of the new day. On the way home he dropped his rabbit to stalk a half-grown bandicoot; and finally, after less than an hour's absence, he returned to the den carrying a rabbit and a bandicoot so that Warrigal might have variety in her breakfast. Being parched with thirst, Warrigal gratefully accepted both kills and without actually eating either drew some sustenance from both. Then with an anxious look at the family, she nudged Finn out of the den with her nose and, leaving him outside on the ledge, turned and raced for the creek, like an arrow from a bow. She was back again inside of two minutes with bright drops clinging to her fur. Finn had sat patiently beside the mouth of the den waiting, and for this Warrigal gave him a grateful glance of appreciation before gliding in to her puppies, who already were beginning to whimper for warmth and nourishment.

Finn took very naturally to the part of father and breadwinner. He lounged about the mouth of the den through the day, creeping in occasionally to see how things went with his mate and returning then to keep guard outside. She allowed him now to touch the odd little creatures who were his children; but they did not like the feeling of his tongue and wriggled away from it in their blind, helpless way. As for Warrigal, she seemed absurdly happy and proud about it all now and assumed considerable airs of importance. She took her food in brief snatches a dozen times during the day, and when Finn left her in the early night for the trails, she looked at him in a meaning way, which said plainly that she attached importance to the matter of food supply, though she could not take to the trails herself. Finn licked her muzzle reassuringly and went out.

The pack had to forage for itself that night, for when Finn made his kill—a fat rock wallaby—he announced in the most unmistakable manner that there was nothing to spare for followers that night and went off mountainward, trailing the whole heavy kill over his right shoulder. In the course of the

night it became known to all the wild people of that range
that the mate of the leader of the pack had other mouths than
her own to feed and that, for the time, Finn would do all the
hunting for the den on the first spur.

25: TRAGEDY IN THE DEN

WHEN Warrigal's puppies were born, Finn, their father, had
been in the Tinnaburra for nearly five months, though he
had only known the Mount Desolation range for some nine
or ten weeks. During the whole of that five months of late
winter and spring, not one single drop of rain had fallen in
the Tinnaburra, and with the coming of Warrigal's children
there came also the approach of summer. Finn, for his part,
gave no thought to this question of weather because he had
quite forgotten that there was such a thing as rain. He had
slept on the earth ever since his escape from the circus, and
he accepted its dryness as a natural and agreeable fact.

But both Finn and Warrigal were rather annoyed when,
just as the puppies began to open their eyes and become a
little troublesome and curious, the creek at the foot of Mount
Desolation disappeared through its shingly bed and was seen
no more. This meant a tramp of three and a half miles to the
nearest drinking place, a serious matter for a nursing mother,
whose tongue seemed always to be lolling thirstily from the
side of her mouth. Warrigal would make the journey to the
drinking place as swiftly as she could and drink till she could
drink no more. Then during the return journey concern for
her children would set the pace for her, and she would arrive
at the den panting and gasping and more thirsty than when
she left it; for the weather was already hot, the air singularly

dry, and Warrigal herself in no condition for fast traveling, with her heavy dugs and body, both amply fed and amply drawn upon in her capacity of nurse-mother. Finn did his part well and thoroughly, and there was no lack of good fresh meat in the den on the first spur, but he could not carry water. And so, during all this time, Finn's mate found herself obliged to run over hard, parched ground at least fourteen miles a day, and often twenty-one, when it would have suited her, and her puppies also, a good deal better to have confined her exercise to strolls in the neighborhood of the den.

One result of this was that Warrigal's children began to eat meat at an earlier stage of their existence than would have been the case if water had been plentiful and near at hand for their mother. From that time on Finn was a very busy hunter. It was probably because of this unceasing demand for fresh meat in the den on the first spur that the leader of the Mount Desolation pack was the first member of it to notice that hunting was becoming increasingly difficult in that region. Finn's quest was necessarily for large meat; and at about this time he was discovering to his cost that he had to go farther and farther afield to find it. It was well enough for the bachelors and spinsters of the pack, the freelancers of that clan. The district was still rich in its supply of the lesser marsupials, rats, mice, and the like, not to mention all manner of grubs and insects and creeping things, among which it was easy for a single dingo to satisfy his appetite. But a giant wolfhound, with a very hungry mate and four ravening little pups, all waiting eagerly upon his hunting, was quite differently situated.

Then Warrigal herself returned to the trails. Finn in no sense failed her as breadwinner, but game being scarce and her children still too young to do any foraging for themselves worth talking about, Warrigal felt that she owed it to her mate to share his burdens with him. The pups had already reached the stage of groveling about outside the den and pursuing the few live things of the insect type that affected that stony spot.

One night Finn had a stroke of luck in stumbling upon a badly wounded wallaby within a couple of miles of the den. In some way this unfortunate creature had managed to get its right hind leg caught in a dingo trap, to which a heavy clog of wood was attached. In the course of time the wallaby would have died very miserably, and already it had begun to lose flesh. But Finn brought a mercifully sudden death to the crippled creature and then proceeded to tear asunder the limb that held the trap. Having accomplished this, he slung the wallaby over his shoulder and set out for the mountain, meaning to allow the family to feast upon this early kill while he took a further look around upon the trails.

Just as Finn, heavily laden, scaled the rocky ledge immediately below the one that flanked the entrance of the den, a shrill cry of mortal anguish fell upon his ears. The cry came from the inside of the den above him, and he knew it for the cry of one of his children in extremity. That gave Finn the most piercing thrill of paternity he had felt up till this time. He dropped his kill and leaped with one mighty bound clear over two boulders and a bare stretch of track to the ledge outside the den. And, in the moment of his leap, a figure emerged from the mouth of the den bearing between its uncovered yellow tusks the body of Warrigal's last-born son, limp and bleeding. This figure, which faced Finn now in the moonlight, was the most terribly ugly one that the countryside could have produced. Gaunt beyond description, ragged, gray, bereft of hair in many places, aged and desperate, old Tasman, the zebra wolf, had his tusks sunk in warm, juicy flesh for the first time in three months and was prepared to pay for the privilege with the remains of his life if need be. Skin, bone, glittering eyes, and savage, despairing ferocity; that was all there was left of Tasman, three months after the death of his son Lupus. He had lived since then almost entirely upon insects, grubs, scraps of carrion dropped by birds, and the like. Desperate hunger and the smell of young animal life and of the proceeds of daily kills had drawn him to the den on the first spur that night; and now, now he was face to face with the master of the range and the outraged father of Warrigal's pups.

The gaunt old wolf dropped his prey on the instant, realizing clearly that his life was at stake. In his day he had slain many dingoes, but that was in the distant past, and this iron-gray monster that roared at him now was different from the dingoes Tasman had known. With massive, bony skull held low and saliva dripping from his short, powerful jaws, the old wolf sent forth his most terrible snarl of challenge and defiance; the cry that had been used in bygone years to paralyze his victims into a condition that made them easy prey for his tearing claws and lancelike tusks. But the horrible sound was powerless so far as Finn was concerned, and the wolfhound gathered himself together now for the administration of punishment that should be as swift as it would be terrible and final. But in that moment he heard a scattering of loose stones behind him, which delayed his spring to allow time for a flying glance over his right shoulder; and that glance changed his whole tactics in the matter of the attack upon Tasman. Even as Finn glanced, an outstretched furry mass flew across his range of vision and landed like a projectile upon the gaunt old wolf's neck. Warrigal also had returned; she also had dropped her kill in the trail below the den, and now Tasman had to deal with the dauntless fury of a bereaved mother. Warrigal was a whirlwind of rage; a revelation to Finn of the fighting force that had given her her unquestioned standing in the pack before ever she set eyes on the wolfhound.

Tasman had his back against the side of the den's mouth now, and he flung Warrigal from him, with a slash of his jaws and a twist of his still powerful neck. But, in the next moment, the underside of that scrawny neck was between the mightiest jaws in the Tinnaburra, and even as the life blood of old Tasman flowed out between Finn's white fangs, the body of him was being literally torn asunder by the furiously busy teeth and claws of Warrigal. Old Tasman was not just killed; he was dispersed, scattered, dissolved, translated within a few minutes into shapeless carrion.

And then, gasping, bleeding, panting, her jaws streaming, Warrigal wheeled about with a savage, moaning cry and shot forward into the den. One son she had seen dead upon the ledge without. Two daughters she found dead within, and while she licked at his lacerated little body, the lingering life ebbed out finally from the other male pup, her sole remaining son. But Warrigal licked the still little form for almost an hour, though it lived for no more than three or four minutes after she entered the den.

Then Warrigal went outside to where Finn sat, alternately licking the one deep wound the old wolf had scored on his chest and looking out dismally across the Tinnaburra. Warrigal sat down on her haunches about two yards from Finn, and having pointed her muzzle at the moon, where it sailed serenely above them in a flawless dark blue sky, she began to pour out upon the night the sound of the long, hoarse dingo howl of mourning. Finn listened for some minutes without moving. By that time the melancholy of it all had entered fairly into his soul, and he, too, lifted up his head and delivered himself of the Irish wolfhound howl, which carries farther than the dingo howl and is more purely mournful than any other canine cry. Also, it has more volume than any other; there is something uncanny and supernatural about its piercing melancholy. And if you were to visit that den today, on the first southeastern spur of Mount Desolation, you would probably find the skeletons of three of Finn and Warrigal's children; for the wolfhound and his mate never entered their old home again.

26: THE EXODUS

IT was rather an odd thing that neither Finn nor his mate ever again entered the lair that had been such a happy home for them since the day of their first meeting. But so it was, and one is bound to assume that the reason for it was grief at the loss of their children. In the early dawning of a blistering hot day they paced slowly down the hill and into the rocky strip of scrub that divided Mount Desolation from the bush itself. Here it was that the rest of the pack lived, and though Finn and Warrigal conveyed no definite news of what had happened during the night, the news must have spread somehow, because before the sun had properly risen, every single member of the pack had climbed the spur and investigated for himself or herself the scattered carrion that had been Tasman.

There was beginning to be considerable distress over the absence of rain, the scarcity of water, and the poor results that attended their hunting. There was no longer any disguising the fact that a very large number of the wild folk, in whom Finn and Warrigal and the rest of the pack were interested, had recently migrated in quest of homes that should be

better supplied with water than the Tinnaburra or the Mount
Desolation range.

Even Finn's prowess as a hunter and a killer was of no
avail in the absence of game to hunt, and during the few days
he and Warrigal spent among the scrub at the mountain's
foot after leaving their den, the wolfhound sometimes traveled from thirty to forty miles without a single kill, being
reduced then, like the rest of the pack, to eat rabbit flesh and
mice and grubs. Already some of the younger members of
the pack had begun to prey upon the flocks of squatters in the
Tinnaburra, and this had brought speedy retribution in the
shape of one young female of their kindred shot through the
head and two promising males trapped and slain, so that
the pack now consisted of no more than fourteen adults and
six whelps, who were hardly capable as yet of fending for
themselves. Men with guns had actually been seen within a
mile of Mount Desolation itself; and owing to the attacks
upon their bark of half-starved small fry, the trees of the bush
were dying by hundreds and thereby opening up in the most
uncomfortable manner ranges that had previously been excellent hunting grounds. The menfolk with guns were most disturbing to Finn, and he was conscious, in sitting down, of a
degree of boniness about the haunches such as he had never
known since the horrible period of his captivity in the circus.
Grubs and mice were not of much use to Finn; and when he
drank, his long tongue had been wont to scoop up more than
twice the amount of water that had served to satisfy any other
member of the pack.

The growing restlessness and discontent that had been
mastering the Mount Desolation pack for weeks now received an immense addition, as far as Finn and Warrigal were
concerned, in the events that led them to forsake their den
on the first spur. It culminated, in Finn's eyes, in the actual
passage through the scrub beside the mountain's foot of a

party of half a dozen mounted men with guns and dogs. This occurred in the late afternoon of a scorching hot day, when most of the pack were sleeping; and if the dogs of the men-folk had not been incredibly stupid in sticking closely to the trail and making no attempt to range the scrub on either side of it, the dingoes would actually have been hunted like hares and some of them, no doubt, would have been killed. As it was, Finn felt as strongly, and perhaps more strongly than any of the elders of the pack, that this event had rendered the range finally uninhabitable. His nostrils twitched and wrinkled for hours after the men had gone; and as soon as darkness fell, he rose in a determined manner, thrust his muzzle meaningly against Warrigal's neck, and took to the open trail. With extraordinary unanimity the other members of the pack began to gather behind Finn. It seemed to be clearly understood that this was no ordinary hunting expedi-tion, and the two mothers of the pack, with their half-grown whelps, whined plaintively as they gathered their small fami-lies about them for journeying.

One very old dog, who had always looked with grudging sullenness upon the great wolfhound and his doings, refused point-blank to be a party to the exodus and croakingly warned the others against following a newcomer and an out-lier such as Finn. The pack paid little heed to the old dingo, and he sat erect on his haunches beside the trail, watching them file along the flank of the mountain. When they were nearly a mile away, the old dingo began to howl dismally; and when Finn made his first kill, seven miles to the north-west of Mount Desolation, old Tufter—he had a sort of mop at the end of a rather scraggy tail—was on hand and yowling eagerly for scraps.

The poor old fellow took great pains to communicate his own discomfort and mistrust to all the other members of the pack, except Finn and Warrigal, whom he ignored, and

pointed out with vehemence that they were heading in the
wrong direction. He was right in a way, for they certainly
were leaving the better country behind them in traveling to
the northwest. South and east of Mount Desolation lay the
fatter and comparatively well-watered lands. Even Finn knew
this, of course; but that way also lay the habitations of men.
Men had tortured him in a cage; the memory of their hot
irons had burned right into his very soul. And, after that,
men, in the person of a certain sulky boundary rider, had
driven him out from their neighborhood with burning faggots and with curses. All this had been brought vaguely to
Finn's mind by the passage through the scrub that day of
horses and men, and the northwest trail was the only possible
trail for him because of that.

From this point on, the pack moved slowly in scattered
formation, each individual member hunting as he went along,
with nose to earth and eyes a-glitter, for possible prey of any
kind, from a grub to an old-man kangaroo. Toward morning,
when they were a good thirty miles distant from Mount
Desolation, they topped a ridge, upon the farther slope of
which a small mob of nine kangaroos were browsing among
the scrub. Finn was after them like a shot, and Warrigal was
at his heels, the rest of the pack streaming behind in a ragged
line, the tail of which was formed by old Tufter and the
whelps. There was a stiff chase of between three and four
miles, and only five dingoes were within sight when Finn
pinned the rearmost kangaroo by the neck and Warrigal
darted in cautiously upon one of its flanks.

Even Tufter got a good meal from this kill, for the kangaroo was a big fellow. The whole pack fed full, and in the
neighborhood of that range they scattered and slept; for in
the gully on the other side of it there was a little muddy
water, and round about there was pleasant cover, which had
sheltered the kangaroos for a week or more. Old Tufter for-

bore to growl, and the young members of the pack were enthusiastic regarding the advantages of migration in the trail of such a hunter as Finn. They did not know that, in a leisurely way, the mob of kangaroos they had flushed were also migrating as a result of drought—but in the opposite direction to that chosen by Finn, who was heading now toward the part of the country the kangaroos had forsaken as being burned and eaten bare and devoid even of such food as bark.

When the dingoes had finished with the little chain of small pools in the gully on the afternoon of that day, there was little left but mud. However, that night's travel brought fairly good hunting, and always among game moving in the opposite direction to that taken by the pack.

For a week now the little pack traveled on in a northwesterly direction, and every day old Tufter growled a little more bitterly and with a little better cause. Game was certainly becoming lamentably scarce, and the country traversed was one that did not at all commend itself to dingoes, being arid, shadeless, and dry as a bleached bone. A long and most exhausting chase did enable Finn to pull down a solitary emu, and of this the pack left nothing but beak and feathers when they passed on, still hungry, in quest of other game.

But for all the shortness of food, which was thinning the flesh over Finn's haunches, it was another cause that led him to swerve from the northwesterly course in a southwesterly direction. He paid no particular heed to old Tufter's continuous growls about the direction taken by the pack under his leadership; but what he was forced to notice was the fact that for two whole days no water had been seen, and the lolling tongues of the young whelps were in consequence so swollen that they could not close their jaws. Throughout one weary night, the pack loped along in dogged silence in a southwesterly direction, their eyes blazing in the keen lookout for game; dry, dust-encrusted foam caked upon their lips, and fierce anxiety was in the heart of every one of them.

Then, in the brazen dawning of a day in which the sun seemed to thrust out great heat upon the baked earth even before it appeared above the horizon, the pack checked suddenly as Blacktip drew Finn's attention to a pair of native companions seen in the act of floating down to earth from the lower limbs of a shriveled red-gum tree. The bigger of these two great cranes had a stature of something over five feet, and his fine blue-gray plumage covered an amount of flesh that would have made a meal for quite a number of dingoes. Yet it was not so much as food, but rather as a guide and indication, that Blacktip regarded the cranes. He knew that they would not be very far from water. The way in which the pack melted into cover in the dim, misty light of the coming day was very remarkable. For several miles now they had been traveling through a country less arid than the plains they had traversed during the previous two days, and now, while seeming to disappear into the earth itself, the members of the pack actually found cover by slinking low amongst a sort of wiry scrub growth with which the ground hereabouts was dotted.

It was thus that Finn saw for the first time the strange dance of the native companion. To and fro and up and down beneath their scraggy gum tree, the two great cranes footed it in a sort of grotesque minuet. And while the native companions solemnly paced through what was really a dance of death for them, Finn and Blacktip and Warrigal stalked them as imperceptibly as shadows lengthen across a lawn in evening time. The three hunters advanced through the scrub like snakes moving in their sleep, and never a leaf or twig made comment on their passage as they slithered down the morning breeze, inch by inch, apparently a part of the shadowy earth itself. The prancing dance of the native com-

panions—these birds mate for life and are deeply and de-
votedly attached one to another—was drawing to its close
when death came to them both like a bolt from the heavens;
such a death as one would have chosen for them, since it left
no time for fear or mourning or grief at separation. Their
necks were torn in sunder before they realized that they had
been attacked. There was less of lordly generosity about Finn's
feeding upon this occasion than he had always shown before.
The great wolfhound realized perhaps that his frame demanded more nourishment than was necessary for the sup-
port of a dingo, and he ate with savage swiftness, growling
angrily when any muzzle other than Warrigal's approached
his own too nearly.

Less than half an hour later the pack was scrambling and
sliding down the high banks of a riverbed, in the center of
which, surrounded upon both sides by a quarter of a mile and
more of shingle and hard-baked mud, there was still a discon-
nected chain of small yellow pools of water. Finn chose a
good-sized pool, and Warrigal tackled it with him; but when
two youngsters of the pack ventured to approach the other
side of that pool, Warrigal snarled at them so fiercely, backed
by a low, gurgling growl from Finn, that the two slunk off and
tackled a lesser pool by themselves.

Where the pack drank they rested. As yet their great thirst
was close to them, and the neighborhood of water seemed too
good to leave. But, in such matters, the memory of the wild
folk is apt to be short. The banks of the riverbed ran due east
and west here; and, though the pack gave no thought to the
question, it was a matter of some importance to each one of
them whether they should eventually leave those banks to
the northward or to the southward; a matter of importance
by reason of the difference in the country to the north and to
the south. But it was chance at last that decided the question

for them. They drank many times during the day, and toward nightfall a small mob of kangaroos was sighted to the northward, and that led the pack to head northward, a little westerly, from the riverbank that night.

27: THE TRAIL OF MAN

IT was exactly a fortnight later when the pack turned despairingly in its tracks, animated by a forlorn desire to reach again the high ragged banks of that shingly riverbed, in which some trace of moisture might be still left, where the muddy pools had been.

But in that fortnight much had happened, and the character and constitution of the pack had undergone notable changes. The six whelps had disappeared, old Tufter and the oldest of the mothers of the pack were no more, and neither the carrion crows nor the ants had profited one atom by these deaths. The pack had not wittingly hastened the end of these weaker ones, but it had left only their bones behind upon the trail. And, now, when one or other of the gaunt, dry-lipped survivors stumbled, a dozen pairs of hungry eyes glittered, a dozen pairs of lips were wrinkled backward from as many sets of fangs, and consciousness of this had a sinister meaning for the stumbler; a meaning that brought a savage snarl to his throat as he regained his footing with quick, threatening looks from side to side and hackles bristling.

The pack was starving. Many times during the past week the thought of turning in his tracks and making for the riverbed had come to Finn, but he had pressed on, fearful of the arid stretch of country he had already placed between himself and that spot. He had no means of knowing that he was in a country of vast and waterless distances. But, acting without knowledge, Finn had turned in his tracks at length, after a fortnight's traveling in which food had been terribly scarce and water even scarcer. Such liquid as they had found would never have been called water by menfolk. Here and there had been a little liquid mud in old water holes and stream beds, and in other places the pack had sucked up moisture through hot sand, after burrowing with feet and nose to a depth of as much as eighteen inches from the surface. Their food had been almost entirely of the grub and insect kind, and Finn, for the first time in his life, had spent long hours in trying to ease the craving within him by gnawing at dry roots.

In appearance, the members of the pack had suffered a wondrous change in these two weeks. Even Warrigal's fine coat had lost every trace of the gloss that had made it beautiful, and the iron-gray hairs of Finn's dense, hard coat had taken on the character of dry bristles. His back, which had been broad and flat, was like the ridge of a gunyah now, from one end of which his neck rose gauntly and appeared to be of prodigious length. His ribs were plain to see on either side of his hollow barrel, and over them the loose skin rolled to and fro as he ran or walked. The eyes of every member of the pack were deeply sunken and ablaze with a dry light, half wistful and half fierce, and more awe-inspiring than any form of full-fed rage could be. They ran in open order now, and when one happened to run unusually close to another, that other would snarl or growl and, sometimes, even snap, with bitter, furtive, half-fearful irritability.

To this rule there was one exception. Warrigal ran steadily in the shadow cast by Finn's big, gaunt frame, her muzzle about level with his elbow. Blacktip kept about the same level on Finn's other side but a good deal farther off, and the others straggled in fan-shaped formation to the rear, scout-

ing at times to one side or the other in quest of insects and
snakes or any other living thing that fangs could crush. No
animal with flesh on its bones and blood in its veins would
have been too big or fierce for the pack to have attacked just
now, for hunger and thirst had made them quite desperate.

It was Blacktip and not Finn, who, on the afternoon of the
second day of the pack's despairing return journey in quest
of the riverbank they had left a fortnight before, called a
sudden halt. Blacktip sniffed hard and long at the ground between his forefeet, and then, raising his head, glared out into
the afternoon sunlight to the southeastward of the track they
were following—their own trail. The whimper that escaped
Blacktip when he began to sniff brought the rest of the pack
about him, full of hungry eagerness to know what thing it
was that had been found. There was something uncanny and
extraordinary about the way in which they glanced one at
another, after, as it were, taking one sip of the scent that had
brought Blacktip to a standstill. Had the scent been of kangaroo or wallaby, rabbit, rat, or any other thing that moves
upon four legs, those curious glances would never have been
exchanged. The pack would have been off hot-foot upon the
trail, without pause for discussion. And there was the scent
of a four-footed creature here, too; but it was merged in, and
subordinate to, the scent over which most wild creatures cry
a halt: the scent of man.

Now in ordinary circumstances the pack would not have
hesitated a moment over such a trail as this. They would have
turned in their tracks and made off in the opposite direction
or gone straight ahead on their own trail and without reference to the man-trail, save to get away from it as quickly as
possible. But these were very far from being ordinary circumstances. The man-trail was the trail of living flesh, of warm
animal life; it was the trail of food. Also, there was merged
in it the trail of a dog; and as each member of the pack ac-

quired that fact, his lips wrinkled backward and a little moisture found its way into his dry mouth.

The pack desired food and drink so urgently that everything else in the world became insignificant by comparison
with food and drink in their minds. The hatred and fear of
man as man was blotted out by the craving for animal food
in any shape whatsoever. Here was a living trail, in the midst
of a dead, burnt-up land of starvation and emptiness. Finn, of
course, had connected men with food all his life long. And
now he was starving. Finn's thoughts could not have been
quite the same as those of the rest of the pack; but they
moved him in the same direction nonetheless, and without
the smallest hesitation, the pack streamed after him when he
took up a new trail and loped off to the southeast, turning
away diagonally from the old track.

As the new trail became fresher and warmer, the leader
was conscious of the warning within him of various conflict-
ing feelings and desires. In appearance Finn was now a
gigantic wolf and one mastered by the fierce passion of
hunger, at that. Apart from appearance, there actually was
more of the wolf than the dog in him now. He belonged very
completely to the wild kindred, and over and above the wild
folk's natural inborn fear and mistrust of men, there was in
Finn a resentment against man; a bitter memory of torture
endured and of the humiliation of having been driven out
into the wild. But Finn's sense of smell was nothing like so
acute as that of the dingoes. He was not so keenly conscious
as his companions that he was on the trail of man. He knew
it; but it was not in his nostrils the assertive fact that it was,
for instance, in the nostrils of Warrigal and Blacktip. There
was in the trail for him a warm animal scent, which gave
promise of food; of food near at hand in that pitiless waste
the pack had been traversing for a fortnight and more. But
every now and again, possibly in places at which the makers

of the trail had paused, Finn would get a distinct whiff of the man scent, and that disturbed him a good deal. He wanted no dealings of any kind with man. But there was nothing else in him just then quite so strong or peremptory as the craving for food and drink; and so, with ears pricked and hackles uneasily lifting, he padded along at the true wolf gait, which devours distance without much suggestion of fleetness.

When night fell, the trail was very warm and fresh, and a quarter of an hour later a light breeze brought news to the pack of a fire not far ahead. This, again, brought pictures to Finn's mind of the encampment from which he had been driven with burning faggots. The pack advanced at a foot pace now and with extreme caution. A few minutes more brought them within full view of a campfire, beside which there were stretched, in attitudes of both dejection and fatigue, two men and a dog; the latter a large, gaunt fox terrier. The men had lighted their fire beneath a twisted, tortured-looking tree, in which there certainly was no life, for every vestige of its bark had gone from it and its limbs were naked as the bones of any skeleton.

The pack drew in as closely as their cover in the scrub permitted and crouched, watching the campfire. Suddenly, a movement on the part of one of them attracted the attention of the fox terrier, and he flew out into the scrub, barking furiously. The pack, in crescent formation, retreated perhaps a dozen paces, saliva trickling from their curling lips. The terrier plunged valiantly forward, hopping the first low bushes, as a terrier will when rabbiting or ratting. It was Blacktip who pinned him to the earth and Warrigal whose fangs next closed upon his body. But Finn smashed the terrier's body in half; and in an instant, the snarling pack surged over the remains. By the time one of the men had risen and moved forward toward the line of scrub, there was not a hair of the dog uneaten. His collar lay there on the ground between two bushes. For the rest, every particle of him, including bones, had been swallowed. From beginning to end the whole operation occupied less than four minutes.

One of the men had not troubled to rise at all. The pack withdrew to a safe distance while the other man rummaged about among the bushes for the better part of a quarter of an hour. The pack, meanwhile, was hidden among the trees a quarter of a mile away. Then the man found the terrier's collar and walked back to the fire with it. He walked slowly and stiffly. When he announced to his companion that there were dingoes about and that they had carried Jock off, the other man only grunted wearily and turned over on his side. So the first man threw some more wood on the fire and lowered himself slowly to the ground, moving painfully and stretching himself out for a sleep.

During the night the pack scoured every inch of the scrub within a radius of one mile from the camp of the two men; and for their reward they obtained precisely nothing at all beyond a few, a very few, grubs and insects, the eating of which served to temper as with fire the keen edge of their hunger. The hours immediately preceding daylight found most of them sitting on their haunches, in a scattered semicircular line in the scrub, glaring through the darkness at the two sleeping men and their now expiring fire. In addition to connecting menfolk with guns and traps and fear of an instinctive and indescribable kind, most of the pack also connected men with food, with sheep, and other domesticated animals, which dingoes can eat. Finn, more than any of them, connected menfolk with food. But, as against that, Finn also connected them with torture and suffering, with hostility and abuse. Finn sat farther from the campfire than any of the others.

When daylight came and one of the men stirred on his elbow and looked up at the sky, the pack retreated slowly backward through the scrub, till more than double that distance separated them from the living food at which they had been wistfully glaring. There was no anger, no savagery, no vestige of cruelty in their minds and hearts. Finn, it is true, cherished some soreness and resentment where men were concerned; but even in his case this brought only the desire to keep out of man's way, while the rest of the pack felt only instinctive dread and fear of man. But now the feeling that ruled the whole pack, the light that shone in their eyes, the eagerness that brought moisture continually to their half-uncovered fangs while they watched—this was simply physical desire for food, simply hunger.

The man who had been the first to stir rose slowly and stretched his arms as though his frame ached, as indeed it did, from a variety of causes. His face had a ten days' growth of hair upon it and was gaunt and haggard, like the rest of him. His clothes hung about him loosely and were torn and soiled and ragged. Under the bronze tan of sunburn on his face and neck there was the sort of pallor that comes from lack of food; in his eyes—deep sunk in dark-rimmed hollows—was a curious glitter not at all unlike the glitter in the eyes of the wild folk who had been watching him during the night It was the same expression that shone out from the eyes of the starved Mount Desolation pack. And the causes behind it were the same.

Presently this man woke his companion, who growled at him, as though he resented the attention.

"Time we were on the move, old chap," said the first man. "We can't afford to wait."

The other man sat up and blinked wearily at the daylight, showing a face as haggard and gaunt as that of his friend.

"By God, I don't know!" he said bitterly. "I don't know whether we can afford to do anything else. Afford! And us carrying a fortune! I said out there that I'd never had good luck before, and—it was right, too. Good luck's not for the likes o' me."

"Oh, yes, it is," said the other man, with an obvious effort at cheerfulness. "You wait till we get our legs under a dinner-table; then you'll tell another tale about luck. Come on! Let's have breakfast and get on. I think you're perfectly right about parting this morning. We can take that to be east, where the scrub gets thick, and that to be south. We'll toss who takes which, and one or other of us will strike something before nightfall—you mark my words—and after that it will be easy to pick up the other's trail. Better make the trail as plain as possible as we go along. Come; buck up, Jeff, old man; this will be our last day hungry. I'm going to take my breakfast now."

Imitating his companion, and with an attempt to look a little more cheery over it, Jeff stood up now and carefully un-corked a canvas-covered water bottle. Each man filled his mouth full from the gurgling contents of his water bottle and stood, swishing the water in his mouth slowly and allowing it to trickle little by little down his parched throat. In this way several minutes were devoted to the swallowing of a single mouthful of water, and that was breakfast.

"If we hadn't chucked the guns away, we might have got a chance at something today," growled Jeff, when his breakfast was done. "I could make a roast dingo look foolish this morn-ing, and I'm none so sure I couldn't eat the brute raw if I got him. You said it was dingoes got Jock last night, didn't you?"

"I suppose it must have been," said the other man. "I don't see what else it could have been. And as to the guns; well, you know, it was that or the stuff. We couldn't carry any more."

"I know. And I'm not sure it's much good carrying that any longer. I reckon I'll dump mine somewhere today before it dumps me. Sixty-six pounds—sixty-six solid pounds o' best pin-fire—and us dyin' for want of a crust. Come on, then! One more try!"

"You've got your revolver still, haven't you?" asked Jeff as he fitted the straps of a big, heavy swag (which had served him for a pillow) about his shoulders, while his companion did the same with his swag.

"Yes," said the other man. "And I tell you what, Jeff; you shall take it today. I've got a jolly good stick here, and I've no use for the revolver, anyhow; couldn't hit a house at a dozen yards, even if I was likely to see one."

They gravely tossed a twig to decide the question of who should head south and who east; and then as gravely they shook hands and parted, Jeff heading south and the other man due east.

Away in the scrub to the northward of the two men, a dozen pairs of eyes more hungry than their own were watching them; or, to be exact, eleven pairs were watching them. Finn lay stretched still at full length beside a bush at Warrigal's feet, while Warrigal peered eagerly through the scrub. Blacktip, followed by three strong young dogs and a bitch, loped off at once, without comment or communication with the rest of the pack, in the direction of the trail of the south-bound Jeff. Warrigal's eyes, as it happened, were fixed upon the shoulders of the other man, and it was his trail that she made for now after rousing Finn with a touch of her muzzle. And so the wild folk divided, even as the menfolk had done, five going south after Jeff, and five others, besides Finn and Warrigal, going east after the other man. But it was broad daylight, and none of them made any attempt to draw near the makers of the trails they followed. They merely followed, muzzles carried low and nostrils and eager eyes questing as they went for any sign of life in the scrub—anything, from an ant to an emu, that by any possibility could represent

food. Meanwhile, the warm trail of the man ahead kept hope
and excitement alive in them, though that man would have
said that he was about as poor a source of hopefulness as any
creature in Australia. To be sure, he had never thought of
himself in the light of food. The dingoes had.

28: IN THE LAST DITCH

It was in the midst of the pitiless heat that comes a couple of
hours after midday and is harder to bear than the blaze of
high noon that the man who was heading due east abandoned
his swag. He had rested for the better part of an hour directly
after noon and had two mouthfuls from his water bottle, one
before and one after his rest. While he rested, the half pack,
headed by Finn and Warrigal, had rested also, and more completely, hidden away in the scrub a quarter of a mile and
more from the man whose trail they followed. Two of them,
Warrigal and another, watched with a good deal of interest
the burial of the swag beneath a drought-seared solitary ironbark. No sooner was the man out of sight—he walked slowly
and with a somewhat staggering gait now—than the pack un-
earthed his swag with quick, vicious strokes of their feet and
laid it bare to the full blaze of the afternoon sunlight. In a
few moments they had its canvas cover torn to ribbons, and
bitter was their disappointment when they came to turn over
its jagged mineral contents between their muzzles and discovered that even they could eat none of this rubbish.

It is fair to suppose that within a couple of hours of this
time the man finally lost the brave remnant of hope with
which he had set out that day. The pack did not reason about
this, but they felt it as plainly as any human observer could

have done, and the realization brought great satisfaction to
each one of them. It was not that they bore the faintest sort of
malice against the man or cherished any cruel feeling for him
whatever. He was food; they were starving; and his evident
loss of mastery of himself brought food nearer to the pack.

The man's course was erratic now; and his trail was altered
by the fact that his feet were dragged over the ground instead
of being planted firmly upon it with each stride he took. The
pack were not alone in their recognition of the man's sorry
plight. He was followed now by no fewer than seven carrion
crows; big, black, evil-looking birds, who circled in the air
behind and above him, swooping sometimes to within twenty
or thirty feet of his head and cawing at him in a half-threat-
ening, half-pleading manner.

When darkness fell, the man lighted no fire this evening.
But neither did he lie down. He sat with his back against a
tree trunk and his legs outstretched; and now and again
sounds came from his lips, which, while not threatening, were
certainly not cries for mercy, and therefore in the pack's eyes
not signals for an attack. The man-life was apparently strong
in him yet; for he sometimes flung his arms about and struck
at the earth with the long, tough stick he had carried all day.
The pack, when they had unsuccessfully scoured every inch
of the ground within a mile of the man for food, drew in
closer for the night's watch than they had ventured on the
previous night. But Finn lay behind a bush and farther from
the man than any of the rest of the pack. He wanted food; he
needed it more bitterly perhaps than any of the others; but
all his instincts went against regarding man himself as food.

The man slept only in broken snatches during this night.
While he slept, Warrigal and the others, except Finn, crept
in a little closer; but when he turned or waved one arm or
when sounds came from his lips, then the dingoes would slink
backward into the scrub, with lips updrawn and silent snarls

wrinkling their nostrils. Toward dawn Warrigal set up a long
howl, and at that the man woke with a great start, to sleep no
more. Presently, others of the pack followed Warrigal's lead,
and staggering to his feet, the man moved forward three steps
and flung a piece of rotten wood in the direction from which
the howls came. Warrigal and her mates retreated for the
better part of one hundred yards, snarling aloud; not from
fierceness but in a kind of wistful disappointment at finding
the man still capable of so much action.

The man's shout of anger and defiance reached Finn's ears.
The voice of man in anger; he had not heard it since the
night of his being driven out from the boundary rider's camp.
The memories it aroused in him were all, without exception,
of man's tyranny and cruelty and of his own suffering at
man's hands. He growled low in his throat but very fiercely.
And yet, it was more than all that. It was the warring within
him of inherited respect for man's authority with acquired
wildness, with his acquired freedom of the wild folk. The
conflict of instinct and emotions in Finn was so ardent as
almost to overcome consciousness of the great hunger that
was his real master at this time, the furious hunger that made
him chew savagely at the tough fiber of a dry root held between his two forepaws.

But the man had taken only three steps, and when he sank
down to the earth again, it was not in the place he had occupied before. He lay down where he had stood when he threw
the billet of wood, and there was that in the manner of his
lying down that boded ill. It was observed most carefully by
three of the crows, who had followed him all the day before;
and upon the strength of it they settled within a dozen paces
of his figure, with an air that seemed to say plainly they could
afford a little more patience now, since they would not have
long to wait.

When full daylight came, Warrigal and her mates were

closer in than ever; hidden in the scrub within forty paces of
the man. Finn retained his old place, some thirty yards farther
back, behind a bush. The crows preened their funereal plumage and waited, full of bright-eyed expectancy. Finn gnawed
bitterly at his dry fragment of scrub root. The splendid pitiless sun climbed slowly clear of its bed on the horizon, thrusting up long, keen blades of heat and light to herald the
coming of another blazing day in the long drought.

Presently, a long spear of the new day's light thrust its
point between the man's curved arm and his face. He turned
on his side so that he faced the sun, and evidently its message to him was that he must proceed with his journey. Slowly
and painfully, he rose as far as his knees and then, with a
groan, drooped down to earth again on his side. The crows
cocked their heads sideways at him. Warrigal and her mates
saw clearly the conclusion the crows had arrived at. They,
also, held that the man was down for good at last. The crows
were safe guides, and one of them was hopping gravely toward
the back of the man. Warrigal, followed by five of her mates,
crept slowly forward through the scrub; and saliva was hanging like icicles from their parted jaws.

Finn saw Warrigal's movement and knew precisely what it
portended. And now Finn was possessed by two opposing inclinations, both terribly strong. Upon the one hand, instinctive respect for man's authority and acquired dislike of man
and all his works bade the great wolfhound remain where he
was. Upon the other hand, two forces impelled him to rise
and join his mate, and those two forces were the greatest
hunger he had ever known and the assertive pride of his
leadership of the pack. There before his eyes his section of
the pack was advancing, preparing for a kill for food, there in
that bitter desert of starvation. And he, the unquestioned
master and leader of the pack, master of all the wild kindred
that he knew; he, Finn, was— Three seconds later, the wolf-

hound had bounded forward, his great shoulders thrusting angrily between Warrigal and the big male dingo who had dared to usurp his, Finn's, place there as leader in concerted action.

For an instant the pack paused, no more than a score of paces distant from the man's shoulders, glaring uneasily. Then the man moved, raising his body slightly upon one elbow. The dingoes drew back a pace, even Warrigal moving back with them, though she snarled savagely in doing so. Finn did not move. Warrigal's snarl told the man of his danger, and with an effort, he rose upon his knees and grabbed at his long stick where it lay on the ground. Again Warrigal snarled, less than a yard from Finn's ears, and her snarl was the snarl that announces a kill. It was not for others to kill when Finn led. And yet something held the great wolfhound's muscles relaxed; he could not take the leap that was wont to precede killing with him. Again Warrigal snarled. The man was rising to his feet. A great fear of being shamed was upon Finn. With that snarl in his ears advance was a necessity. He moved forward quickly but without a spring. And in that instant the man, having actually gotten to his feet, swung around toward the pack with his long stick uplifted, and Finn gathered his hindquarters under him for the leap that should end this hunting—this long, strange hunting in a desert of starvation.

The wolfhound actually did spring. His four feet left the ground. But, with a shock that jarred every nerve and muscle in his great frame, they returned to earth again, practically upon the exact spots they had left. His sense of smell, never remarkable for its acuteness in detail, had told Finn nothing, save that his quarry in this strange hunting was man. But the wolfhound's eyes could not mislead him, and in the instant of his suddenly arrested spring—the spring that it had taken every particle of strength in his great body to check—he had

known, with a sudden revulsion of feeling that positively
stopped the beating of his heart, that this man the pack had
trailed was none other than the Man of all the world for him;
the man whose person was as sacred as his will to Finn; the
Master, whose loss had been the beginning and the cause of
all the troubles the wolfhound had ever known.

There had been the beginning of the killing snarl in Finn's
throat when he sprang, and as he came to earth again at the
man's feet, possessed and almost paralyzed by his amazing
discovery, that snarl had ended in as curious a cry as ever left
the throat of four-footed folk since the world began. It was
more like human speech than that of the wild people. It
welled up into the air from the very center of that in Finn
which could be called his soul.

And in that same instant, too, recognition came to the
Master, and he knew his huge assailant to be no creature of
the wild, no giant wolf or dingo, but the wolfhound of his
own breeding and most careful, loving rearing. It was from
some central recess of his own personality that the Master's
cry of "Finn, boy!" answered the strange cry with which the
wolfhound came to earth at his feet.

But behind them was the pack, and in the pack's eyes what
had happened was that their leader had missed his kill; that
fear had broken his spring off short and that now he was at
the mercy of the man who, a moment before, had been mere
food. For a dingo, no other task, not even the gnawing off of
a limb caught in a trap, could require quite so much sheer
courage as the attacking of Man in the open—man erect and
unafraid. But Warrigal had never in her life lacked courage,
and now, behind her courage and her devotion to her mate,
there was hunger, red-toothed and slavering in her ears;
hunger stretching her jaws for killing, with an eagerness and
a ferocity that could not be denied. In the next instant Warrigal had flown at the man's right shoulder with a fierce snarl

that called those of her kind who were not cowards to follow
her or be forever accursed.

Warrigal's white fangs slashed down the man's coat sleeve
and left lines of skin and blood where the cloth gave. For one
moment Finn hesitated. Warrigal was his good mate, the
mother of his dead children, his loving companion by day and
night, during long months past. She concentrated in her own
being all the best of his kinship with the wild. As against all
this, Warrigal's fangs had fastened upon the sacred flesh of
the Master.

Next instant, and even as the biggest male dingo of the
pack flew at the man's other side, Finn pinned his mate to
earth and, with one tremendous crunch of his huge jaws,
severed her jugular vein and set her blood running over the
parched earth.

In that moment, the pack awoke to realization of the
strange thing that had befallen them. They had been seven,
pitted against a single man, and he apparently in the act of
ceasing to be erect man and becoming mere food. Now they
were five—for Warrigal's life ebbed quickly from her—pitted
against a man wakened to erectness and hostility and their
own great leader, the great wolf, who had slain Lupus, their
old fierce master, and even Tasman, his terrible sire. It is certain that at another time the pack would not have hesitated
for one moment about turning tail and fleeing that place of
strange, unnatural happenings. But this was no ordinary
time. They were mad with hunger. Blood was flowing out
upon the earth before them. One of them had the taste of
man's blood on his foaming lips. This was not a tracking or a
killing in prospect but a fight in progress. The pack would
never turn tail alive from that fight.

The man had his back to the withered ironbark now, and
besides the long stick in his right hand, he held an open knife
in his left hand, as a long, fierce bitch found to her cost when

she leaped for his throat, fell short, and felt cold steel bite
deep in her flank as she sank to earth. And now the great
wolfhound warmed to his work, with a fire of zeal mere
hunger itself could not have lit within him. He was fighting
now as never before since his fangs met in his first kill in
faraway Sussex. A tiger could hardly have evaded him. His
onslaught was at once terrible and swift as forked lightning.
It seemed he slashed and tore in five separate directions at one
and the same time. But that was only because his jaws flashed
from one dingo's body to another with such rapidity that the
passage between could not be followed by the eye. This
meant that his fangs could not be driven deep enough for
instant killing. There was not time. But they went deep,
nonetheless; and blood streamed now from the necks of the
dingoes that succeeded one another in springing at the man
and the wolfhound.

Two of the dingoes owed their deaths to the long knife
blade of the man; but even as the second of them received
the steel to the hilt below his chest bones, the man sank,
utterly exhausted and bleeding freely, on his knees, and from
there to the ground itself. This drew the attention of the
three surviving dingoes from the leader, who in some mysterious manner had become an enemy, to the fallen man
who was now, clearly, a kill. Mere hunger, desperate hunger,
was uppermost in the minds of the three. They quested flesh
and blood from the kill that lay helpless before them.

It was then that Finn outdid himself; it was then that he
called into sudden and violent action every particle of reserve
strength that was left in him; so that, almost within the passage of as many seconds, he slew three full-grown dingoes,
precisely as a game terrier will slay three rats, with one crushing snap and one tremendous shake to each. Starved though
they were, these dingoes weighed over forty pounds apiece;
yet when they met with their death between Finn's mighty

jaws, their bodies were flung from him, in the killing shake, to a distance of as much as five yards.

And then there fell a sudden and complete stillness in that desert spot. Finn licked the Master's white, blood-flecked face where it lay on the ground. And at that, the waiting crows settled down upon the bodies of the outlying dingoes. After long licking, or licking that seemed to him long, Finn pointed his nose to the brazen sky and lifted up his voice in the true wolfhound howl, which is perhaps the most penetratingly saddening cry in Nature.

29: BACK FROM THE WILD

FOUR men were riding together through the low, burnt-up scrub, and in front of them, holding their horses at a smart amble to be even with his jog trot, a naked aboriginal was leading the way on his own bare feet.

"Blurry big warrigal 'e bin run here!" said the aboriginal suddenly, as he stooped to examine a footprint in the trail they were following. He counted the different footprints and announced to the horsemen that seven dingoes had followed the trail they were following at that moment. He explained that these dingoes, led by the "blurry big warrigal," must have been terribly badly in want of food, and that he did not think much of the chances of the man they had followed.

One of the riders—it was Jeff—nodded his head dolefully over this.

"I reckon all the plaguy warrigals in this country must 'a' gone crazy," he said. "You know I told you there was half a dozen on my track. But we're goin' right; you can be dead sure o' that, for that was his swag we found all right, and you

could see the dingoes had been at that. My oath! To think o'
them brutes scratching up a fortune that way an' leaving it
there!"

Another three miles were covered, and then, suddenly, the
native halted, with one hand raised over his head, which was
turned sideways in a listening attitude. He explained, a moment later, that he could hear howling, such as a "blurry big
warrigal" might produce. The party pushed on, and two or
three minutes later they were all able to make out the sound
the fellow had heard. But the fellow shook his head now and
informed them that no warrigal ever made a howl like that;
that must be "white feller dog."

"Well, that's queer," said Jeff, "for Jock was killed the
night before we parted. But, say, whatever it is, that's a most
ungodly sort o' howl, sure enough!"

Five or six minutes later the native gave a whoop of
astonishment as he topped a little ridge and came into view
of the Master lying prone upon the ground, with Finn sitting
erect beside his head. One of the riders pulled out a revolver
when he caught sight of Finn's shaggy head.

"Well, may I be teetotally jiggered!" he growled. "What
sort of beast do ye call that?"

The riders galloped down the slope and flung themselves
hurriedly from their horses. The leading man waved his whip
at Finn to drive him off. And then it was seen that Finn's
assiduous licking had been sufficient to restore the man to
consciousness. The Master raised his head feebly and said:

"For God's sake don't hurt the dog! He saved my life.
Killed six dingoes in front of me. God's sake don't touch
the—"

And with that he lapsed again into unconsciousness, while
Jeff propped up his head and another man produced a spirit-
flask and the native gazed admiringly around upon the dead
dingoes and the huge wolfhound who sat there, with hackles

raised and lips a little curled by reason of the proximity of the menfolk. But Finn was perfectly conscious that the Master was being helped, and he showed no inclination to interfere. He was watchful, however, and would not retreat for more than a few paces.

The party had brandy and water and food in plenty with them; and it was not long before the Master was sitting up and munching soaked bread and sipping brandy and water, while one of the men cleansed and bandaged his arms where the dingoes had torn them. Another of the men tossed a big crust of bread to Finn, and seeing the way the wolfhound bolted this, he realized that the hound was as near to starving as the man. After that, Finn had food and drink in modest quantities; and presently the Master called to him and placed one arm weakly over his bony shoulders, while telling the men, in as few words as might be, something of the manner in which Finn had fought for him and the origin of their relationship.

Exactly a week later, Finn lay on the balcony of a country town hotel, with his nose just resting lightly on the Master's knee. The Master was still weak. He lay on a cane lounge, with one hand on Finn's shoulder. Beside him, in a basket chair, was the Mistress of the Kennels, and now and again her hand was passed caressingly over Finn's head. There was still a good deal of gauntness about the great wolfhound; but he was strong as a lion now, and his dark eyes gleamed as brightly as ever through their overhanging eaves of iron-gray hair.

"Well," said the Master, looking across at his companion over Finn's head. "I'm not very certain about most things. It takes some time to get used to being rich, doesn't it? I suppose we may be called rich. They say the claim is good enough for half a dozen fortunes yet; and sixty odd pounds

of gem opal is no trifle, of itself." (As a matter of fact, the
Master's swag brought him an average price of just over
twenty pounds to the ounce, or £21,250 for the lot, apart
from his share in a very rich claim.)

"One thing I am dead sure about, however, and that is
that, come rain or shine, there isn't money enough in all Australia to tempt us into parting with Finn boy again. Finn,
boy!"

The wolfhound raised his bearded muzzle and softly licked
the Master's thin brown hand. It was his weakness, no doubt,
that produced a kind of wetness about the man's eyes.

"It's 'Sussex by the sea' for us, Finn, boy, in another month
or so; and, God willing, that's where you shall end your days!"

As he responded, after his own fashion, to the Master's assurance, there was small trace in the great wolfhound's eyes
of his relationship with the wild kindred of the bush.

Ingram Content Group UK Ltd.
Milton Keynes UK
UKHW020347300523
422541UK00005B/140

9 781017 940725